The working classes
in Victorian fiction

by the same author

Working-class stories of the 1890s

1 Scene outside London Public House, *c.* 1890

The working classes in Victorian fiction

P. J. Keating

Lecturer in English Literature,
University of Leicester

London   Routledge & Kegan Paul

First published 1971
by Routledge & Kegan Paul Ltd
Broadway House, 68–74 Carter Lane
London EC4V 5EL
Printed in Great Britain
by Cox & Wyman Ltd,
London, Fakenham and Reading
© P. J. Keating 1971
No part of this book may be reproduced
in any form without permission from
the publisher, except for the quotation
of brief passages in criticism

ISBN 0 7100 6991 X

Contents

List of illustrations

To Connie

Preface

The main purpose of this book is to examine the presentation of the urban and industrial working classes in Victorian fiction. Although the period covered is from 1820 to 1900, I have paid especially close attention to the last two decades of the century with fiction published earlier than this (in particular the industrial novels of the 1840s and 50s, and the work of Dickens) being used to provide constant points of comparison. I have concentrated almost exclusively upon those writers who tried to describe working-class life in a realistic manner and have given less attention to those who wrote *about* working-class life. There is, consequently, more on Kipling than Carlyle, more on Arthur Morrison than William Morris. In order to follow as consistent a policy as possible I have omitted Utopian fiction from my discussion, as well as novels which are set in the historic past – novels, that is, in which the recreation of past social conditions is of central importance. This rule has, however, been necessarily relaxed in certain cases, most notably that of *Felix Holt*. I have also made no attempt to deal with the novel of Jewish life in the East End.

In order to avoid periphrasis, terms such as 'working-class fiction' and 'working-class novelist' have been used to refer solely to subject matter, and indicate either fiction about, or a novelist writing about, the working classes. Where an author's class background has some special significance this has been emphasized in the text. I have also used the term 'working class' throughout in preference to 'proletariat' and the prefixes 'urban' and 'industrial' to indicate the two principal working-class groups studied here, as well as the different literary traditions to which they belong: further definitions and classifications are examined in the opening chapter. I have omitted entirely fiction about agricultural workers and (allowing for one or two special cases) domestic servants. *Jude the Obscure* is not included, partly because it needs to be considered (in some senses at least) in relation to other fiction about agricultural life, and partly because the working-class aspects of this remarkable novel seem to me to demand a kind of social and literary analysis very different from that which I have employed.

Fiction published after 1900 is not discussed in any detail and I have tried to resist the temptation to make frequent comparisons between Victorian and twentieth-century novels. There is some justification for adhering with reasonable rigidity to this upper time limit. Many of the late-Victorian novelists discussed here continued to publish well into the twentieth century, but by 1900 they had either stopped writing fiction centred upon working-class life, or their work had settled down into comfortable stereotypes. The various literary and social forces examined (especially the sociological investigation of the working classes, the discovery of the East End, and the initial impact of French naturalism) had also served their pioneering purposes by the close of the century. In addition, one of the most striking features of twentieth-century working-class fiction (beginning shortly after the year 1900) is that much of it is by authors who are themselves of, or from, the working classes. This fiction deserves serious study, but as one of my principal points of concern was the ways in which the Victorian working classes are presented by mainly middle- and upper-class writers, this was not the place for it.

During the course of my research I have been most fortunate in the advice and encouragement I have received. At the University of Sussex I would particularly like to thank Professor David Daiches and Professor Asa Briggs for guidance on matters extending far beyond the writing of this book, and Dr Patricia Thomson for originally supervising my research and for making countless criticisms and suggestions which were always valuable. At the University of Leicester I have been given every opportunity by the Victorian Studies Centre to discuss and revise my ideas, and I would like to thank all those who contributed to these discussions from which I have derived great benefit. I am especially grateful to Professor Philip Collins and Dr H. J. Dyos for their constant encouragement and help. I am also indebted to the Trustees of the London Library for a generous grant towards the cost of membership which enabled me to use their excellent collection of nineteenth-century literature, and to the Research Board of the University of Leicester for financial aid in preparing the final manuscript of this book. To my friend Dr Richard Price, of the University of Northern Illinois, it is impossible even to specify my thanks. From first to last there is hardly an idea expressed here that did not grow out of, or benefit from, discussions with him.

P. J. Keating

Acknowledgments

The author and publishers wish to thank the following for permission to reproduce the illustrations listed below:

'Scene outside London Public House, c. 1890' and '"The Jago", Boundary Street, c. 1890' reproduced by permission of the Greater London Council Photographic Library.

'"Mean Streets", Tent Street, Bethnal Green, c. 1900' reproduced by the courtesy of the London Borough of Tower Hamlets Libraries Committee.

'"Street Arab", c. 1900' reproduced by courtesy of Dr Barnardo's.

1

The two traditions,
1820-80

I

'If you look for the working classes in fiction,' wrote George
Orwell in 1940, 'and especially English fiction, all you find is a
hole.' He goes on to qualify this statement:

> For reasons that are easy enough to see, the agricultural
> labourer (in England a proletarian) gets a fairly good showing
> in fiction, and a great deal has been written about criminals,
> derelicts and, more recently, the working-class intelligentsia.
> But the ordinary town proletariat, the people who make the
> wheels go round, have always been ignored by novelists.
> When they do find their way between the covers of a book, it
> is nearly always as objects of pity or as comic relief.[1]

It is important to distinguish between the quantitative and qualitative judgements being made by Orwell. On the one hand, it is
simply untrue that the urban working classes ('the people who
make the wheels go round') have always been ignored by novelists.
There is, in fact, a considerable body of English fiction which
deals with, or purports to deal with, not merely the exceptions
acknowledged by Orwell but 'the ordinary town proletariat'. In
the Victorian period alone there were some hundreds of novels
written on this very subject. On the other hand, Orwell's objection
to the presentation of the working classes 'when they do find their
way between the covers of a book', while a slight exaggeration, is

more just. For there are few English novels which deal with working-class characters in a working-class environment in the same sense as there are novels about the middle or upper classes in their own recognizably real settings: in other words, novels which treat of the working class as being composed of ordinary human beings who experience the range of feelings and emotions, social aspirations and physical relationships, that it is the special province of the novelist to explore.

Most working-class novels are, in one way or another, propagandist. They are usually written by authors who are not working class, for an audience which is not working class, and character and environment are presented so as to contain, implicitly or explicitly, a class judgement. The author may wish to show, for instance, that the working classes are basically no different from other people, or that they are, in a spiritual sense at least, more fortunate than other social groups: or that they are not at heart violent and so long as their just complaints are listened to sympathetically the middle and upper classes have nothing to fear from them. Or even more directly, that they need help, that they shouldn't drink, that more schools, hospitals or workhouses – as the case may be – should be built for them. Put simply the most important single fact about the fictional working man is his class.

The historical reason for this is easy to see. During the nineteenth century there were two periods when a significant number of novelists seriously attempted to present the working classes in fiction. Both were times of social upheaval when real or imagined class fears compelled people to look afresh at the basic social, economic and political structure of society. In the 1840s and 50s the motivating force was the outcry over the condition of industrial workers, together with the middle-class panic engendered by Chartist politics: in the period 1880-1900 it was the problem of urban slum conditions and the widespread public debate on Socialism. The fictional response in both periods was almost entirely non-working class. For the novelist who wished to write about the working classes but was not himself from a working-class background, the publicity arising out of these moments of crisis enabled him to create a social framework for his fiction within which he could present a way of life in every respect alien to his own, and closed to him at moments of greater stability. In both periods the fictional response trails behind political and social reform movements. The industrial novel develops only after the Blue Books and Chartism have paved the way, and the urban novel of the 1890s has a similar dependence on reform agitation of the previous decade. This is one reason for the narrow range of working-class experience presented in fiction, and it also explains why the fiction of each period is dominated and restricted by the single image of a Victorian city. In the earlier period Manchester is used to symbolize both the greatness and shame of Industrial England;[2] in the later period the East End of London serves the same dual function for Imperial England. In both cases novelists were following rather than anticipating the forces making for change. When the crisis declined the interest of novelists declined also.

In so far as it is possible to talk at all of a genuine working-class literary tradition in the Victorian age, it is to be found in certain regional poets (both dialect and non-dialect), in a considerable mass of Chartist verse and doggerel, and most interestingly in the memoirs of working men who rose to positions of eminence in public life. Apart from a few Chartist novels imaginative prose is non-existent.[3] A critical search in Victorian literature for a working-class tradition leads inevitably to the pessimistic conclusion reached by William Empson: 'It is hard for an Englishman to talk definitely about proletarian art, because in England it has never been a genre with settled principles, and such as there is of it, that I have seen, is bad.'[4]

Theoretically, of course, it is not necessary to be of the working class to write an outstanding novel about the working class, as Émile Zola's great trilogy, *L'Assommoir* (1877), *Germinal* (1885) and *La Terre* (1887) indicates. Nor does it follow that a working-man turned novelist will be able to write a good novel about his own class. Thomas Wright and Robert Blatchford are perfect examples of working-class writers who produced important documentary studies of working-class life and very poor novels on the same subject. Nor again is it a matter of sympathy for or hostility towards the workers as a class. This is almost totally unimportant. The crucial point is whether the novelist is effectively committed to artistic principles or to an overt class viewpoint. Most Victorian novelists come into the second category, and their presentation of working-class characters can be seen to become more successful as they themselves retreat from a position of authorial didacticism. This was very much the point made by Engels in his famous letter to Margaret Harkness:

> I am far from finding fault with your not having written a purely socialist novel, a *Tendenzroman*, as we Germans call it, to glorify the social and political views of the author. That is not at all what I mean. The more the author's views are concealed the better for the work of art. The realism I allude to may creep out even in spite of the author's views. Let me refer to an example.

Engels's example is Balzac, whose sense of realism was so intense that it compelled him 'to go against his own class sympathies and political prejudices'.[5] What Engels is praising in Balzac is his analysis of social relationships, not his treatment of working-class characters – there are in fact no urban or industrial workers in the *Comédie humaine*. With the partial exception of Dickens, this sense of realism is not applicable to the English novelists, who usually present working-class characters in relation to a specific social issue, and are therefore pre-eminently concerned with a form of realism analogous to a sociological document or parliamentary report. In their work we do not feel the realism creeping through in spite of the author's personal views. Rather, the reverse is true – we are too often conscious that the author's concern with social antidotes has weakened the power of his documentary realism. The constant presence of social purpose in the working-class novel leads to a manipulation of the characters' actions, motives and speech, in order that they may be used finally to justify a class theory held by the author. However hard the novelist tries to suppress his sympathy, or hostility, his own class viewpoint becomes transparently clear, and the artistic value of the particular work suffers. This is obvious enough when applied, for instance, to a temperance reform tale, but it is also true, in varying degrees, of most working-class novels written in the nineteenth century. Too often individual working-class scenes in Victorian novels are praised for their historical accuracy, while the total pattern and effect of the novel is either ignored or excused. When we look more closely at how exactly working-class characters are treated in relation to characters of other classes, we find time and time again that the novelist has unconsciously set into motion a process

2 Thomas Rowlandson: 'Love and Dust', 1788

3 I. R. and G. Cruikshank: 'Lowest *Life in London*'. Tom, Jerry and Logic, among the unsophisticated sons and daughters of Nature, at 'All Max' in the East. Pierce Egan, *Life in London*, 1821

4 Phiz: 'Kit Nubbles at Home', *The Old Curiosity Shop*, 1841

of avoidance which prevents him from dealing with his professed subject – the working classes.

This central weakness is most apparent in the imposition of unnatural values and attitudes upon working-class characters, allowing them free expression and a full life only in so far as this fits in with the author's preconceived, socially desirable image of them. William Empson's observation that 'proletarian literature usually has a suggestion of pastoral, a puzzling form which looks proletarian but isn't',[6] is very relevant here. For although it is not my intention to use the phrase 'proletarian literature' in the sense that Empson uses it ('the propaganda of the factory-working class which feels its interests opposed to the factory owners'), his perceptive exploration of the ways that pastoral conventions may be subconsciously employed to hide latent radical or political ideas has a worth beyond the Marxist frame within which he places it. The technique, or to use Empson's terminology again, the 'trick' of pastoral, appears under many strange guises in Victorian working-class fiction, and just because a novelist will often vehemently defend his working-class scenes on the grounds of realism, this should not allow us to ignore the fact that what is carefully observed class reality to the author may well come over as pastoral to the reader.

Any attempt to show how the working classes are portrayed in Victorian fiction must return again and again to the apparent difficulties experienced by novelists in trying to establish a balance between commitment to a class viewpoint and artistic form. Prior to 1880 the problem is there but novelists seem barely conscious of it: after 1880 it becomes an issue of central importance and is most successfully resolved, I shall argue, in the short stories and ballads of Rudyard Kipling. Before looking in detail at the attempts by late-Victorian writers to solve this and other problems, it is necessary, if we are to be sure of what is new and what inherited in their work, to place them in a wider nineteenth-century setting.

II

The industrial novel of the 1840s and 50s is the only type of English working-class fiction to have received much attention from literary and social historians. In comparison the novel of non-industrial urban working-class life has been totally ignored. Ever since Orwell's common-sense rejection of Dickens as a 'proletarian writer' (a critical approach which differed little from that of Gissing forty years earlier), it has generally been accepted that the 'people who make the wheels go round' hardly exist in fiction, and certainly cannot be said to constitute a viable literary tradition. It is only in recent years that the work of George Gissing and Rudyard Kipling has been treated with the respect it deserves and so far this revaluation has produced little that is new on their contributions to working-class fiction. The slum novelists of the nineties have received even less favourable treatment, and are usually dismissed by literary historians as inferior imitators of either Zola or Dickens, according to the historian's point of view.

This prejudice in favour of the industrial novel is particularly surprising because not only were there far more novels written during the Victorian period which deal with the urban rather than the industrial working class, but in qualitative terms there is little to choose between the two. The industrial novels have retained a lasting interest largely because of their unusual subject matter, but hitherto the same critical allowance has not been given to the urban novel. Yet the fiction produced by writers such as Augustus Mayhew, Gissing, Kipling, Arthur Morrison, Henry Nevinson or Somerset Maugham is as successful as anything in the industrial tradition with the possible exception of *Hard Times*, the first half of *Mary Barton* and *North and South*. And if this fiction is considered for its presentation of the working classes then *Hard Times* also disappears and we are left with Mrs Gaskell as the sole representative. One major reason for this discrimination is the difficulty of defining what exactly is meant by the two words 'working' and 'class'. This can be clarified by examining how the meanings differ when applied to two separate literary traditions – the industrial and the urban.

To talk of the industrial tradition is to mean a handful of novels written primarily in the fourth and fifth decades of the nineteenth century. The earliest is Harriet Martineau's *A Manchester Strike* (1832). This is followed by Mrs Trollope's *Michael Armstrong* (1839-40); *Helen Fleetwood* (1839-40) by 'Charlotte Elizabeth' [Mrs Tonna]; Disraeli's *Coningsby* (1844) and *Sybil* (1845); Mrs

Gaskell's *Mary Barton* (1848) and *North and South* (1855); and Dickens's *Hard Times* (1854). There the tradition virtually ends until the twentieth century. As has already been suggested, interest in industrialism as a subject for fiction was closely related to the rise and decline of Chartism, and once public concern with this particular form of conflict abated so did the novelist's ready-made frame of reference. In the 1860s and 70s the old framework was no longer valid, and novelists, lacking the kind of personal involvement that might have led them to write naturally of working-class life, simply waited until a new social framework was created for them. Then there was a resurgence of working-class fiction.

Of later industrial novels there is George Eliot's *Felix Holt* (1866), the only important novel written in response to the agitation for working-class enfranchisement in the sixties, and more concerned with this than industrialism; Charles Reade's attack on Trade Union villainy, *Put Yourself in His Place* (1870); Gissing's *Demos* (1886), in which the workers are urban rather than industrial; and William Morris's dream utopia *News From Nowhere* (1891), in which no recognizably real worker of any kind appears. The only late-Victorian industrial novel which deserves a place beside those of Mrs Gaskell and Disraeli is W. E. Tirebuck's now totally forgotten *Miss Grace of All Souls* (1895), certain passages of which Tolstoy was reported to have described as among 'the best examples of modern English fiction'.[7]

There is no difficulty about defining the worker in these novels. He is part of a composite portrait called Labour and is shown to be in bitter conflict with a further composite portrait called Capital. The Oxford English Dictionary gives as a definition of 'working class': 'The grade or grades of society comprising those who are employed to work for wages in manual or industrial occupations'; and defines 'class' as: 'A number of individuals . . . possessing common attributes, and grouped together under a general or "class" name.' The industrial worker fits perfectly into both of these definitions. In each novel the workers share in common skills, occupations, wage levels, and most important of all, interests and attitudes. Each worker is part of the same instantly recognizable whole. This is not to say that all workers are presented as identical or interchangeable types. Indeed, it is a constant preoccupation of the industrial novelist to show that within the working-class world there exist social hierarchies almost as rigid as those

B

in society as a whole. In *Mary Barton*, for instance, Job Legh, John
Barton, Jem Wilson and Davenport are completely unlike each
other so far as intelligence, wage-earning capacity, occupational
skill and moral strength are concerned, but they all appreciate
that these distinctions are nothing compared with the class attitudes that bind them together. In the industrial novel the
difference between a respectable artisan and the poor is decided
by such factors as unemployment, the relative size of the family
to be supported or personal character weakness. However high
one may rise, or however low another may fall, each recognizes
the possibility of himself in the other. They do not represent two
separate worlds.

This sense of class oneness is conveyed more than anything
else by the stark hostility of the industrial-town landscape (varied
only by areas of appalling slums), and by the uniform tone of
seriousness adopted by the novelists. Just as the novels were
written because of a social problem, so are the characters treated
with a moral intensity that is always directed towards heightening
the tragedy of the working-class situation. Where there are efforts
to present a more inclusive view of working-class life, these take
the form of lingering remnants of an older, more communally
centred, rural culture which is rapidly being subverted by the mass
regimentation of industrialism. Families are still shown helping
each other in moments of distress; they may join together for
conversation or supper; they may even be entertained by a song
or have a drink in the pub, but the most striking thing about such
gatherings is the atmosphere of solemnity that prevails.[8] Rarely
do these characters exhibit any feeling of spontaneous joy or
happiness. Nobody in an industrial novel laughs, makes jokes or
dances, and nowhere is this negative characteristic more apparent
than in Dickens. The difference in treatment can be clearly seen
by comparing the presentation of Rachael, in *Hard Times*, with a
woman who is her almost exact urban working-class equivalent,
Mrs Plornish in *Little Dorrit*. In financial terms Rachael is probably better off than Mrs Plornish and the social positions they
occupy in their respective communities are about the same, but
it would be impossible to imagine Rachael, or indeed any industrial worker, being given the speech patterns and personal idiosyncrasies that belong to Mrs Plornish. These qualities are allotted
by the novelist, and to be seen to manipulate such a serious subject

as an industrial worker in order to make the reader laugh would
have been considered an act of bad faith, or even taste. This is
partly due to the acute awareness in both author and reader of
social crisis, but also, and more fundamentally, to the entirely
different kinds of convention and attitude that governed the literary
treatment of the industrial and urban workers.

In real life the industrial labourer was the product of a new
kind of environment. No one really comparable with him had
existed before, and in writing about him novelists had no literary
tradition to draw on. The urban working class, on the other hand,
was the product of a radically changed environment, and, in however altered a form, had played a variety of parts in centuries of
English literature. Unlike their industrial counterparts, the late-
Victorian urban novelists can be seen in relation to several lines
of tradition. Apart from the debate on French naturalism, in
which they found themselves often unwillingly involved, they
could look back to the attempts of earlier-Victorian writers,
dominated by Dickens, to present the working classes in fiction,
and beyond, to an age-old tradition of London low-life scenes in
English literature. In literary forms as diverse as the picaresque
novel, the literature of roguery, criminal biography, eighteenth-
century poetry and drama, Elizabethan and Jacobean drama, and
in the early fiction of writers such as Deloney and Nashe, there
can be found many scenes in which lower-class town 'types' or
'characters' play parts of varying extent and importance. It is
mainly the darker sides of town life that are examined – the tavern,
brothel, criminal conclave, or the smart urban confidence trickster
fleecing the innocent country bumpkin – but neither the poor nor
the more respectable members of the lower classes are ignored.[9]

What has always fascinated the writer on London low life is the
existence within the same basic environment of widely disparate
social groups and individuals, seemingly independent of each
other and yet, when compared with the middle and upper classes,
seen to be bound together by their relative poverty. On 12 April
1783, Boswell records that Dr Johnson 'talked to-day a good deal
of the wonderful extent and variety of London, and observed, that
men of curious enquiry might see in it such modes of life as very
few could even imagine. He in particular recommended us to
explore Wapping, which we resolved to do'. Nine years later Boswell carried out this resolution but 'whether from that uniformity

which has in modern times, in a great degree, spread through
every part of the metropolis, or from our want of sufficient
exertion, we were disappointed'.[10] Save for the absence of class
terminology this exchange might well have been made exactly a
century later. The different responses of the sympathetic and the
sensation-seeking slummer is a very common late-Victorian
experience, but it is by no means peculiar to that period, nor
indeed to post-Industrial Revolution society. Both before and
after Johnson, 'men of curious enquiry' writing about London have
always noted the existence of 'such modes of life as very few could
even imagine'.

This point is of some importance when we consider the presentation of the urban working classes in fiction. In historical terms
the nineteenth century is cut off from earlier centuries by the
whole complex of social changes connected with the Industrial
Revolution – unprecedented urban development, the gradual
transformation of the English economy from a rural to an industrial base, the breakdown of old types of relationship between
employer and employee, and the rise of organized working-class
politics. The class terminology we use today is a product of those
changes:

> There was no dearth of social conflicts in pre-industrial
> society, but they were not conceived of at the time in straight
> class terms. The change in nomenclature in the late eighteenth
> and early nineteenth centuries reflected a basic change not
> only in men's ways of viewing society but in society itself.[11]

In the eighteenth century the words used to describe social divisions were 'rank', 'order', 'state', 'station' or 'degree'; and when
referring to specific economic groups, 'interests'. The lower classes
in this sense did not constitute an 'interest' but existed as separate,
occupational groups, largely isolated from each other, both
ideologically and geographically. As Diana Spearman has pointed
out: 'There is no evidence that these groups considered themselves
to belong to one class; indeed it is most unlikely that they did, for
there was nothing to unite them: their interests were not identical
and there was no theory to persuade them they were.'[12] The term
'working class' (as distinct from 'lower class' which had existed
earlier) seems first to have appeared around 1815, and by 1824 the
word 'class' was firmly established as a social label.[13]

The sense of social turmoil indicated by the changing nature of class terminology is most clearly seen in the vast growth of cities during the nineteenth century. In 1800 there was no town outside of London with a population of 100,000; by 1891 there were twenty-three. During the century the populations of towns such as Liverpool, Birmingham, Manchester and Sheffield multiplied tenfold. London increased phenomenally from under 1 m. in 1801 to $4\frac{1}{2}$ m. a century later, when it contained approximately 14 per cent of England's population. By 1891 almost a third of the total population lived either in London or in cities containing more than 100,000 inhabitants.[14]

The great changes in the basic structure of working-class life brought about by the twin forces of urbanization and industrialism are reflected in entirely different ways in the two literary traditions. While the industrial novel adopts the idea of town life as comprising two large, economically interdependent, conflicting class groups, the urban novel stresses more than ever before the variety and mystery of the London streets. It highlights individual types, especially the bizarre and grotesque, and concentrates on what distinguishes lower-class groups from each other rather than what unifies them, on the idea of contrast rather than conflict.

The most important pre-nineteenth-century influence on the urban novelists is Hogarth. Keith Hollingsworth, referring to the 'Newgate' novel, has noted that 'in the twenties and thirties one finds his name constantly',[15] and the same is true of the Victorian age as a whole. The two most significant urban working-class novelists, Dickens and Gissing, both greatly admired Hogarth. In the 1841 Preface to *Oliver Twist*, Dickens allowed Hogarth to be his only predecessor in treating of the 'miserable reality' of lower-class criminal life; and in a remarkable conversation preserved by Forster, Dickens speaks at some length about Hogarth's work.[16] One of the details Dickens noted with special interest was the way Hogarth created slum environments which seemed as much alive as their wretched inhabitants, a technique Dickens himself was to use with wonderful effect. Just as Dickens looked back to Hogarth in order to find a parallel with his own 'realism', so Gissing, drawing comparisons from a time which gave a more specific definition to the term, stated his preference for the painter above the novelist because Hogarth 'gives us life – and we cannot bear it'. As a child Gissing had spent many hours poring over a book of Hogarth's plates, and in his first novel, when Mr Tollady takes Arthur Golding on a tour of the slums, he advises the painter to 'be a successor of Hogarth, and give us the true image of *our* social dress'.[17]

Yet even these acknowledgments give little indication of the extent of Hogarth's influence on Victorian literature. It is essential to distinguish between two aspects of his low-life scenes. First, the detailed portrayal of the suffering poor in urban slum environments, and secondly, the strong element of caricature he employs to heighten the meaning of his social message. The bodies of Hogarth's characters are bent and twisted, their faces distorted and grotesque. In the midst of appalling poverty there is a milling vigour, a sense of continual movement and life, however debased. Hogarth aimed to evoke sympathy by means of repulsion, a technique diametrically opposed to that of the industrial novelists who tried to evoke sympathy through pity.

Ready to learn from Hogarth were the great English engraver-caricaturists of the late-eighteenth and early-nineteenth centuries. In the work of Gillray, Rowlandson and the two Cruikshanks, Hogarth's detailed environments receive less attention and his sense of caricature more. The low-life figures swell to gigantic proportions filling the whole canvas; the obscenely bloated bodies with their bumpy, deformed heads, rubbery lips and protruding teeth, eclipse both metaphorically and literally the environments they inhabit. Furthermore, with Hogarth it was the narrative content of his paintings that eighteenth- and nineteenth-century novelists found so attractive; the paintings existed as works of fiction in their own right. The later caricaturists, however, concentrated on coloured prints rather than paintings and became increasingly involved in book illustration, using their talents to interpret someone else's words. In the literature of sport and travel that was so popular for the first forty years of the nineteenth century, the caricaturists combined with writers to produce imaginative guides to English country and town life. The various partnerships that were established proved unequal to say the least: the writers being, in the main, little better than hacks and the illustrators men of genius. In works such as the *Dr. Syntax* tours and *The Microcosm of London* (1808) the drawings completely dominate the written commentary; while Rowlandson's superb 'Characteristic Sketches of the Lower Orders', originally commissioned to accompany *The New Picture of London* (1820), take on a life of their own. Here the characters and types have little to do with changing social conditions. They are timeless street figures, selling their wares, berating passers-by, or scrounging a tip: in artistic terms they are a mixture of Hogarth's debased urban creatures and the traditional cartoon portrait of Hodge. Yet their power is undeniable. The distorted bodies coloured in pastel shades create at one and the same time a sense of suppressed humanity and colourful, vigorous life.

The imbalance between illustration and text was only corrected with the appearance of Pierce Egan, Surtees and Dickens, who rejected the feeble travelogue style in favour of an imaginative, humorous treatment of the traditional subjects. Like their illustrators, Egan, Surtees and Dickens possessed a taste for the farcical incident, mysterious urban character, and contrasting modes of London life, and it was these qualities they passed on to their successors throughout the middle years of the century. Dickens, of course, immediately surpassed the humble efforts of Egan and Surtees, and proceeded to develop themes and techniques which the lesser writers could hardly have imagined, but when considering his presentation of working-class characters it is always important to remember the literary tradition to which *Sketches by Boz* and *The Pickwick Papers* belong.

The archetypal urban novel of the early-nineteenth century is Pierce Egan's *Life in London* (1821). This novel, which John Camden Hotten called 'the most popular work in British literature',[18] is a hymn of praise to the variety of life to be found in London, or as Egan himself describes it, 'a Camera Obscura View of the Metropolis':[19]

> POUSSIN never had a more luxuriant, variegated, and interesting subject for a landscape; nor had SIR JOSHUA REYNOLDS finer characters for his canvas than what have already had a sitting for their likeness to embellish LIFE IN LONDON.[20]

As befits its subject matter it is an extravagant and uneven work that moves swiftly from high to low society, from East to West London, from one social oddity to another. The simple narrative is interspersed with songs and ditties, poetic invocations and extensive footnotes, all directed to prove one single thought:

LONDON! thou comprehensive word,
What joy thy streets and squares afford!
And think not thy admirer rallies
If he should add your *lanes* and *alleys*.[21]

What fascinates the Corinthians on their rambles through the
metropolis is the omnipresent urban culture. The traditional
literary use of a journey (as used, for instance, by Fielding and
Smollett), was to introduce various aspects of society by moving
from town to town, or more customarily from country to town,
thus contrasting rural and urban ways of life. In Egan the visitor
from the country provides a starting point but no more, for life
in London is all life, everywhere and of every kind. The diversity
of manners, morals, colourful slang, speech patterns, and human
types is to be found, Egan frequently stresses, in nowhere but
London. If, however, the Corinthians are bewildered by the infinite
variety of London life, they are quite sure where *real* life is to be
found:

'Yes my dear Coz. It is a motley group,' replied Tom; 'but it
is a view of real life; and it is from such meetings as these,
not withstanding they are termed very *low*, that you have a
fine opportunity of witnessing the difference of the human
character. In the circles of fashion you will scarcely meet with
any contrast whatever.'[22]

This is after they have been to watch a pit-fight between a monkey
and a dog, and it takes several other encounters with lower-class
London ('Chaffing Peter' the dustman, a costermonger and his
donkey, a visit to the docks, a dance with the prostitutes and
sailors in a 'sluicery', and an initiation into the methods of the
'Cadgers' in the 'back slums of the Holy Land'), before the class
moral of the metropolitan rambles is stated: "It is," said LOGIC
to TOM, "I am quite satisfied in my mind, the LOWER ORDERS
of society who really ENJOY themselves."[23] This sense of enjoyment is graphically conveyed by the Cruikshanks' illustrations.
While the slim, elegantly tailored figures of Tom and Jerry stroll
through London, they are surrounded by leering, cavorting lower-
class characters dressed in picturesque rags.

Life in London represents a real starting point in the history
of the urban novel. Egan looks back to the London low-life

tradition and forward to the 'Newgate' novel, Mayhew's extensive gallery of street types, and also to Dickens's equally varied gallery of eccentric characters who, while they may be classified under the general heading 'lower class', often possess vague, undifferentiated social backgrounds. Yet if Egan does concentrate on the picturesque elements of lower-class life, there is to be found in his novel an awareness of poverty (which for Egan is no problem), and a line of distinction drawn between those who work for their living and those who beg or thieve. Most important of all, *Life in London* is the first novel in which we find directly stated the division of the London classes into two topographical blocks, with the lower classes living in the East and the upper classes in the West. Much later in the century it was the general realization of this fact which was to provide the urban equivalent of the industrial novel's Labour and Capital conflict. Egan still presents this contrast in picturesque terms (Almacks and ALL-MAX, 'the COVES in the *East* – and the SWELLS at the *West*'), but the class potential is strongly there.

Where the novelists who succeed Egan differ from him is in their return to an Hogarthian slum environment peopled mainly by the suffering poor; though an environment rendered more horrific and brought up to date by Carlyle's penetrating vision of the signs of the times, and humanized by Dickens. Egan's city had been constructed on a simple linear principle which allowed him to focus attention on Tom and Jerry moving leisurely from sight to sight. For both Carlyle and Dickens the city is organic, a total world of contrasting yet interdependent parts. This much their interpretations share, but differ entirely in mood and tone. Carlyle's city is symptomatic of a social malaise, a 'wasp-nest or bee-hive', in which all is confusion and turmoil, with human activity a revolting compound of 'wax-laying and honey-making, and poison-brewing and choking by sulphur'. Diogenes Teufels-dröckh has no need or desire to ramble through Weissnichtwo: he can sit at his attic window and from there 'see the whole life-circulation of that considerable City'. By removing, as it were, a communal roof, he can reveal the myriad, teeming, ironically independent cells of the modern city organism:

Upwards of five-hundred-thousand two-legged animals without feathers lie around us, in horizontal positions; their heads all in nightcaps, and full of the foolishest dreams. Riot cries aloud, and staggers and swaggers in his rank dens of shame; and the Mother, with streaming hair, kneels over her pallid dying infant, whose cracked lips only her tears now moisten. All these heaped and huddled together, with nothing but a little carpentry and masonry between them; – crammed in, like salted fish in their barrel.[24]

This does not describe the city of Dickens's early sketches and novels. Like Egan he was concerned primarily with London, and like Carlyle he was fascinated by the turmoil and confusion of modern city life, but he transcended both Egan's view of London as a playground for the upper classes and Carlyle's tone of personal disgust. London is defined, almost exclusively, in terms of its streets, the veins of the city organism. It is not simply that many of the most memorable characters in *Sketches by Boz*, *Pickwick Papers* and *Oliver Twist* literally 'belong' to the streets, though contemporary reviews abounded with praise and criticism of Dickens for revealing so much of this side of London life. It is rather that street life is realized so vividly – its variety, activity and manners made so central to Dickens's view of society – that everything else seems pallid in comparison. Even the respectable middle-class characters are continually drawn to the streets; their homes are merely temporary stopping places or final havens of rest in which no one can really believe. The moral worth of such characters is determined by the amount of sympathy they are capable of feeling for those worse off than themselves; though they must also be willing to prove the genuineness of their feelings, for sympathy expressed but not acted upon Dickens always inter- prets as hypocrisy. The streets of London become their proving- ground where they make contact with other classes and act out their concern in the public gaze. Tom and Jerry's leisurely stroll gives way to a mood of urgency and rush. One contemporary reviewer wrote:

Reading Boz's Sketches is like rattling through the streets of London in a cab: the prominent features of the town strike upon the eye in rapid succession, new objects perpetually effacing the impression of the last; all is bustle and movement, till the jerk of the stoppage announces that the 'fare' or the 'sketch' is ended.[25]

This captures very well the external nature of Dickens's London, though it neglects his special power of investing the ordinary and the mundane with an air of mystery and strangeness; employing the London streets to reveal a life with which everyone was familiar but which no one actually knew. Gissing fully appreciated this aspect of Dickens's early work: 'Never had been known,' he wrote of *Sketches by Boz*, 'such absorbing interest in the commonplace.'[26]

The enormous impact of Dickens largely accounts for the predominance of London in Victorian working-class fiction. Apart from Manchester (briefly in the late forties), and until the emergence of the East End in the 1880s, no other city established a distinctive enough image in fiction to challenge London's supremacy. But Dickens's influence extends far beyond this. He determines the very tone of the urban novel, and his influence on the presentation of working-class characters in fiction is felt even today, though it is difficult to see precisely why this should be so. Gissing decided that Dickens 'treats at once of the lower middle class, where he will be always at his best; with the class below it, with those who literally earn bread in the sweat of their brows, he was better acquainted than any other novelist of his time, but they figure much less prominently in his books.'[27] This observation is perfectly just. Excepting the shadowy Daniel Doyce, the intellectual working man and the superior artisan are entirely absent from his novels, and even if we place the widest interpretation on the 'respectable' working class the only representatives are the Plornishes, Toodles, Mrs Nubbles and Betty Higden. One group sharing many qualities in common can be defined as criminal or debased working class (Bill Sikes, the Artful Dodger, Nancy, Rogue Riderhood, Gaffer Hexam, Mrs Brown and Magwitch), but characters such as Mrs Gamp, Sam Weller, Silas Wegg, Venus, Bailey Junior, the 'Marchioness', Boffin, Rob the Grinder and Deputy, are almost impossible to define in meaningful class terms. Some of these can be described as working class on the strength of their occupations or slum backgrounds, but they are no more offered as working-class representatives than the criminals. On the other hand, the Toodles, Plornishes, Betty Higden and Jo, do play class roles in their respective novels, as do Stephen Blackpool and Rachael in *Hard Times*. The greater proportion of Dickens's lower-class characters belong to the Hogarth-Rowlandson-Egan line of tradition. Together with an even more extensive gallery of characters who can be classified rather uneasily as 'lower middle class', they are products of the labyrinthine streets of the modern city. They differ from the lower-class characters of Rowlandson and Egan because of Dickens's Carlylean awareness of rapidly changing social conditions, but the difference is still a matter of degree rather than kind; an impression which gains strength when we consider the great care Dickens took to pick the right illustrators for his novels. The best of these, Cruikshank and Phiz, possessed a sense of caricature that descended straight from Hogarth.

If, however, Dickens rarely deals extensively with the poor or working classes, an overwhelming sense of their existence is never absent for long. Even at moments when the novel is not dealing with a lower-class theme we are suddenly made aware of a horrifying backcloth of rickety houses, crowded alleys and filthy humanity-packed courts. No opportunity is missed to address the reader on the state of the poor; no effete aristocrat or pompous merchant is presented without a lower-class comparison being implied; no genuine social grievance is allowed to pass without Dickens championing its reform. Most prevalent of all is his loathing of all kinds of oppression or suffering. A vast number of minor characters are orphans or former workhouse inmates who appear briefly and then pass out of the novel, leaving behind them only the information that they were orphans or workhouse inmates and that their lives can never be clean because of it. The blackest mark against Bounderby is his imagined slum childhood, romantically embellished and employed to give himself strength of character. Dickens's own view of the effects of such a childhood is non-Smilesian and environmentalist. Magwitch, Bradley Headstone, even Uriah Heep can evoke sympathy when they talk of their past lives:

Father and me was both brought up at a foundation school for boys; and mother, she was likewise brought up at a public, sort of charitable, establishment. They taught us all a deal of umbleness – not much else that I know of, from morning to night. We was to be umble to this person and umble to that; and to pull off our caps here, and to make bows there; and always to know our place, and abase ourselves before our betters. And we had such a lot of betters![28]

This sense of oppression, helplessness, suffering or unhappiness, permeates Dickens's novels, and not merely the working-class sections of them. The presentation of characters such as Florence Dombey, Caddy Jellyby, Little Dorrit, Little Nell, Tom Pinch, or Smike, plays a large part in making it seem as though Dickens's novels are concerned almost exclusively with the working classes.

More directly, Dickens reinforces this generalized humanitarian concern with a series of superb class confrontations in which representatives of the wealthy or oppressing classes are defeated by representatives of the poor or oppressed. In the early, exuberant *Pickwick Papers*, Sam Weller's victory over Serjeant Buzfuz is straightforward; the result of verbal dexterity and greater knowledge of life. But in the confrontations between Mr Dombey and Toodle or Captain Cuttle; Bounderby and Stephen; Mr Dorrit and John Chivery; Joe Gargery and Miss Havisham, the working-class representatives are largely inarticulate and the victory takes place only in the mind of the reader. It entails both a moral and a class judgement.

There is, of course, a further and occasionally contradictory side to Dickens's treatment of working-class life. A strong feeling for its humanity and vitality needs to be set against the suffering and oppression. A comparison of two slum descriptions, one by Charles Kingsley, the other by Dickens, can demonstrate this most clearly. Here, Sandy Mackaye takes the young, idealistic poet, Alton Locke, on a sight-seeing tour of working-class London:

> It was a foul, chilly, foggy Saturday night. From the butchers' and greengrocers' shops the gaslights flared and flickered, wild and ghastly, over haggard groups of slip-shod dirty women, bargaining for scraps of stale meat and frost-bitten vegetables, wrangling about short weight and bad quality. Fish-stalls and fruit-stalls lined the edge of the greasy pavement, sending up odours as foul as the language of sellers and buyers. Blood and sewer-water crawled from under doors and out of spouts, and reeked down the gutters among offal, animal and vegetable, in every stage of putrefaction. Foul vapours rose from cow-sheds and slaughter-houses, and the doorways of undrained alleys, where the inhabitants carried the filth out on their shoes from the backyard into the

court; and from the court up into the main street; while
above, hanging like cliffs over the streets – those narrow,
brawling torrents of filth, and poverty, and sin, – the houses
with their teeming load of life were piled up into the dingy,
choking night. A ghastly, deafening, sickening sight it was.
Go, scented Belgravian! and see what London is![29]

Kingsley's sole intention is to describe to the reader the horrors
of working-class life; to recreate the feeling of repulsion experienced by himself. Even allowing for our knowledge (drawn from
other sources) that conditions in St Giles's were appalling, it is
notable that Kingsley has deliberately chosen what would normally be a fairly gay scene – a street market at its busiest moment,
Saturday evening – and that he makes no attempt whatsoever to
present it from a working-class viewpoint. The gaslights are
'wild and ghastly', the shoppers are 'haggard groups of slip-shod
dirty women', and odours from the food stalls are 'foul'; the
food is all adulterated and everyone is swearing. The roads are
obviously never cleaned as the 'blood and sewer water' mingles
with 'offal, animal and vegetable, in every stage of putrefaction'.
The streets are 'narrow, brawling torrents of filth, and poverty,
and sin'.

There is no vitality, humour, banter or laughter, and there are
no family shopping outings. The horror belongs entirely to Kingsley. And the final sentence makes it clear that this scene has been
chosen as typical of working-class London as a whole: it is not
simply an isolated plague spot. This kind of slum description is
the most common in Victorian fiction before the eighties. They are
not incidental but hold a central place in the novels, in that they
are being used to grip the reader and stir his conscience. Almost
everything else that happens in the novel depends upon such
scenes for its validity. To show the shoppers laughing or joking,
in this example, would defeat Kingsley's main purpose in writing
the novel, as would any suggestion that the participants might
express other opinions about it than his own. There is nothing
indeed to be said in its favour. It is all foul and should be swept
away by progressive legislation, and meanwhile if we wish to
praise a working man, we can do so by showing him as someone
fit for middle- and upper-class society; someone who has no kin-
ship with the 'slip-shod dirty women' of St Giles's.

It is not difficult to find similar scenes in Dickens, though his awareness of their potency as class propaganda is much sharper than Kingsley's, and his sense of subtlety in discriminating between different kinds of working-class environment is infinitely greater. One technique peculiar to Dickens is to give a minimum of physical description, and instead merely suggest a slum environment by suddenly bringing before the reader a tumbling mass of inhabitants who are by no means squalid or lacking in humour. This example is from *Bleak House*; it follows on the discovery of Nemo's dead body:

> By this time the news has got into the court. Groups of its inhabitants assemble to discuss the thing, and the outposts of the army of observation (principally boys) are pushed forward to Mr. Krook's window, which they closely invest. A policeman has already walked up to the room, and walked down again to the door, where he stands like a tower, only condescending to see the boys at his base occasionally; but whenever he does see them, they quail and fall back. Mrs. Perkins, who has not been for some weeks on speaking terms with Mrs. Piper in consequence for an unpleasantness originating in young Perkins' having 'fetched' young Piper 'a crack,' renews her friendly intercourse on this auspicious occasion. The potboy at the corner, who is a privileged amateur, as possessing official knowledge of life and having to deal with drunken men occasionally, exchanges confidential communications with the policeman and has the appearance of an impregnable youth, unassailable by truncheons and unconfinable in station-houses. People talk across the court out of the window, and bare-headed scouts come hurrying in from Chancery Lane to know what's the matter. The general feeling seems to be that it's a blessing Mr. Krook warn't made away with first, mingled with a little natural disappointment that he was not. In the midst of this sensation, the beadle arrives.[30]

What is so striking about this passage is not that the working-class participants have become human beings – on the contrary, they still possess the two-dimensional qualities of cartoon figures – but that the slum itself has been humanized. It has not corrupted, deformed, degraded or in any significant way imposed itself upon the inhabitants; rather, this normal process has been reversed, and the vitality and vigour of the inhabitants have been used to create and define their environment. /Variations of this technique are used to present some of Dickens's most memorable working-class settings – Bleeding Heart Yard, Mrs Gamp's Holborn and Staggs's Gardens. Where we do get physical descriptions of slums they are often of the 'filth, putrefaction and poverty' variety (in *Bleak House* alone there are Tom-All-Alone's and the brickmaker's house to set against and contrast with the above scene), but unlike Kingsley, Dickens refused to believe that this represented the whole of working-class life. /

Indeed, it is more common to find criticisms of Dickens for painting working-class life in too glowing terms, than of Kingsley for painting it too bleakly. For just as Hogarth painted a 'Beer Street' to complement his 'Gin Lane', so Dickens, especially in his early novels, emphasized certain moral positives in working-class life which he shows as flourishing in even the foulest rookery. Today little attention is paid to this side of his work, but in the late-nineteenth century it was often considered the most charac-teristic and successful feature. The famous *philosophie de Noël* scenes usually involve the middle classes, but many of the qualities that characterize the Christmas attitude are permanently embedded in Dickens's respectable working men and women. All of the characters who can be classified in this way, and most of the suffering poor as well, are strongly endowed with honesty, moral strength and good-neighbourliness – virtues which are usually rewarded by individual philanthropy. And if death comes before earthly reward is possible, then there is the consolation that 'hearts may count in heaven as high as heads'.[31] So firm is Dickens's conviction that the poor are distinguished from other classes by their kindness to each other, that, in *David Copperfield*, as first Emily and then Mr Peggotty wander throughout Europe, there emerges a sense of this quality as providing the foundation stone for an International Brotherhood of the Poor.[32] Even in a novel as late as *Great Expectations* when Dickens's view of society had changed considerably, it is Joe Gargery and Biddy who represent the most pure moral values to be found in the book. And in his next, far more ambiguous novel, *Our Mutual Friend*, many of the same qualities are given, without qualification, to Betty Higden. This image of the 'good' working man, as a model either to copy or react against, was to prove Dickens's most influential legacy to late-Victorian working-class fiction.

Apart from Dickens, interest in street types and the suffering poor as the two representative aspects of urban working-class life was further kept alive during the mid-Victorian period by *Punch*, the vaguely reformist tone of which achieved its strongest expression in the drawings of John Leech: 'A Court for King Cholera' (1849) and 'St. James turning St. Giles out of his Parks' (1850). While Leech spoke for the poor, the cartoons of Charles Keene served to foster the idea of the urban workers as being individuals rather than a class. His drunken cabbies, street urchins and housemaids with their pert charm and ever-ready wit, did much to establish the image of the cheerful cockney. Keene's cockney characters look back to Sam Weller and forward to Phil May and E. J. Milliken's 'Arry – a line of tradition which attains some importance in the eighties and nineties. In addition to these pictorial images of the working classes made popular by *Punch*, mention should also be made of a similar kind of subject matter employed by mid-Victorian narrative painters. The idealized view of the working classes held by the Pre-Raphaelites is epitomized, at least in its non-medieval aspect, by Ford Madox Brown's 'Work' (1865), which glorifies working-class muscle in a manner that anticipates Socialist-Realism. More typical of Victorian genre painting are Frith's panoramic views of English society: 'Ramsgate Sands' (1851), 'Derby Day' (1858) and 'The Railway Station' (1862). Other similar paintings are Erskine Nicol's 'Waiting for the Train' (1864), George Elgar Hicks's 'Billingsgate' (1861) and Arthur Boyd Houghton's 'Holborn in 1861'. Like the mid-Victorian working-class novelists, these painters were fascinated by the interrelationship of different classes in English society, but by the time we come to Sir Luke Fildes's 'Applicants for Admission to a Casual Ward' (1874), the social compromise has fallen apart, the poor are now a separate group, isolated and outcast, and we move from Dickens's to Gissing's world.

As we have seen, it is extremely rare to find in early- or mid-Victorian literature a sense of the urban working classes as comprising people who 'work' or wish to work, or who, taken collectively, constitute a social class. The whole sweep of the urban tradition had acted against the establishment of a class image of the kind found in the industrial novel. The vastness of London; the many

different grades of wealth and poverty to be found in close
proximity, and the tradition of presenting colourful street types
in sharp pictorial outline, or as literary props for romantic low-life
scenes, all tended to encourage an awareness of what diversified
the urban workers rather than what united them. Yet if we place
together the inhabitants of Egan's 'back slums', Mayhew's street
tradesmen and characters, Dickens's seething slum populations
and Kingsley's craftsmen, then it is possible to reach a viable, if
necessarily broad, definition of the urban working class. But first,
in order to summarize the argument so far, as well as to make it
more inclusive, it is worth attempting a classification of the different
types of working-class novel written before 1880, and then a
further classification of the different kinds of working-class
characters who appear in them.

III

It is possible to distinguish between five distinct types of novel in
which the working classes play more than a fleeting part:

1 The novel dealing with a cross section of English society in
which the working classes appear as just one part of a total social
pattern. The 'ramble through the metropolis' is the most traditional formula. In its nineteenth-century form this is established
by Egan's *Life in London,* and Dickens's early novels belong to the
same tradition; his later novels represent a more profound treatment of the same formula.
2 The romance. This differs from type 1 in that working-class life
is presented as ugly and debased, and serves either as a starting
point for the working out of a tortuous, often criminal, plot, or for
the rise from rags to riches of a low-born, or supposedly low-born,
hero. Once this purpose has been served the working-class theme
is gradually faded out. The class structure of the romance is
usually based on a direct relationship between the very rich or
aristocracy and the poor. Apart from an occasional, sentimentally
presented exemplary working man, the poor are shown to be
morally and physically inferior to other classes, their way of life
something to escape from as soon as possible. Examples in the
'Newgate' tradition are: Bulwer Lytton's *Paul Clifford* (1830),

Harrison Ainsworth's *Jack Sheppard* (1839), Renton Nicholson's *Dombey and Daughter* (1850) and Douglas Jerrold's *St. Giles and St. James* (1851). Examples in the 'rags to riches' tradition: Maria Cummins's *The Lamplighter* (1854), F. W. Robinson's *Owen: A Waif* (1862) and *Mattie: A Stray* (1864).

3 The non-romantic novel of working-class life set entirely in a working-class environment. This type of novel hardly exists before the eighties, though it becomes much more common later. The earlier-Victorian equivalent is the novel of street life which is influenced by Dickens and Mayhew, and bound together with a dash of Newgate crime. While the plot is largely romantic there is a considerable feel for the complex structure of working-class life, and much detailed sociological observation. Good examples are: Augustus Mayhew's *Kitty Lamere* (1855) and *Paved with Gold* (1858); James Greenwood's *The True History of a Little Raga-muffin* (1866); Thomas Wright's *Johnny Robinson* (1868) and *The Bane of a Life* (1870).

4 The 'Condition of the People' novel. Social propaganda directed at a non-working-class audience with the intention of transforming middle- or upper-class attitudes. The working-class scenes are in the main realistic, though heavily weighted towards the more poverty-stricken aspects of industrial and urban life. As we have seen, the industrial novels come under this heading, as does *Alton Locke*. Other similar novels in the urban tradition are: William Gilbert's *Dives and Lazarus* (1858), a semi-fictional account of a slum doctor's experiences which contains slum descriptions of the Kingsley variety, and which is virtually unique in describing the work of the Medical Inspectors of Health; and J. E. Jenkins's *Ginx's Baby* (1870), a bitter satire on the workings of mid-Victorian philanthropy.

5 Novels directed at a working-class reading public with the intention of transforming manners or habits. These are mainly brief, exhortatory homilies published in great numbers by religious and Temperance Tract societies. They possess little literary interest, and here only temperance reform fiction will be discussed. Probably the most influential writer of temperance fiction was Mrs Clara L. Balfour, and two tracts by her, *Scrub: or the Work-house Boy's First Start in Life* (1860), and *Toil and Trust: or The Life Story of Patty the Workhouse Girl* (1860), are characteristic of the genre. The full-length temperance novel was not directed

exclusively, or perhaps even mainly, at the working classes, but was used to urge the middle and upper classes to change their intemperate ways and help reform the workers. A good example of a full-length temperance novel, middle class in setting but containing working-class scenes, is Mrs Henry Wood's *Danesbury House* (1860). The differences between fiction of this kind aimed at working- and non-working-class reading publics, were less a matter of content and style than of publishing price and format.

In these five types of novel we can distinguish between six kinds of working-class character:

1   Respectable. He is usually a skilled artisan who is shown to be devoted to his family, or, if unmarried, to his neighbours' welfare. He represents the highest social rank in working-class fiction, though very rarely does he quite correspond to the 'aristocrat of labour' or the 'educated working man' as described by Thomas Wright in his fascinating studies of the mid-Victorian urban working classes. In temperance fiction he is used as an idealized contrast to the drunkard; in the 'Condition of the People' novels he acts as a stabilizing force between revolutionary sentiment and middle-class orthodoxy, unless morally corrupted by unemployment or victimization. In Chartist fiction he is the idealized hope of revolutionaries. In romances he is the recipient of upper- or middle-class philanthropy which enables him to escape from his own class background.

2   Intellectual. The kind of working man who plays such a prominent part in histories of working-class movements, sociological studies of the reading public, or who presents himself in memoirs, is almost totally absent from pre-1880 fiction. The only two figures who can be called working-class intellectuals are Felix Holt and Alton Locke. Felix Holt is an interesting example as his personal attitudes (especially his determination to retain his connections with the workers rather than use his education to escape from them) foreshadow those of many later heroes, especially in twentieth-century literature. But the working-class theme of the novel is explored in a very shallow manner. George Eliot's attitude is similar to the 'Condition of the People' novelists, while the tortuous plot places *Felix Holt* firmly as a working-class romance. Alton Locke retains more interest as an intellectual working man

because through him we see a side of London life which Dickens never touches. Kingsley's treatment of working-class characters is close to that of the industrial novelists (with whom he is usually categorized) in that he explores the physical and moral relationships between the respectable, politically conscious craftsmen and the debased creatures of an East End Sweater's Den and the Bermondsey slums. Crossthwaite and Jemmy Downes (like Higgins and Boucher in *North and South*) do not belong to different social groups. They epitomize contrasting degrees of moral strength in responding to what is essentially the same situation.

3 Poor. The most common type of Victorian working-class character. Unskilled, often illiterate, poor through no fault of his own, he is an object of social pity. He is usually shown to possess a high standard of morality and good-neighbourliness, and is helped over immediate material problems by individual philanthropy. He may be adopted, or have his life transformed, by wealthy patrons; but more often his death, or the death of his wife or child, is employed as a conscience-stirring moment of pathos.

4 Debased. The second most common type in pre-1880 novels. He is defined in terms of drunkenness, brutality or moral viciousness. These are really character traits and the debased working man is distinct from the criminal whose anti-social activities are to some extent rationalized. His debased qualities may sometimes be regarded as having been caused by his poverty, though more frequently he is criticized by the author for tarnishing the image of the more respectable sections of working-class life. In romances he is beyond help, a wife- and child-beater, taking their money to buy beer, and may be used as a device to drive the working-class child from home, the first step from rags to riches. He is the obvious target for temperance reformers.

5 Eccentric. He is working class by virtue of his environment, but is defined primarily in terms of personal idiosyncrasies; especially an out-of-the-way occupation, or a bizarre, humorous manner of speech.

6 Criminal. More properly termed 'low' than working class, he plays a minor role in 'Newgate' novels (the major criminals usually being upper-class changelings), and in novels of street life. The debased working man may become a criminal, by murdering his wife or child when drunk, for instance, but usually

working-class criminals belong to the literature of roguery. They are petty robbers, pick-pockets, confidence-tricksters or fences, and are often presented as corruptors of children.

IV

However disparate the various kinds and groups of urban working-class characters discussed so far appear to be, they did share a common culture. Louis James has mentioned how surprised Thackeray was to discover, through reading some fiction aimed at a working-class audience in 1838, the extent and inclusiveness of this sense of shared urban values: 'Moreover, it was not just a continuation of the old popular cultures which expressed them-selves in broadsheets, chapbooks, and popular drama – it was new, and had formed itself in the past decade. It was quite cut off from the middle and upper classes.'[33] James goes on to show that the authors and readers of this literature were very conscious of what it meant to belong to an urban working class:

> It is interesting to note how directly these periodicals were the expression of the new life of the towns. Their existence relies on interest in events and people in a particular urban society – the suffix 'in London,' 'in Liverpool,' and so on, is important. Most of these periodicals were neither scandal sheets, nor general gossip magazines drawing on the appeal of glamour in the fashion of modern 'society' columnists. They tried to reveal the organism of town life, claiming omniscience.[34]

If these workers were linked culturally by an awareness of the organism of town life, they also shared the economic insecurity inherent in servicing the consumer demands of a huge, non-industrial city. For Victorian novelists the urban working man is pre-eminently a Londoner, and the industrial worker is nearly always a northerner. London factory life is virtually ignored throughout the period, and, as has just been noted, the highly skilled, steadily employed urban artisan receives far less attention from novelists than the poor and the debased.

Gissing's workers 'who literally earn bread in the sweat of their brows', and Orwell's 'people who make the wheels go round', are obviously the same. They can be divided into two main occupation groups. First, those who follow a skilled or semi-skilled trade, or who provide a service for the benefit of the community as a whole (e.g. house painter, tailor, cab driver); and secondly, those who work at an unskilled, manual job (e.g. casual labourer, dock worker, road sweeper). To these must be added the large number of street traders in the nineteenth century (e.g. costermongers, fish sellers, flower girls, newsboys) who provided a service for both their own communities and those of the middle and upper classes. Furthermore, within a specifically working-class area the social distinction between, for instance, the small shopkeeper and his customers, is less sharp than in predominantly middle- or upper-class areas. The sense of class association resulting from this produces a separate category of people. They have been well described by Richard Hoggart: 'Some are self-employed; they may keep a small shop for members of the group to which, culturally, they belong or supply a service to the group, for example as a "cobbler," "barber," "grocer," "bike-mender," or "cast-off clothing dealer."'[35]

This point is important. For what largely determines whether or not we can call many urban characters working class depends not merely on the environment they inhabit (the sunken aristocrat living in the slums and so loved by romantic novelists is obviously not working class), nor does it necessarily depend upon how much money someone earns, for this may vary as much as their occupations. What does matter is how far that person associates himself, in terms of status, values and attitudes, with his working-class environment. Thus, depending upon their psychological or social presentation, a publican or a domestic servant may or may not be regarded as working class. Orwell's angry rejection of the 'criminal' and 'derelict' is a reaction against those writers who see such types as representative members of the working class, but he is really being over-sensitive. The criminal, derelict, fence or prostitute may, according to circumstances, be working class, just as they may, in other circumstances, be middle or upper class. In so far as it is possible to establish an upper dividing line, over which anyone who steps ceases to be regarded as working class, that line is represented by the office worker. Allowing for the obvious exceptions mentioned above, Gissing's social classification of *The Nether World* as comprising 'the two great sections of those who

do, and those who do not, wear collars',[36] will be followed throughout this book.

What needs further emphasis about these different kinds of
worker is the precariousness of their individual financial situations.
Victorian philanthropists liked to distinguish between the respectable working man and the poor, but in many cases the distinction
was more imagined than real. Mayhew subtitled his great work,
'Those that will work, those that cannot work, and those that will
not work', thus clearly drawing several important distinctions.
And his brother Augustus went to some pains to make the same
point – that there is little sense in discriminating between the
working class and the poor, for the transient nature of their
employment quite easily leads to a reversal of their positions:

> Not to speak of the really destitute and the outcast, the
> well-to-do in London are surrounded by thousands whose
> labour lasts only for the summer – such as brickmakers,
> market gardeners, harvest men, and the like; besides
> multitudes of others, such as navigators and ground
> labourers, who can ply their trade only so long as the earth
> can be made to yield to the spade and the pick; and others
> again, as the dock labourers and 'longshore men, who depend
> upon the very winds for the food and fuel of themselves and
> families.[37]

The fact that many Victorian novelists show urban working-class
characters as continually unemployed is not necessarily a bar to
calling them workers. In such uncertain economic conditions,
unemployment may be frequent and of varying duration. The
important point is that when, or if, the working man does work it
is at one of the kinds of job discussed here. His wife and children
are subject to the same qualifications. In Victorian fiction the
street urchin employing his strength or wits to earn a few coppers,
and the long-suffering wife making matchboxes at home, are very
common urban types. Almost all of the people considered here
can be described, in Gissing's words, as 'that class of city population just raised above harsh necessity'.[38]

2

New lines and continuing traditions

I

In the eighties, the two writers most associated with the novel of working-class life were Walter Besant and George Gissing. The first was immensely popular, his best-selling novels widely discussed and influential in serving the cause of philanthropic schemes, as well as encouraging the tone of a new kind of working-class romance. The other was almost entirely ignored by the general reading public, and although his novels were praised by a small group of London intellectuals, and acknowledged by Charles Booth as being especially valuable for their trustworthy picture of working-class life,[1] they appear to have had little practical or literary influence. Twentieth-century critical opinion has reversed this bias. Besant's peculiar amalgam of aristocratic slum missionaries and cheerful, misunderstood working men, eliminating class divisions in a Palace of Delight, seems for the modern reader to be totally inappropriate, and has been largely ignored by critics. On the other hand, Gissing's studies of isolated intellectuals waging uneasy war with ubiquitous social and democratic forces, have been increasingly recognized as reflecting an important stage in the development of twentieth-century literature and thought.

But if, during the eighties, Besant's work received more attention than Gissing's, the fact that the two novelists represented contrasting approaches to the same subject was not ignored. In

April 1888, *Murray's Magazine* published an article by Edith
Sichel called 'Two Philanthropic Novelists: Mr. Walter Besant
and Mr. George Gissing'. Miss Sichel argued that it was the day
of the philanthropic romance and divided adherents into two
schools with Besant representing the Optimists and Gissing the
Pessimists. In the comparisons she draws between the two Gissing
comes off the better, but he does not escape unscathed. In one
sense pessimism is more praiseworthy than optimism: 'Mr.
Gissing writes us a realistic jeremiad, whilst Mr. Besant gives us a
Bowdlerised Whitechapel – a family edition of the East-End,
which is wholesome for our hopes, but often not so true a picture
as the other.' But both pictures are unbalanced, with Gissing's
'resolute wailing' working as much against the attainment of a
total view as Besant's 'persistent glee about non-existent joys'.

These various observations are extremely sound. Gissing and
Besant, in their total dissimilar ways, were making the most
conscious attempts to write novels centred upon working-class life
since Mrs Gaskell and Kingsley. They anticipate in several
respects the slum novelists of the nineties, but their influence
upon them was indirect, and the writer who forms a link between
the two last decades of the century is not Gissing or Besant, but
Rudyard Kipling. But until the late eighties these two writers
were alone in trying to bring about new departures in working-
class fiction. Those of their contemporaries who were producing
work in the same area need to be seen in relation to several
continuing lines of tradition. Many of them had been writing
since the 1860s and in their work can be found attitudes and
techniques which recur throughout the century, and which writers
coming to prominence in the eighties and nineties either moulded
to suit the changed conditions or rebelled against. Three main
lines of tradition can be discerned, two of which have already been
mentioned briefly in the previous chapter – the literature of social
exploration; didactic literature, represented here by temperance
reform fiction; and working-class romance.

II

The image of the working-class novelist as an explorer is common
in both the industrial and urban traditions. Drawing upon the

reader's familiarity with the literature of foreign travel popular throughout the period, the novelist presents himself, or one of his central characters, as someone who undertakes a dangerous voyage of discovery into an uncharted working-class world, from which he eventually returns with a fully documented report of his adventures. As the reader is being invited to share these adventures, and to learn from them, the usual starting point is a state of ignorance about working-class life, and on its simplest level the imagery of exploration and discovery is employed ironically to rebuke the reader for his lack of knowledge or concern – while he may not be able to visit Tahiti or India, there is no good reason why he should not know what conditions are like in Manchester or Drury Lane. But rarely does this kind of imagery work in so straightforward a manner. Indeed, novelists were attracted to it largely because of its ability to evoke a variety of simultaneous, and often ambiguous, connotations. The novelist's own confession of recent ignorance, for instance, makes more dramatic the role he has played, and therefore lessens the severity of his rebuke to the reader, while at the same time it presses home the message that now an exploratory voyage has been made and the true condition of the people brought to light, such a state of affairs must not be allowed to continue. On another level it encouraged a literal rather than metaphorical interpretation. For author and reader alike, it *was* dangerous to allow the working classes to gather together in dark, little-known areas of the country and major cities: there *was* something tribal, primitive and unchristian about it. Writers were not slow to compare the moral fervour aroused by campaigns to abolish Negro slavery or to send missionaries to convert the heathen with the relatively bland indifference to the condition of English workers, equally enslaved and heathen. Variations on Mrs Jellyby's 'telescopic philanthropy' abound in the literature of social exploration.

It was comparatively easy for the industrial novelists to pass as genuine explorers. With the exception of Mrs Gaskell, none of them knew the north of England at first hand, and their choice of industrialism as a subject for fiction necessarily involved them in travel to a distant part of the country (either literally or via Blue Books and other published reports), observation of an alien way of life and eventually the responsibility of reporting as truthfully as possible what they had seen and experienced. Like the explorer of primitive foreign countries, their principal task was to reveals for the reader's entertainment and instruction, the habits, custom, and environment of a strange, unsophisticated people; the double irony being that they were really exploring one, not two, nations, and that while the element of instruction was to be set in fictional form, the traveller's tales were to be accepted as absolute, verifiable truth:

> Let no one suppose we are going to write fiction, or to conjure up phantoms of a heated imagination, to aid the cause which we avowedly embrace . . . vivid indeed, and fertile in devices must be the fancy that could invent a horror beyond the bare, every-day reality of the thing! Nay, we will set forth nothing but what has been stated on oath, corroborated on oath, and on oath confirmed beyond the possibility of an evasive question.[2]

Not all of the industrial novelists approached the problem so crudely as Mrs Tonna, but they were all conscious of the need to combat the possible incredulity of their readers. The special position they claimed for themselves imposed special responsibilities which they were not always able to bear. Disraeli expected his readers to believe that: 'Infanticide is practised as extensively and as legally in England, as it is on the banks of the Ganges,' which he knew to be true from his 'own observation', and at the same time managed to make this sound mundane by claiming that he had been obliged to omit from his report 'much that is genuine'.[3] Mrs Gaskell, frightened at having actually reproduced John Barton's thoughts on the upper classes, hurriedly apologizes for being realistic: 'I know that this is not really the case; and I know what is the truth in such matters; but what I wish to impress is what the workman feels and thinks.'[4] In this sentence the dilemma of the industrial explorer-novelist is captured perfectly. He needed to present the workers as distant beings, but not too distant; as comprising a separate nation, but not too separate; as having ideas of their own, but not too much their own; as representing a threat, but not too serious a threat. A mixture, in short, of fact and fiction.

The wonder of exploration also had a part to play. Sidonia's advice to Coningsby to visit the living glory of Manchester rather than the dead splendour of Athens and Rome; Disraeli's own

description of the Mowbray warehouses as being no less remarkable than the palaces of Venice; and Dickens's 'Fairy palaces' in
Hard Times,[5] are all used ironically, to heighten the misery of the
workers' condition, and positively, to express a rather naïve pride
in the miracle of English industrial supremacy. An examination
of the relationship between these two attitudes lies at the very
heart of *North and South*, the most subtle and complex of the
industrial-explorer novels. Margaret Hale, by gradually
shedding her prejudices against the north of England, and by
growing to recognize that it is there that the future is being
moulded, ceases to be an outsider and becomes an inhabitant. In
having her own eyes opened she helps open the eyes of others,
and this gives the role she has to play an extra dimension. For it is
not only the southerner for whom the industrial worker is like a
member of an unknown tribe. Neither Mr Bounderby nor Mr
Gradgrind has any idea how to get to Pod's End, the down-town
area of Coketown, and Louisa Gradgrind has been brought up in
a similar state of ignorance: 'For the first time in her life Louisa
had come into one of the dwellings of the Coketown Hands; for
the first time in her life she was face to face with anything like
individuality in connexion with them.'[6] Scenes similar to this, in
which leading members of an industrial town are suddenly made
aware of the existence of their workers, occur in all the industrial
novels. They are moments when the analogy between the novelist-
explorer and his more exotic counterpart breaks down. For ultimately the novelist is unable to return home and write his report
as though he has been simply describing a distant foreign tribe
that can now be forgotten. By transferring the explorer spirit to a
local, preferably wealthy or influential, inhabitant, he is accepting
that it is not two nations he has been exploring, but two halves of
the same nation.

One further fundamental belief shared by the industrial novelists
was that in order to observe the *working* classes it was necessary to
travel north: London had no such sight to offer. This is apparent
from the exploratory journeys made by the novelists themselves
(Dickens to Preston, Mrs Trollope to Manchester and Bradford,
Disraeli to Willenhall), and is expressed unequivocally by their
explorer-characters. Egremont explains that in order to learn
something of the People's condition he was obliged to travel north
because: 'That is not to be done in a great city like London. We

all of us live too much in a circle.'[7] And Margaret Hale, returning to Milton after a stay in London, is more impressed than before with the industrial activity of the north: 'There might be toilers and moilers there in London, but she never saw them; the very servants lived in an underground world of their own, of which she knew neither the hopes nor the fears; they only seemed to start into existence when some want or whim of their master and mistress needed them.'[8] This attitude reinforces the point already made, that while a class image of the industrial worker was firmly established by the 1840s, a similar mass identity of the urban worker was not established until forty years later. But long before this the explorer attitude had permeated urban literature.

In 1862 an anonymous reviewer of Mayhew's *London Labour and the London Poor* wrote: 'Mr. Mayhew's work comprises an amount of information upon the London poor, their histories and habits, that entitles it to a foremost rank in that peculiar literature which is now becoming so common, the literature not of common life only, but the commonest, oddest, and most out of the way.'[9] And Mayhew himself had described his work as 'supplying information concerning a large body of persons, of whom the public had less knowledge than of the most distant tribes of the earth'.[10] Mayhew's words could have been used by an industrial novelist, his reviewer's could not. The industrial worker was taken far too seriously for his way of life to be described as 'common', 'odd', or 'out of the way', and there was nothing 'peculiar' (as the word is used here) about the literature devoted to him; but all of these words would have been considered apt when applied to the London working man.

It is not always possible, or sensible, to distinguish in this 'peculiar literature' of urban life between fiction, non-fiction and semi-fiction. The immediate reference here is to writers such as Mayhew, John Hollingshead, George Godwin, Charles Manby Smith and John Garwood, who most consciously employed the language of social exploration and played an important part in keeping the condition of the London poor in the public mind during the mid-Victorian period. But what is said of them is also often applicable to their immediate predecessors and contemporaries in the field of fiction, especially Dickens (whose *Sketches by Boz* did much to establish the pattern of one kind of semi-fictional urban exploration), Kingsley and Augustus Mayhew; and to a vast number of other urban explorers – journalists, slum priests and tract distributors – writing throughout the century, whose work varies greatly, from the passionately committed to the sensation-seeking. Ruth Glass has noted two important qualities the best of these writers shared – the 'sympathy and anger' that inspired their work, and a 'virile, lucid' prose style.[11] They also shared an approach to the subject which was qualitative rather than quantitative (though they occasionally showed themselves to possess a greater sense of systematic analysis than is allowed them by modern sociologists), and a willingness to argue their points of view by means of dramatically presented case studies, and highly emotive language:

> Deep are the 'Mysteries of London,' and so environed by difficulties, that few can penetrate them. The condition of large sections of its inhabitants is wholly unknown to the majority of those above them in the social pyramid, the wide base of which is made up of poverty, ignorance, degradation, crime and misery.[12]

The urban differed from the industrial explorers in that they were trying to open the eyes of their readers to what was near at hand and over-familiar, rather than to what was distant and strange; to the great variety of London life and its perplexing social stratification, rather than to a simple Capital-Labour conflict: 'Owing to the vastness of London . . . owing to the moral gulf which there separates the various classes of its inhabitants – its several quarters may be designated as assemblages of towns rather than as one city . . . the rich know nothing of the poor.'[13] The voyage of exploration necessary to correct this state of affairs need only consist of a ten-minute walk from St James's to St Giles's, the most favoured of many such comparisons. And even this amount of trouble was not really necessary, for the streets of London are 'an open book, in which he that runs to and fro may read as he goes along, gathering not merely amusement and excitement, but valuable instruction too, from its ever varying pages'.[14] Each and every man is capable of being an urban explorer once his conscience has been smitten and his eyes opened.

If the language of urban exploration gained one kind of effect by carefully playing down the special nature of the explorer, it also achieved compensation by emphasizing the explorer's willingness to delve below the surface, and the courage he required 'to brave the risks of fever and other injuries to health, and the contact of men and women often as lawless as the Arab or Kaffir'.[15] As with the language of industrial exploration, the imagery employed by the urban explorers was calculated to appeal partly to the reader's social conscience, and partly to his class fears. Possible retribution for neglect is constantly threatened, but because the crucial urban relationship is between rich and poor, rather than Capital and Labour, retribution is conceived of in terms of contamination rather than physical violence. Two images used by George Godwin to describe areas of London known only to the very poor are especially revealing. These 'dark and dangerous places', within easy reach of fashionable London, are seen as 'swamps' and 'shadows' – 'the festers and malignant sores with which the body of society is spotted'.[16] These images are used to suggest a society which hides the fact that it has contracted a serious disease by an outward show of prosperity. Such an attitude is foolish because antidotes are still possible – 'bridges' can be built over swamps, 'light' can dispel shadow. But if bridges are not built and light is not cast, then the unknown forces that thrive in swamps and shadows will wreak vengeance.

Of the urban explorers who link the mid- and late-Victorian periods, James Greenwood and George R. Sims may be taken as characteristic. They were both journalists, unbelievably prolific, and interested in writing fiction based on their urban adventures. Greenwood's best work is to be found in his early factual reporting, often written under the pseudonyms 'One of the Crowd' and 'The Amateur Casual', which belongs properly to the school of Mayhew. At best these reports combine astute observation, an inexhaustible curiosity, and strong humanitarian feeling, making his low-life studies valuable social documents. After the sensation caused by *A Night in a Workhouse* (1866) – a piece of social exploration that anticipates Jack London's *The People of the Abyss* (1903) and Orwell's *Down and Out in Paris and London* (1933) – Greenwood's name alone was sufficient to gain him entrance to lower London, and to reach those places where his name meant nothing he travelled in disguise. From these journeys he sent back detailed reports on various aspects of working-class and criminal life, ranging from hop-picking to a 'knock-out auction', from thieves' kitchens to slum missions, always carefully noting peculiarities of dress, behaviour and speech. His talents are best seen in *The Seven Curses of London* (1869) and *The Wilds of London* (1874). Throughout the eighties and nineties he continued to publish collections of articles, sketches and short stories which testify to the fervour of his explorer spirit, but to little else. Like so many other writers he was incapable of successfully employing his considerable knowledge of working-class life to write convincing working-class fiction. In his early novel *The True History of a Little Ragamuffin* (1866) he had tried to achieve a balance between everyday working-class life and the more sensational, criminal life of the streets, but his later fiction, *Almost Lost* (1883), *Jerry Jacksmith of Lower London* (1890) and *Fair Phyllis of Lavender Wharf* (1890), showed no artistic development. It remained a mixture of the domestic sentimentality of Dickens and the more brutal and bizarre elements of the 'Newgate' novel.

George R. Sims is remembered today for two main reasons. First, for his dramatic documentary study *How the Poor Live* (1883), which will be discussed later:[17] and secondly, as the author of the ballad 'In the Workhouse, Christmas Day', the popular transformation of which might well stand as a classic example of genuine working-class response to superimposed middle-class sentiment. Like Greenwood, Sims was able to bring working-class characters alive in his factual reports, but quite incapable of repeating this success in fiction, and the vast number of short stories he wrote during this period are of little interest. Occasionally they centre upon the poor, but are dominated by the same ambiguous attitudes, at times bordering on the vicarious, that one finds in the sentimental-melodramatic mixture already noted as characteristic of Greenwood's work. Because of his close association with the theatre Sims tended to deal with a kind of lower-class limbo land where few social distinctions are made between chorus girls, clowns, coachmen, ragamuffins and maidservants. All the standard plot patterns that bedevil working-class fiction can be found in his slight stories – the loving couple dying beautifully of starvation, the discovery of noble relatives, the poor inheriting a fortune, the Dick Whittington hero, and violent murder as a way of life. His great love of London also led him to write a number of books of the 'mysteries of the streets' variety such as *Tales of Today* (1889) and *In London's Heart* (1900).

D

It would be wrong to undervalue the sympathy for the poor felt by Greenwood and Sims, and the parts they played in publicizing slum conditions, but neither made any original contribution to working-class fiction. They kept alive the image of the urban explorer in the seventies and early eighties by searching out pockets of London life which were odd, distressing or quaint, but lacked the profound social understanding of the best of their predecessors in this field, and were too rooted in the literary conventions they had adopted to benefit from the new frame of reference created in the eighties and nineties. By the mid-eighties, with many years of publishing before them, the work of Greenwood and Sims was made out-of-date by the discovery of the East End and the creation of a new kind of urban-explorer image.

III

Temperance fiction is discussed briefly here as a type of didactic literature, most common during the middle years of the century but still published in the eighties and nineties, in which repeated attempts were made to present working-class life. Temperance reformers justified their use of fiction on the grounds that a dramatized real-life situation, in which the drunkard saw mirrored the foulness of his degraded state, was likely to have more effect than dull sermonizing. This belief was, of course, ages old and one which late eighteenth- and early nineteenth-century reformers had found particularly attractive. In 1832, glancing back at Hannah More and Mrs Trimmer, Harriet Martineau had sung a premature, and unconsciously ironic, elegy over fiction with a scarcely veiled moral purpose: 'It is many years since we grew sick of works that pretend to be stories, and turn out to be catechisms of some kind of knowledge which we had much rather become acquainted with in its undisguised form.'[18] Her own *Illustrations of Political Economy*, for the modern reader perfect examples of such fiction, are excluded from censure because of the scientific certainty of their informing principles. Fiction is thus allowed because it is really fact. The same specious reasoning was later to be used by the temperance novelists.

It is tempting to see these 'moral purpose' writers and tract distributors as an army of Mrs Pardiggles ruthlessly forcing literature fit only for babies on poverty-stricken, illiterate labourers; and certainly enough conceit and condescension can be found in their various published memoirs to support such a view. But it is also clear that they were often genuine social explorers. Catherine Marsh trying to convert the Crystal Palace navvies, Mrs Wightman working among the drunkards of Shrewsbury, Mrs Bayly organizing mothers' meetings in the East End of London, and Mrs Ranyard selling Bibles to the women of St Giles's, are not comic figures. Their determination to confront working-class life face to face, and to write frankly of their experiences, turned their memoirs into best-sellers, and like the publications of the less ideologically committed urban explorers, helped draw attention to the neglected poor and encouraged others to undertake similar work. Allowing for a certain lack of subtlety, the tone of voice and role adopted are the same as those of Mayhew, Godwin, Sims or Greenwood:

> Reader, are you disposed for a walk into one of the lowest parts of London – into a region which people of the better class seldom or never see . . . Novelists, and still more truly City Missionaries and Scripture Readers have, perhaps, painted it in words to us before today; but now we are going to see it for ourselves, as it existed in the month of June, 1857, for 'seeing is believing.'[19]

It is less easy to be kind about the tracts they distributed or the full-length temperance novels they inspired others to write. While such literature did not deal solely with the working classes, it was the poor who provided the most flagrant examples of the degrading effect of alcohol, and who, through the media of charitable institutions, abstainer-priests, and slum visitors, were most accessible to propaganda. Temperance novels were usually very short and designed to illustrate the causal relationship between drunkenness and poverty, and the social wisdom of total abstention. All characters are seen in relation to these basic ideas which are clearly expressed by James Yeames in 'Pot, Pipe, and Poverty, or, the three P's'. An abstainer-priest surprises a parishioner having a quiet drink and smoke, and says to him: 'I know, now, why you are so distressed, and why you are clad in rags; *there* is the cause of all your poverty.'[20] The rigidity of this belief allowed the existence of only two working-class types – on the one hand, the respectable working man who epitomizes all that is good, simply because he abstains and is therefore able to spend his money on a home and family; and on the other, the drunkard who beats his wife and rolls senseless in the gutter. There can be no intermediate stages between the man who drinks a companionable glass of beer with his dinner and the chronic alcoholic, for the former will surely turn into the latter. The man who drinks is always physically and morally gross, as in this description by M. A. Paull:

> He was a heavy, coarse, bloated, vicious-looking man, with swollen distorted features: a large red nose, bleary eyes, and a mouth that was suggestive of nothing so much as bad language and brutal sensuality.[21]

If this man should even now sign the pledge then there is a good chance of his being able to save both home and family, as does the hero of Paull's *The Pearl of Billingsgate* (1890). The father in this novel is a drunken street trader. When he falls ill his daughter Pearl takes over his job, wandering the streets with the heavy barrow convinced that Jesus will protect her virtue. She is so successful that her father is smitten with remorse for his past brutality and signs the pledge. Shortly after the family is able to move to a better neighbourhood where they live soberly happy ever after.

One member of the working classes given prominence in temperance fiction is the slum child. Partly because of the drunken violence used against him by debased parents, and partly because he himself might take to drink at an early age, temperance novelists attached a special importance to the slum child and employed him in their fiction as a convenient symbol of purity and innocence. Having been influenced by temperance lecturers either at school or in the streets, he returns home to preach to his drunken parents, denouncing them in a manner reminiscent, for the modern reader, of the children in *1984* who act as agents for the Thought Police. But Orwell's children are themselves shown to be corrupt. This is not so in temperance fiction, where even the lovable ragamuffin common in the literature of roguery becomes angelic and radiant, someone, as it was often useful to claim, no different from the children of other classes. Mrs Stanley Leathes adopted this idealistic approach and defended it on the grounds of realism:

Many of the stories are quite true, for during many years of London life I have watched carefully the little darlings that toddle about the pavements, sit on the doorsteps, and play on the narrow stairs of their comfortless houses; and I have found there are as many sweet little pets among those we are prone to look upon as nuisances in our paths, as among those in the higher classes of life.

Her intention was 'to help the children of the rich to look with love and interest on the children of the poor',[22] but like all such novelists she felt that 'love and interest' could only be engendered if the rich and poor children were presented as identical beings.

IV

The romantic novelists, unlike the temperance reformers, did not belong to one school of thought, but they did all adhere to certain basic literary conventions governing the presentation of the working classes in fiction, and this makes it possible to consider them as a group. While their novels may still possess an element of social propaganda, they lack the informing seriousness of purpose found in the 'Conditions of the People' novels; and differ from temperance fiction in their willingness to allow the working man to rise in the world by means of individual philanthropy rather than self-help. In order to heighten the dream-like drama of personal release the romantic novelists created slum environments in which brutality, drunkenness, wife-beating and sordid poverty are accepted as normal features of working-class life. The following novels may be considered characteristic of the genre: David Christie Murray's *A Life's Atonement* (1880), A. T. Winthrop's *Wilfred* (1880), Silas K. Hocking's *Her Benny* (1879) and *Cricket: A Tale of Humble Life* (1880), M. A. Curtois's *Athlos* (1886) and William Barry's *The New Antigone* (1887). In these novels the narrow-minded idealism of the temperance reformers is replaced by romantic realism.

William Barry, for instance, would not have agreed at all with Mrs Leathe's view of slum children as 'little darlings that toddle about the pavements'. In his eyes 'the typical child . . . was ugly, deformed, ailing, accustomed to stripes and blows, full of premature greed, a thing of rags and disease, old in sin, and steeped in impurity'.[23] The tone of outraged horror is typical of the romantic approach, as is the following description:

> Beyond these walls . . . lies the anarchy of London. Rags, hunger, nakedness, tears, filth, incest, squalor, decay, disease, the human lazar-house, the black death eating its victims piecemeal, – that is three fourths of the London lying at these doors.[24]

What is even more typical is that a novelist capable of seeing London in these terms should have chosen his principal characters from the remaining quarter of the city. Yet *The New Antigone* is by no means a negligible novel. It retains some historical interest because of William Barry's attempt to explore the reasons for, and the meaning of, the anarchism that attracted so much public, though little worthwhile fictional, attention in the late-Victorian period.[25] But what concerns us here is the process of avoidance unconsciously employed by Barry when writing of the working classes. The slum setting is established, albeit rather hysterically, and is shown to be teeming with neglected humanity, but the author then follows the adventures of an intellectual engraver, an idealized exponent of free love who turns to slum work in repentance for her sins, and an aristocratic anarchist, with the result that the novel is concerned less with the working classes than with a country-house romance.

This process of avoidance is what most typifies the working-class romance which contains, in varying proportions, four main elements. First, a central character not himself working class who is brought into contact with slum life, in, for instance, an attempt to redeem his wasted life, as a fugitive from justice or as an aristocratic changeling. Secondly, several rhetorical descriptions of slum life. Thirdly, the manifestation of some vague philanthropic concern. And fourthly, one or two scenes of death, suffering or violence. The main action of the novel does not usually deal with the working classes who appear in a thematically relevant sub-plot, or are shadowy figures whose problems are discussed by the central characters.

All four elements are featured in *A Life's Atonement*. The hero is a young nobleman on the run from the police who goes to live in Bolter's Rents. He is befriended by a doctor who, out of sympathy for the poor, offers his services free to the slum dwellers.

On one visit to Bolter's Rents the doctor takes his wife with him and shows her the various sights:

> One or two women unutterably coarse and frowsy, stood in a little patch of moonlight with their hands under their aprons, and their hair in wild disorder. They lolled against the wall, or stood uprightly vacant, or shambled loosely from side to side, but said nothing, and were without occupation.[26]

At another point the doctor describes Bolter's Rents as: 'A haunt of thieves, and worse – a haunt of cadgers, tramps, crossing-sweepers, the riff-raff of the London streets; a tumble-down fever den; a brick-and-mortar ulcer.'[27] Thus even in a work by a novelist so sympathetic to the working classes as David Christie Murray no attempt is made to present the workers as normal human beings.[28] They are merely a coterie of grotesques who provide a backcloth for the solution of the ultimate problem – will the debased nobleman, known to the 'riff-raff' as the 'Dook', be recognized by his old friend who has come to Bolter's Rents to set a vast philanthropic scheme into motion? Meanwhile the reader has been shuttled between high life in the country and a couple of violent deaths in the slums.

Every working-class romance written at this time employs a variation on this process of avoidance. *Wilfred* is about a French boy living in an English slum who is 'obviously the son of a gentleman'. One day he meets a friendly aristocrat in the park who on hearing his story immediately sets out to find the boy's ancestors. *Athlos* is a fairly conventional 'rags to riches' tale in which a young orphan is sent to work in a pawnbroker's shop, then in an office ('Johnnie had been educated in roughness, but he was not rough by nature') until eventually overcoming all the obstacles placed in his way, though helped a little by some upper-class friends, he ends up as a wealthy banker. The novels by Silas K. Hocking are unusual in that they deal with slum life in Liverpool rather than London, and superior to the other romantic novels discussed so far in that a genuine attempt is made to portray the life of street arabs, but which descend into mawkish improbability. In *Cricket*, for example, the young hero, inspired by his girlfriend little Cricket, attends a ragged school, and by the close of the novel is running a prosperous book shop which specializes in rare editions.

Enough has been said to show that while the novels by Sims, Greenwood, the temperance reformers and romantic novelists, purport to be about the working classes, very few genuinely working-class characters ever appear in them; and in the rare case when a working-class man or woman is made a central character the action is presented in such a way as completely to nullify the class meaning of the book. It is important to note that this process of avoidance of main issues is not peculiar only to minor, or indeed very minor novelists, but applies to most English working-class fiction written before the eighties. It is not so much a matter of degrees of talent, as a refusal or inability to break away from the literary and social conventions governing the role that a working man could be allowed to play in a novel. Most examples given so far have been from novels of little intrinsic worth, but if we examine one of the outstanding novels of the eighties, *The Princess Casamassima*, we shall find that exactly the same conventions that forced Barry or Greenwood to avoid dealing directly with the working classes apply to Henry James's sole excursion into working-class fiction.

While working on *The Princess Casamassima* James wrote in his notebook: 'I have never yet become engaged in a novel in which, after I had begun to write and send off my M.S., the details had remained so vague.'[29] He was referring mainly to the problems he had created for himself by trying to write *The Bostonians* at the same time, but he was also running into difficulties which the alien subject matter of *The Princess Casamassima* had forced upon him. Like Dickens, Besant, Gissing and many others before him, he could claim that 'this fiction proceeded quite directly, during the first year of a long residence in London, from the habit and interest of walking the streets',[30] and to this experience he brought a wealth of literary associations, for as Leon Edel has pointed out, 'the image of the depressed side of London had been with him ever since his childhood reading of Dickens'.[31] In spite of this, James obviously felt that neither his literary nor his personal experiences were sufficient, and he deliberately set out to examine certain aspects of lower-class life. His notebooks and letters show how fascinated he was by the possibility of a working-class revolution breaking out. Disillusioned with English politics, he planned a visit to Ireland in order to see 'a country in a state of revolution', and also visited Millbank Prison where he was taken on a guided tour by officials, and began to note down 'Phrases of the People', heard on his London walks, phrases such as 'that takes the gilt off, you know', 'he cuts it very fine' and ''ere today, somewhere else tomorrow, that's 'is motto'.[32]

The preface he later added to the novel shows exactly the kind of difficulty James felt himself faced with. It is the most explicit defence of the need, in writing about the working classes, to employ an exceptional working man as hero, and therefore a perfect example of the avoidance of main issues. While quite aware that Hyacinth Robinson was not a representative working man, one feels James regretted this had to be:

> This in fact I have ever found rather terribly the point – that the figures in any picture, the agents in any drama, are interesting only in proportion as they feel their respective situations; since the consciousness, on their part, of the complication exhibited forms for us their link of connexion with it. But there are degrees of feeling – the muffled, the faint, the just sufficient, the barely intelligent, as we may say; and the acute, the intense, the complete, in a word – the power to be finely aware and richly responsible.

It could be well argued that the whole history of the attempts by generations of writers to present the working classes in fiction, is concerned with just this problem – how to write about 'the muffled, the faint, the just sufficient, the barely intelligent'. James acknowledged the problem but chose the alternative, a hero who was someone like himself but 'with every door of approach shut in his face'. When he says that Hyacinth Robinson 'sprang up for me out of the London pavement', he does not mean, as one might expect, that he was a ragamuffin or street arab, but instead, 'some individual sensitive nature or fine mind, some small obscure intelligent creature whose education should have been wholly derived from [the London streets] capable of profiting by all the civilisation, all the accumulations to which they testify, yet condemned to see these things only from the outside'. This choice, as James goes on to point out, was inevitable, for 'we care, our curiosity and our sympathy care comparatively little for what happens to the stupid, the coarse and the blind; care for it and for the effects of it, at the most as helping to precipitate what happens to the more deeply wondering, to the really sentient'.[33]

Yet even allowing for all this James could still not bring himself to make Hyacinth – however 'deeply wondering' he might be – a genuine product of the London slums. Like the romantic novelists James made his hero not merely exceptional in intellect but in birth also – his mother was French and his father an aristocrat. *The Princess Casamassima* is not really a story of the frustrated sensibility of a working-class boy but is rather about the uncertain social position of a classless intellectual, and in this sense George Ford's remark that Gissing's *Workers in the Dawn* was a more likely influence upon *The Princess Casamassima* than Dickens, is surely plausible.[34]

Like Gissing James was unable to avoid the emergence of rather ambiguous attitudes whenever it was necessary for him to place his hero in a working-class environment. The two aspects of his being – the superior intellect and working-class background – needed to be continually balanced against each other:

> There was something exotic in him, and yet, with his sharp
> young face, destitute of bloom but not of sweetness, and a
> certain conscious cockneyism that pervaded him, he was as
> strikingly as Millicent, in her own degree, a product of the
> London streets and the London air.[35]

In a straight physical description like this the two aspects can just be balanced, but when human relationships are involved his 'sensitive nature' and 'fine mind' produce disturbing, and unintentional, judgements: 'Hyacinth had long ago perceived that his adoptive mother had generations of plebeian patience in her blood, and that though she had a tender soul she had not a truly high spirit.'[36] This also brings James close to Gissing who repeatedly denigrated characters for their lack of aesthetic sensitivity, even though, apart from this failing, they were shown to be wholly admirable human beings. Hyacinth is further continually made to proclaim his own superiority. He confides to the Princess that he 'thought the people in his own class generally very stupid – distinctly what he should call third-rate minds'.[37] But it is never clear why he should even consider them to be of the same class as himself. When Lady Marchmont calls on the Princess at her country home the visitor naturally accepts Hyacinth as an aristocrat, and the Princess compliments him on this achievement: 'You have come out of the poor cramped hole you've described to me, and yet you might have stayed in country-houses all your life.'[38] Even Paul Muniment calls Hyacinth 'A duke in disguise'[39] and in doing so states the dominant psychological drive in Hyacinth – a desire to kill and yet at the same time preserve his unknown aristocratic father, symbolized in the final choice of suicide above assassination.

Hyacinth's view of the social alternatives possible for him is also revealing. When, towards the close of the novel, he is tormented by his change of heart (by his new-found belief in the preservation of the beautiful rather than the destruction of the social structure), he sees the 'lower classes' as totally incapable of providing any satisfactory alternative kind of society:

> There were nights when everyone he met appeared to reek
> with gin and filth and he found himself elbowed by figures as
> foul as lepers. Some of the women and girls in particular
> were appalling – saturated with alcohol and vice, brutal,
> bedraggled, obscene.[40]

These presumably are the kind of people the Princess wants to meet and about whom Hyacinth has to confess he knows nothing. They are also the people James obviously felt comprised the masses, for when Pinnie dies Hyacinth acknowledges that she had saved him from his 'natural portion' – 'the workhouse and the gutter, ignorance and cold, filth and tatters, nights of huddling under bridges and in doorways, vermin, starvation and blows'.[41] The alternatives are thus a debased or a country-house life; the position of the respectable artisan to which the central group of workers belongs is ignored as a meaningful way of life.

The Princess Casamassima is, of course, a political novel and it is natural that the anarchists should be presented, as Irving Howe has pointed out, 'as skilled artisans rather than factory proletarians',[42] but the book makes a larger claim than this implies. In Leon Edel's description it is about 'the plight of the London working class and its nascent revolutionary impulse',[43] and this is correct save that the working class, in the sense of the term as used by Edel and Howe, never appears. It is, however, often described as in the following much-quoted passage:

> They came oftener this second winter, for the season was
> terribly hard; and as in that lower world one walked with

one's ear nearer the ground the deep perpetual groan of London misery seemed to swell and swell and form the whole undertone of life. The filthy air reached the place in the damp coats of silent men and hung there till it was brewed to a nauseous warmth, and ugly serious faces squared themselves through it, and strong-smelling pipes contributed their element in a fierce dogged manner which appeared to say that it now had to stand for everything – for bread and meat and beer, for shoes and blankets and the poor things at the pawnbroker's and the smokeless chimney at home.[44]

The only time the people described here make an appearance in the novel is at a meeting in the Sun and Moon public house, and it was for the presentation of these characters that James reserved his 'Phrases of the People':

A little shoe-maker with red eyes and a greyish face, whose appearance Hyacinth deplored, scarcely ever expressed himself but in the same form of words: 'Well, are we in earnest or ain't we in earnest? – that's the thing *I* want to know.' He was terribly in earnest himself, but this was almost the only way he had of showing it; and he had much in common (although they were always squabbling) with a large red-faced man, of uncertain attributes and stertorous breathing, who was understood to know a good deal about dogs, had fat hands and wore on his forefinger a big silver ring containing some one's hair – Hyacinth believed it to be that of a terrier snappish in life. He had always the same refrain: 'Well now are we just starving or ain't we just starving? I should like the v'ice of the company on that question.'

When the tone fell as low as this Paul Muniment held his peace save for whistling a little and leaning back with his hands in his pockets and his eyes on the table.[45]

The difference in tone between these two passages is quite remarkable. When the complaints of the People are described indirectly then James strikes a pose of sympathy which gives some meaning to the political aims of Paul Muniment and Hyacinth; but when the ordinary working-class members of the group express for themselves this same vague, yet pitiful sense of bewilderment at social conditions, they are dismissed as unimportant by both James and his substitute working-class heroes. The concentration on the men's gross physical details, stage cockney accents, and their vulgar jewellery and hobbies; together with James's sneering comments – 'He was terribly in earnest himself' – and the open scorn shown by Paul and Hyacinth, all serve to make nonsense of any argument that would claim *The Princess Casamassima* as a successful working-class novel.

But there is one important qualification to be made, for in the portrait of Millicent Henning, James transcended his normal limitations and created an isolated working-class character more convincing than either Paul or Hyacinth. George du Maurier, a good judge of cockney character, proclaimed her 'the best character in the book', and singled out as her refreshing qualities: 'her freedom, her readiness for a row, her potentiality for barricades or triumphal processions (in spite of her hands and feet).' As Leon Edel remarks, after quoting this passage: 'It is doubtful whether Millicent had a potential for barricades: but du Maurier describes her essential qualities.'[46] What is even more impressive is the way James manages to relate these qualities to Millicent's slum background. The Henning home in Lomax Place is shown as makeshift and undisciplined, a place of bustle and unavailing effort against the forces of dirt and growing children. It is dominated by a mother who likes her gin, but is not presented as debased, and who keeps her family alive by good-natured sponging on her neighbours. Millicent's upbringing is as unlike Hyacinth's as it is possible to be, and if Hyacinth's background is similar to that of a Gissing hero, the presentation of Millicent's family owes everything to Dickens. When the Henning family is finally evicted from Lomax Place they take with them that sense of working-class vitality so lacking in the remainder of the novel:

> Lomax Place had eventually, from its over-peeping windows and doorways been present at the seizure, by a long-suffering landlord, of the chattels of this interesting race and at the ejectment of the whole insolvent group, who departed in a straggling, jeering, unabashed, cynical manner, carrying with them but little of the sympathy of the street.[47]

When Millicent reappears 'in the wantonness of her full-blown freedom',[48] she carries with her all the force and vigour of her class, providing a striking contrast to the sensation-seeking Princess and the philanthropic Lady Aurora.

We can thus see that the four elements which define the working-class romance appear just as strongly in the work of Henry James as in that of, for instance, William Barry or David Christie Murray. As a novelist James was infinitely superior: as a novelist of working-class life he was really little different.

The novels of Gissing and Besant should be seen in relation to the three main lines of continuing tradition discussed here, especially that of working-class romance. Gissing is the first Victorian novelist, whose efforts can be traced through a series of novels, to struggle seriously with the artistic problems involved in the presentation of the working classes in fiction. Besant is hardly concerned with these problems at all. At one and the same time he dispenses with the old romantic formula and by taking the process of avoidance to farcical lengths, succeeds in producing a new, equally facile, pattern for working-class romance. He also helps give a fresh impetus to the urban-explorer image. Working-class romance of the kind discussed in this chapter does not die out. As throughout the nineteenth century it remains extremely susceptible to fluctuations in literary taste and social issues, maintaining its basic form but varying its constituents according to the development of more original working-class fiction produced in the late eighties and nineties.

3
George Gissing

I

George Gissing wrote five novels which deal specifically with
working-class life: *Workers in the Dawn* (1880), *The Unclassed*
(1884), *Demos* (1886), *Thyrza* (1887) and *The Nether World*
(1889). When studied in chronological order they testify to a
consistently serious attempt to break with static literary conventions; a struggle with the problem of how to establish a balance
between a personal social viewpoint and artistic objectivity when
writing about the working classes. These were tasks for which
Gissing felt himself peculiarly fitted. 'I have a book in my head,'
he wrote in 1886, 'which no one else can write, a book which will
contain the very spirit of London working class life.'[1] This sense
of personal association with the working classes was unlike that
experienced by any other novelist so far discussed. Gissing's own
background was conventionally middle class, but the series of
events which began with his expulsion from Owen's College in
1876 and culminated in the publication of his first novel four
years later, turned him into a social outcast, a position which he
seemed uncertain whether to glorify or deplore. Married to an
alcoholic prostitute and forced to live in the slums (at least partly
because of genuine poverty), he tended to view his own intellec-
tually outcast position and the suffering of the slum populations
as brought about by the same hostile society. His flirtation with
social-reform movements was brief but deeply felt. As the author

of *Workers in the Dawn* he proclaimed himself 'a mouthpiece of the advanced Radical party',[2] and vowed to use his novels to arouse public interest in social issues:

> I mean to bring home to people the ghastly condition (material, mental and moral) of our poor classes, to show the hideous injustice of our whole system of society, to give light upon the plan of altering it, and, above all, to preach an enthusiasm for just and high *ideals* in this age of unmitigated egotism and 'shop.'[3]

But Gissing's fervid radical spirit soon disappeared. Three years later he had completely reversed his earlier position, and rejected all concern with social reform:

> My attitude henceforth is that of the artist pure and simple. The world is for me a collection of phenomena, which are to be studied and reproduced artistically. In the midst of the most serious complications of life, I find myself suddenly possessed with a great calm, withdrawn as it were from the immediate interests of the moment, and able to regard everything as a picture . . . Brutal and egotistic it would be called by most people. What has that to do with me if it is a fact?[4]

In theory Gissing sounds convinced enough, but in practice the distinterested aesthete did not supplant the social reformer. The two were grafted together. Gissing's best working-class study, *The Nether World*, is the result of this devotion to objective truth inspired by a powerful sense of horror or even disgust at the condition of the poor. From the beginning his championship of the working-class cause had been equivocal, but a strong sense of social pity had kept his doubts in check. Now, as his own material position improved, and as he grew more conscious of the isolated position of the artist in late-Victorian society, he not only dissociated himself from the working classes but became a confirmed anti-democrat. An entry in his diary, made during a trip to Paris in 1888, is especially revealing: 'I experience at present a profound dislike for everything that concerns the life of the people . . . All my interest in such things I have left behind in London. On crossing the Channel, I have become a poet pure and simple, or perhaps it would be better to say an idealist student of art.'[5] The phrase 'at present' is misleading as even in his earliest novels it is possible to distinguish elements of his anti-democratic attitude, and in *Demos* his hostility to the working classes had been openly expressed. What is especially interesting about this particular statement is that it was made between *Thyrza* and *The Nether World*, which are respectively the gentlest and the most virulent of his working-class novels. Throughout the eighties Gissing alternated between feelings of pity and loathing for the working classes and this personal confusion is apparent in his novels.

No earlier writer had faced this particular dilemma. Dickens, Mrs Gaskell and Kingsley had been as horrified by slum conditions as Gissing, and the reformist aims of their novels were little different from those expressed by the author of *Workers in the Dawn*. But their treatment of working-class characters and environments had been so handled as to inspire in the reader the maximum possible amount of sympathy, and in order to achieve this it was necessary that only certain aspects of working-class life should be shown. To allow, for instance, a non-debased working man to swear, get drunk, abuse the government or indulge in any form of violence, without condemning him (either overtly or by means of some fearful retribution), would have tended to undermine the very sympathy which the author was trying to evoke. Many of the limitations of early-Victorian working-class fiction are attributable to this kind of misapplied sympathy. After *Workers in the Dawn* Gissing suffered from no such inhibition. When he says that he has rejected social purpose and become an 'idealist student of art', he does not mean that he has rejected the working classes as subject matter, only that he would no longer be their champion; that they had become for him, 'a collection of phenomena . . . to be studied and reproduced artistically'. In one sense his 'dislike' of the workers gave him an advantage over his predecessors as he no longer felt it necessary to explore working-class themes in terms of a straight moral conflict. He was able to criticize working-class life without feeling that he was somehow betraying the weak and helpless. But Gissing only enjoyed this advantage so long as he could maintain strict artistic control over his own class bias. Once the balance tilted (and it often did) then his hostility towards the workers weakened the quality of his novels in much the same way as the excessive sympathy of earlier writers had weakened the quality of theirs. At these moments the idealism

E

of Mrs Gaskell or Kingsley is transformed into the class pettiness of Gissing; a niggling concern with the inferior eating habits, pronunciation and intellect of his working-class characters; temporarily forgetting their humanity and employing them as pawns in a cultural war.

But this weakness, central as it is to a total view of Gissing's work, should not be allowed to obscure his genuine achievements. His first novel had been written during the bitterly unhappy years of his first marriage, and the hysterical slum descriptions and reformist aims of *Workers in the Dawn* were the result of his attempt to find some kind of class affiliation to alleviate his outcast position. His personal involvement with working-class life had prevented him from attaining the objective truth he now regarded as his paramount artistic duty, and in search of material he turned to those sections of life of which he had little first-hand knowledge. Significantly it was in working-class districts that he was forced to do his research. He was amused when reviewers took him for a working man:

> Why, it is the *other* kind of life that I have had to make a study of – the low, not the middle class life.[6]

The tightly controlled and sociologically exact scenes of *Demos* and *Thyrza* were possible only after a painstaking study of his chosen subject:

> I spent an evening in the east end on Saturday. It is a strange neighbourhood, totally different from the parts of London in which my walks generally lie. The faces of the people are of an altogether different type, and even their accent is not quite the same as that of the poor in the west end. I rambled till midnight about filthy little courts and backyards and alleys, and stumbled over strange specimens of humanity.[7]

While 'toiling fearfully over the construction' of *Thyrza*, he was worried because the actual writing was delayed while he gathered more material: 'I have to go over a hat factory, a lunatic asylum, and other strange places; also to wander much in the slums.'[8] And during the same period he wrote to his sister: 'I am living at present in Lambeth, doing my best to get at the meaning of that strange world, so remote from our civilisation . . . I have the strangest people and scenes floating in my mind. Tomorrow, a

Bank Holiday, I must spend in the street; there is always much matter to be picked up on such days.'[9] A year later, still searching for slum material, he noted scenes which particularly disturbed him: 'Last Sunday evening I spent on Clerkenwell Green – a great assembly-place for radical meetings and the like. A more disheartening scene is difficult to imagine – the vulgar, blatant scoundrels!'[10] His distrust of radicalism was closely related to his vision of the socially aloof artist, as is seen from his attitude towards William Morris's involvement with Socialism: 'Why cannot he write poetry in the shade? He will inevitably coarsen himself in the company of ruffians.'[11]

In spite of his ever increasing personal distrust of the subject he was so carefully studying, Gissing continued, throughout the eighties, to gather details of working-class speech and behaviour which he used to give a sense of sociological exactitude to his novels. Such a technique, even when developed with Gissing's care and skill, offers, of course, no guarantee of success, and it is an important point to remember when considering Gissing's working-class novels, that his knowledge came from his experience as a lodger and a reporter. The significance of this did not escape Frank Swinnerton:

> Very few educated people have lived among the poor for any reason but that of benefiting them or 'studying' them. Gissing both lived among the poor and 'studied' them; but he lived among them by reason of the most lamentable necessity, and he studied them without ever learning their spiritual language. He was always a stranger, homeless and miserable. Is it any wonder that what he saw was as lugubrious as his own mood?[12]

It is true that Gissing was rarely able to get really inside his working-class characters; to give them that sense of oneness with their environment which is the special quality of the great novelist. His is an observed world and he has much greater success with descriptive and analytical passages than with working-class characterization. Yet it is his faith in the scientific observation of working-class life that sets him apart from earlier writers. The qualities he possessed were rare and valuable – an essential honesty, a refusal to compromise with publishers, reading public, critics or his own conscience, and, most of all, an unshakable trust in Art.

The development of Gissing's artistic and social v   ιe
eighties, as reflected in his five working-class novels, i   ly
complex, but certain phases can be indicated. In artisti   s
development is easy to chart. The first of these novels is
the last is the best; while the three intervening novels r
gradual artistic progression. Gissing's development as a
however, must be closely related to his changing attitude
the working classes. In *Workers in the Dawn* and *The Uncl*
appears as a social reformer, pointing out the suffering of the poor
and acting as their champion. In *Demos* he becomes openly critical
of the working classes, with the result that their suffering receives
less attention and their revolutionary aspirations more. In *Thyrza*
an unusual tone of gentleness prevails. The workers in this novel
are not presented as the suffering poor, nor are they subjected to
anti-democratic criticism. Then, just as Gissing's early marriage to
Nell Harrison had been largely responsible for the tone of his
first novel, so her miserable death reawakened in him all the pity
for, and distrust of, working-class life which he had so carefully
controlled in *Thyrza*, and inspired him to write *The Nether
World*.

In order to indicate the full extent of Gissing's break with earlier
working-class fiction, three aspects of his novels will be studied
here. First, his treatment of slum environments; secondly, the
role played by the substitute working-class hero; and thirdly, his
presentation of working-class characters. Finally, a study of *The
Nether World* will show how Gissing at last fully succeeded in
writing a novel which contained what he regarded as 'the very
spirit of working-class life'.

II

The changes that took place in Gissing's attitude towards the art
of fiction and the role of the artist in society are directly reflected
in his descriptions of slum environments. In *Workers in the Dawn*,
as Frank Swinnerton has pointed out, 'horror is the chief note
sounded whenever the poor are under observation'.[13] The long
opening chapter is a grim portrait of a street market in the Barbican
which belongs to the 'filth, putrefaction, and poverty' tradition
of early-Victorian fiction. It is very similar in both tone and

setting to the passage from *Alton Locke* which was discussed in Ch. 1, but this does not necessarily mean that Gissing was plagiarizing Kingsley. Here at the start of his career he was adopting the most common literary approach to slum descriptions; an approach which he was to reject almost immediately, and which later novelists were to react strongly against. Gissing is the guide:

> Walk with me reader, into Whitecross Street. It is Saturday night, the market-night of the poor; also the one evening in the week which the weary toilers of our great city can devote to ease and recreation in the sweet assurance of a morrow unenslaved. Let us see how they spend this 'Truce of God'; our opportunities will be of the best in the district we are entering.

The buildings and streets are described in such a way as to re-create the feelings of repulsion experienced by the guide. The superabundance of inexact adjectives and a rhetorical tone scarcely avoiding hysteria emphasize that, like Kingsley's St Giles's, this is not one particular part of London but rather a social evil symptomatic of a diseased society:

> The fronts of the houses, as we glance up towards the deep blackness overhead, have a decayed, filthy, often an evil look; and here and there, on either side, is a low, yawning archway, or a passage some four feet wide, leading presumably to human habitations. Let us press through the throng to the mouth of one of these and look in, as long as the reeking odour will permit us. Straining the eyes into horrible darkness, we behold a blind alley, the unspeakable abominations of which are dimly suggested by a gas-lamp flickering at the further end.

The Barbican is Hell and the people who throng the market are grotesque. They arc presented only in terms of debased qualities. The tradesmen 'abuse each other with a foul-mouthed virulence surpassing description'; the crowd around the whelk stall are 'miserable looking wretches'; and the bundles of second-hand clothes 'piled up in foul and clammy heaps' attract buyers who 'ogle the paltry rags, feverishly turn their money in their hands, discuss with each other in greedy whispers the cheapness or otherwise of the wares'. The reader together with the guide is accosted by a little girl, 'the very image of naked wretchedness, holding up, with shrill, pitiful appeals, a large piece of salt for which she wants one halfpenny'. Should the guide allow his imagination to dwell upon the domestic circumstances of these people he would merely encounter further vileness. For the child, 'failure to sell her salt will involve a brutal beating when she returns to the foul nest which she calls home'. The trashy trinkets sold on other stalls are merely things 'such as may tempt a few of the hard-earned coppers out of a young wife's pocket, or induce the working lad to spend a shilling for the delight of some consumptive girl, with the result, perhaps, of leading her to seek in the brothel a relief from the slow death of the factory or the work-room'.

To the filth and the meanness, the total lack of any kind of taste or understanding, is added the foulness of the gin-shop:

> Here a group are wrangling over a disputed toss or bet, here
> two are coming to blows, there are half-a-dozen young men
> and women, all half drunk, mauling each other with vile
> caresses; and all the time, from the lips of the youngest and
> the oldest, foams forth such a torrent of inanity, abomination,
> and horrible blasphemy which bespeaks the very depth of
> human – aye, or of bestial – degradation.

In the midst of this Hell, Gissing does allow one cheerful note to creep in, though any thought that this might represent a positive value is immediately rejected:

> It must be confessed that the majority do not seem unhappy;
> they jest with each other amid their squalor; they have an
> evident pleasure in buying and selling; they would be
> surprised if they knew you pitied them. And the very fact
> that they are unconscious of their degradation afflicts one
> with all the keener pity. We suffer them to become brutes in
> our midst, and inhabit dens which clean animals would shun,
> to derive their joys from sources from which a cultivated
> mind shrinks as from pestilential vapour.[14]

Workers in the Dawn is the only one of Gissing's novels of slum life in which the descriptions are of this virulence. In the novels that followed, working-class districts are often portrayed in a plain journalistic style, as though directly transcribed from note-book jottings:

Litany Lane was a narrow passage, with houses on one side; opposite to them ran a long high wall, apparently the limit of some manufactory. Two posts set up at the entrance to the Lane showed that it was no thoroughfare for vehicles. The houses were of three storeys. There were two or three dirty little shops, but the rest were ordinary lodging houses, the front-doors standing wide open as a matter of course, exhibiting a dusky passage, filthy stairs, with generally a glimpse right through into the yard in the rear. In Elm Court the houses were smaller, and had their fronts whitewashed.[15]

In *The Unclassed* and in *Demos* this gradual development of restraint is observable, although occasionally the old bitterness breaks through. But by *Thyrza*, Gissing's method of creating a slum portrait had completely changed. Here the activity of the streets is no longer a public exhibition of a sub-human race, but the genuine expression of a way of life. A comparison of the Lambeth Walk street-market scene in *Thyrza* with that of the almost identical scene in the Barbican, discussed earlier, is especially revealing:

The market-night is the sole out-of-door amusement regularly at hand for London working people, the only one, in truth, for which they show any real capacity. Everywhere was laughter and interchange of good-fellowship. Women sauntered the length of the street and back again for the pleasure of picking out the best and cheapest bundle of rhubarb, or lettuce, the biggest and hardest cabbage, the most appetising rasher; they compared notes and bantered each other on purchases. The hot air reeked with odours. From stalls where whelks were sold rose the pungency of vinegar; decaying vegetables trodden underfoot blended their putridness with the musty smell of second-hand garments; the grocers' shops were aromatic; above all was distinguishable the acrid exhalation from the shops where fried fish and potatoes hissed in boiling grease.[16]

Thyrza possesses an exactness of locality and sympathy of presentation unique in Gissing's working-class novels. Not only is the atmosphere of Lambeth successfully conveyed but it is favourably contrasted with the Caledonian Road, where Thyrza works for a while as a waitress. Just as Gissing came to understand that the inhabitants of the slums were more human than their external appearance suggested, so he came to feel that in spite of the squalor, slum areas generated their own sense of individuality.

Gissing frequently noted that one of the most urgent problems of working-class life was the lack of any kind of privacy, which led to the normal intimacies of life being acted out in public. In *Thyrza* these scenes no longer excite his disgust, and no longer is there emphasis solely on the debauchery of the streets. The role that music plays in the novel is a good example of his improving technique.

The children dance to a barrel organ in the streets and Gissing sees the vulgar yet emotional music as symbolizing 'the half-conscious striving of a nature which knows not what it would attain'.[17] Old Mr Boddy plays the violin in his shabby room, and will doubtless be remembered by future generations for this idiosyncrasy, just as Matthew Trent is remembered in Paradise Street for his fine tenor voice. As Thyrza and Lydia sit looking out of the window on a Sunday afternoon they hear the strains of Mr Jarmey's accordion playing a selection of tunes varying from 'popular hymnody to the familiar ditties of the music-hall',[18] and Thyrza herself, the pure and idealized heroine, sings at a 'Friendly Lead' in the Prince Albert to a rapturous and relatively sober reception; later she sings in the beautiful home of Mrs Ormonde where Annabel's piano-playing is such as Thyrza had never imagined to exist. Egremont hears Thyrza sing before he actually meets her; and when Gilbert Grail takes the two sisters to the St James's Hall for a special treat, Egremont is also there to point out that the performance, blissful as it seems to Thyrza, does not represent music of the very highest quality. Throughout the novel music symbolizes both the passion and calm of the story, and in so far as it is capable of bringing the classes closer together or forcing them further apart, is both a divisive and a communicative force.

During these middle years of the eighties Gissing's conviction that he alone of the novelists of his time possessed the ability to write books containing 'the very spirit of London working-class life', is finally justified and it is in *Thyrza* that this special knowledge is most sympathetically employed. The rather facile acceptance of individual philanthropy which spoils the ending of *The*

Unclassed is now seen to have been a mistake; the snobbishness of
Demos is held in abeyance, and the long, vague slum descriptions
of *Workers in the Dawn* are replaced by brief sketches of photographic exactness. Thus Paradise Street:

> The name is less descriptive than it might be. Poor
> dwellings, mean and cheerless, are interspersed with
> factories and one or two small shops; a public house is
> prominent, and a railway arch breaks the perspective of the
> thoroughfare midway.[19]

To this simple outline there are added details and images of working-class life, so that the street becomes a reality by virtue of the
activity of its inhabitants. The busy market place, the gossiping
housewives, the sounds of church bells and street vendors, the
music and dancing, and the voices of married couples quarrelling
when the pubs turn out, are all used to bind together the complex
class structure of the book. The subdued tone of *Thyrza* comes
largely from an increasingly skilful use of the material of everyday
life, a retreat from melodrama, and a willingness to see working-
class life as something other than a social disease.

III

Gissing's often quoted description of his own special type of
hero as being 'well-educated, fairly bred, *but without money*'[20]
refers properly only to those novels he wrote after *The Nether
World*, for in the earlier novels one further quality is required – a
strong social conscience. Of these heroes only Richard Mutimer,
in *Demos*, can be genuinely called a working man. Arthur Golding
(*Workers in the Dawn*), Osmond Waymark (*The Unclassed*) and
Walter Egremont (*Thyrza*) are all displaced intellectuals. The
basic conflict in each of these novels comes from the hero's need
to choose between a public and a private life, and in every case the
development of the self is seen as of more importance than
devotion to philanthropy.

Arthur Golding is a good example (similar to Hyacinth Robinson
in *The Princess Casamassima*) of the way in which the special
problems involved in placing a working-class character at the
centre of a novel may be unconsciously side-stepped by the

author. Although Arthur Golding is not working class by birth (his father is an Oxford graduate who dies of alcoholism in the slums), his upbringing is almost entirely so. A friend of his dead father takes him to stay in the country but after a brief period Arthur returns to the London streets where, at first, he is preyed upon by the lowest of the slum dwellers. At this stage of his life he is totally illiterate but the slums have not corrupted him:

> Arthur had already several times given indications of what in a child of higher birth we might, perhaps, be allowed to call chivalrous feeling; as it is, I suppose we must content ourselves with allowing the poor lad a negative commendation, and say that he was in some degree distinguished from other boys of his position by a certain want of brutality, an absence of vulgar selfishness.[21]

It is at his own insistence that he learns to read and write, and although he is later helped by his more respectable working-class friends, it is also largely by his own exertions that he develops his natural talent as an artist. The inevitable legacy is eventually forthcoming, leaving the way clear for him to choose between a public and a private code of values.

In the novels of Walter Besant the heroes and heroines are aristocrats disguised as working people who literally act out an elaborate part in a slum masquerade. Gissing is never so foolish as this, but in this case his preoccupation with an exceptional member of the working classes leads him into a position which is equally false. When Mrs Frederick Harrison read Gissing's first novel she asked her husband, 'Where are the Workers in the Dawn?'[22] and her confusion is understandable for the title does not refer to the working class at all: 'It is a novel . . . of social questions, and the principal characters are earnest young people striving for improvement in, as it were, the dawn of a new phase of our civilisation'.[23]

Although one of the avowed aims of the book was to show truthfully the pitiful condition of the poor, the 'earnest young people striving for improvement' are not themselves of the poor, nor are their personal problems really concerned with poverty. The moral issue that confronts Arthur Golding is whether he should devote his energy and money to social work or to developing his artistic talents. His love for the ethereal and wealthy Helen

Norman, and his marriage to Carrie Mitchell, an unregenerate prostitute, are presented in such a way as to leave him no meaningful choice at all. For by virtue of his exceptional sensitivity he stands outside a working-class way of life, and just as the slums seem to have played no part in the formation of his character, so they now exert no real influence on his final decision. As an artist he possesses a yearning for the ideal which is symbolized by the unattainable Helen Norman: 'She much resembled some sweet and placid-faced Madonna gazing herself into beatific reverie before an infant Christ.'[24] Slum reality is marriage to Carrie Mitchell: 'She was emphatically a child of the town, dreaming of nothing but its gross delights, seeing in everything pure and lovely but a sapless image of some town-made joy.'[25] The differences between the two women are not merely those of beauty and wealth, but of culture. Carrie's response to her environment is working-class and Arthur Golding cannot take it. To Carrie Mitchell his moral dilemma is meaningless, and it is Helen Norman who eventually makes up his mind for him. She herself is a slum worker but she has no doubt that Art must take priority: 'The feelings of infinite compassion for the poor which work so strongly in your mind are most natural, but you must not allow them to lead you astray.'[26]

Arthur Golding's main task in the novel is to join the divided classes in a bond of understanding and sympathy. Because of the special qualities he possesses he is able to move from high to low society in a way that would be impossible for a more representative working man. Gissing, like many earlier novelists in this respect, is very much aware of the need for the proper type of spokesman. Shock tactics are one possibility:

What if Bill Blatherwick himself, bestially drunk as he now is, were to be transported bodily into one of these mansions and then thrown down upon the carpet – a novel excitement for these Christmas guests! Would it strike any of them, with the terrific force of a God-sent revelation, that to them individually was due a share of the evil which has bred such an unutterable abomination?[27]

But Blatherwick would only excite disgust or ridicule. Will Noble, the leader of the Working-Men's Club, who is decently dressed, well spoken, politically moderate and self-educated, would be a better representative, but he lacks that cultured air which is peculiarly upper class. If communication is to be made at all then like must speak to like. The result is that Arthur Golding, in a sense different from a Besant hero, becomes an aristocrat masquerading as a working man.

In *Workers in the Dawn* Gissing imposes upon his characters a static set of values which serves to destroy the very sympathy he is trying to build up. Because Arthur deserves the best he must seek outside his own class, and when his search appears to be frustrated he turns back to the very worst within his own social group. Thus his marriage to Carrie Mitchell is doomed as much by his nature as hers. The mixed motives of social pity and sexual attraction that lead to the marriage conflict are nullified by her relapse into drunkenness and prostitution; a fall which is due partly to habit but also in a large degree to the boredom and frustration brought about by Golding's attempts to make her worthy of himself:

> At first he had always taken Carrie with him when he went
> on these evening walks, but by degrees her commonplace
> chatter, her vulgarisms of thought and language, her utter
> insensibility to the impressions of the season and the hour,
> rendered her company at such times intolerable to him.[28]

By making Arthur Golding an artist Gissing places him as superior, not merely to his social background, but to even the best of the working-class characters such as Will Noble. The artist, for Gissing, stands beyond society; he represents spiritual aspirations which by their very nature obliterate the slum background. Even the pavement artist who first teaches Arthur the rudiments of drawing:

> Was an idle, drunken, good-for-nothing fellow enough, but
> now and then he had a few ideas somewhat above the level of
> of his surroundings, and Arthur found unceasing pleasure in
> his conversation.[29]

For the Gissing hero the way out is through an understanding of Art. He escapes from the slums by appreciating a culture which is alien, not only to the working man, but to the vast mass of mankind; for, ironically, those qualities which make Arthur Golding

exceptional in the slums, make him just as outstanding in the
West End world of Mr Gresham and Helen Norman.

In *The Unclassed* and in *Thyrza* Gissing avoided the problems
that Arthur Golding's working-class upbringing had given by
making both Osmond Waymark and Walter Egremont financially
independent. The former, an aspiring novelist, is university
educated and supplements a small private income by working first
as a school teacher and later as a rent collector in the slums. The
latter is a wealthy intellectual who is brought into contact with
slum life when he gives a series of lectures on English literature
to a select group drawn from 'the upper artisan and mechanic
class'.[30] Julian Casti, Osmond Waymark's companion, is a shop
assistant, whose spare time is devoted solely to self-education and
the writing of poetry on classical themes.

Here once again we find that same absorption in the condition
of the poor by people who are not themselves part of the scene
they discuss. This is especially noticeable in Waymark's literary
theories which are almost identical to those of Gissing quoted
earlier:

> The fact is, the novel of every-day life is getting worn out.
> We must dig deeper, get to untouched social strata. Dickens
> felt this but he had not the courage to face his subjects; his
> monthly numbers had to lie on the family tea-table. Not
> *virginibus puerisque* will be my book, I assure you, but for
> men and women who like to look beneath the surface, and
> who understand that only as artistic material has human life
> any significance.[31]

And later:

> Art, nowadays, must be the mouthpiece of misery, for misery
> is the keynote of modern life.[32]

Julian Casti's praise of the novel strikes just the right note to
please Waymark:

> 'It is horrible,' he exclaimed; 'often hideous and revolting to
> me; but I feel its absolute truth. Such a book will do more
> good than half a dozen religious societies.'[33]

Waymark's novel is, of course, *Workers in the Dawn*, and as we
have seen, that misery which 'is the keynote of modern life' is

not so much the misery of the suffering poor (although this is no facile romance and the reader is made fully aware of the reality of working-class poverty), as the intellectual torment of a substitute working-class hero.

In this respect the most interesting aspect of *The Unclassed* and *Thyrza* is the type of heroine chosen by Gissing. In his first novel Helen Norman had been a goddess. Supremely beautiful, virtuous, intellectual, wealthy, irreligious and possessed of a strong social conscience, she was in class terms far above Arthur Golding, though in spite of this, no less than he deserved. But in these two later novels the Arthur Golding–Helen Norman relationship is reversed, and it is the heroines who are given working-class backgrounds. They are neither wealthy nor intellectual: Ida Starr is a prostitute and Thyrza a factory girl. Yet they are still treated in a manner similar to Arthur Golding. They are provided with qualities of beauty and character which make them independent of, or indeed out of place in, a working-class setting. Ida Starr is perfectly at ease with the money that eventually comes to her, and by the close of the novel has successfully made the incredible journey from unconventional prostitute to conventional Lady Bountiful. Thyrza too, after some grooming, is more at home with Egremont's upper-class friends than with her own relatives in Paradise Street.

The presentation of Ida Starr and Thyrza indicates an important problem that Gissing, at this stage of his development, was unsure how exactly to handle – the sexual attractiveness of working-class women. In his first novel he had made it quite clear that Carrie Mitchell's hold over Golding was largely sexual, but the full force of this issue was avoided by making her a prostitute. Furthermore he had employed the idealized image of Helen Norman as a continual contrast to the gross Carrie Mitchell. Helen refuses, in spite of her constant praise of the free and unconventional life, to live with Golding while his wife is alive, and he returns to Carrie. Both decisions are openly approved by Gissing. The working-class girl, despite her cultural deficiency, is good enough to serve as a sexual partner for Golding, while the upper-class girl remains a sexually attractive but morally aloof paragon. As a way out of this unsatisfactory dilemma Gissing allowed working-class heroines such as Ida Starr and Thyrza to be sexually attractive only in proportion as they possessed upper-class qualities. This was, of course, the traditional solution. In earlier novels the more ordinary working-class characters do not seem to have a sex life at all. On the one hand there is the coy courtship, and on the other, the slum father or mother surrounded by children. The exceptional working-class hero, however, as exemplified by Alton Locke or Felix Holt, is attracted only to upper-class women, who in turn offer themselves to him as a reward for his class superiority. Gissing's presentation of Thyrza and Ida Starr is a variation on this literary convention. It was not until *The Nether World* that he was to dissent completely from it.

That Gissing realized he was here dealing with exceptional people is frequently apparent. The very title *The Unclassed* establishes the social fluidity of Casti, Waymark and Ida Starr, and even Gilbert Grail, the working man Thyrza throws over when she realizes that she is in love with Egremont, is not allowed to be typical: 'We have every reason to think highly of Mr. Grail,' Annabel remarked. 'He must be as exceptional in his class as she is.'[34] And Gissing gives to Gilbert Grail the highest praise possible:

> To Gilbert, a printed page was as the fountain of life; he
> loved literature passionately, and hungered to know the
> history of man's mind through all the ages. This distinguished
> him markedly from the not uncommon working man who
> zealously pursues some chosen branch of study . . . Taste for
> literature pure and simple, and disinterested love of historical
> search, are the rarest things among the self-taught.[35]

Where this constant stress on characters who are classless falls down is that the issues naturally raised are repeatedly avoided. Like many earlier novelists Gissing continually pressed home the argument that the slums corrupt humanity and are therefore evil, but at the same time he was unwilling to face the necessary implications of his belief – that if the novel is to deal with working-class life then it must place at the centre working-class men and women who are representative of and not superior to their social environment.

Demos, Gissing's 'savage satire on working-class aims and capacities',[36] represents one way of solving this problem. Richard Mutimer is a 'mechanical engineer' who unexpectedly inherits a fortune from a distant relative. He uses the money to set up an industrial town run on firm Socialist principles, but is corrupted by the upper-class life he enters, recognizing it to be in all ways superior to that offered by his own class.

What is especially revealing here is the type of character given to Richard Mutimer:

> Richard represented – too favourably to make him anything but an exception – the best qualities his class can show. He was the English artisan as we find him on rare occasions, the issue of a good strain which has managed to procure a sufficiency of food for two or three generations.[37]

Physically he equalled the 'natural ease and dignity . . . of the picked men of the upper class';[38] but it is in the intellectual sphere that he becomes inferior. As so often in Gissing we see the worth of a man evaluated by the type of books he has in his library:

> Without exception they belonged to that order of literature which, if studied exclusively and for its own sake – as here it was, – brands a man indelibly, declaring at once the incompleteness of his education and the deficiency of his instincts. Social, political, religious, – under these three heads the volumes classed themselves, and each class was represented by productions of the 'extreme' school. The books which a bright youth of fair opportunities reads as a matter of course, rejoices in for a year or two, then throws aside for ever were here treasured to be the guides of a lifetime.[39]

It is an extremely significant chapter. The implications are clear. Richard Mutimer is to be out of place in upper-class society because he has not read the right books. He will fail to help the Socialist cause and his character will be corrupted because he does not possess the key to Paradise – a knowledge of imaginative literature:

> English literature was to him a sealed volume; poetry he scarcely knew by name; of history he was worse than ignorant, having looked at this period and that through distorting media, and congratulating himself on his clear vision because he saw men as trees walking.[40]

Gilbert Grail had possessed the very sensibility which Mutimer lacks, but he had been uninterested in social issues, while Mutimer prepares to set himself up as a leader of men. In order to fight for his class Mutimer must enter into conflict with those upper-class men he physically equals; but sensitivity is also required and Mutimer possesses only the kind of intellect peculiar to his class. Gissing is apologizing that Mutimer is not something better. Society may be to blame but the obvious conclusions are shirked:

> The bent of his mind would have led him to natural science, but opportunities of instruction were lacking, and the chosen directors of his prejudice taught him to regard every fact, every discovery, as *for* or *against* something.[41]

When we first meet the Mutimer family, Richard, although 'never having suffered actual want',[42] lives in a slum district, is a Radical lecturer at Working-Men's Clubs, and has just lost his job because of his socialist sympathies. He is naturally defined in terms of 'for' and 'against'. Although Gissing sympathizes with this he is unable to treat Mutimer other than satirically. The result once again is an avoidance of main issues and a romance of corrupted character and inter-class love, which is doomed because the working man is not worthy of his wife. For unlike Golding, Waymark, Ida Starr or Thyrza, Richard Mutimer is inferior to his new environment, and it is for this that Gissing apologizes.

The working man's attitude to life around him is merely one type of response. To the best of the slum novelists of the nineties such attitudes constituted an integral part of working-class expression. The slum novelists felt justified in criticizing social conditions, but not in criticizing attitudes produced by those conditions. Gissing never drew such a distinction. Because of his stress upon the supreme worth of a highly developed aesthetic sense, he could recognize only one type of response; all others were not different, but wrong:

> One evening, while he was standing on the bridge admiring the Thames gleaming with glorious colours in the sunset, he noticed a workman near him enjoying the spectacle and was delighted to think that the poor man was able to respond to the beauty of the scene. But the man turned to him with the remark, 'Throws up an 'eap of mud, don't she?'[43]

As Jacob Korg has pointed out, this real life experience provided the model for Carrie Mitchell's description of a beautiful sunset

as being 'almost as pretty as the theaytre',[44] but it has an importance far beyond this. As we have seen, Gissing's heroes would
never be allowed to respond to such a situation in this way.
Golding, Waymark, Egremont, Ida Starr, Julian Casti, even
Thyrza and Gilbert Grail; none of these could ever have been so
vulgar, and Richard Mutimer is corrupted because he certainly
could have been. Thus the one group of heroes is treated sympathetically and Mutimer alone is the object of Gissing's heavy
satire. At this point Gissing clearly believed that the working man
was not fitted for an heroic role.

IV

Gissing's repeated use of a substitute working-class hero as the
focal point of his novels does not lead, as one might expect, to a
direct confrontation between the very rich and the very poor. On
the contrary, his extreme sensitivity to class distinctions made it
possible for him to present in his novels a wider cross section of
lower-class society than any other English novelist. Of the
different types of working-class characters discussed in Ch. 1,
only the criminal is really absent from Gissing's novels, although
Bob Hewett in *The Nether World* is probably best classified thus.
The respectable, intellectual, poor, debased and eccentric are
all represented, and within this basic classification numerous
variations are exercised.

In his first novel Gissing exaggerated both the substitute hero
and the vileness of the slum environment, and as a natural result
of this he concentrated on working-class characters who were
either debased or respectable. Of the ordinary poor only Ned
Quirk and the Rumball family come to life and they are employed
simply to help move Arthur from the clutches of the debased; an
essential step towards the ultimate discovery of his social and
intellectual equals.

The small group of respectable working men that centres upon
Mr Tollady, the printer, are similar figures to Crossthwaite in
Alton Locke. By virtue of an elementary utilitarian education and
a tendency towards the kind of reading that, as we have already
seen, Gissing regarded as producing well intentioned but culturally
deficient men, they are naturally attracted to atheism, radical

politics and the Working-Men's Club. Mrs Frederick Harrison's remark that 'the finer type of London workman has never been so truly drawn'[45] is understandable, but the excessive emphasis on their fine qualities tends to set them apart from the physical and spiritual struggles inherent in their social position. They are sincere, honest to a fault, and deeply concerned about the condition of those less fortunate than themselves; they are moderate in their political beliefs, and have some savings behind them mainly because they are strict teetotallers. It is significant that the Working-Men's Club they run declines because the ordinary members prefer to spend their spare time drinking and listening to a less rational kind of political discussion than Will Noble will countenance. It is also significant that the only revolutionary among them, Pether, suffers a particularly gruesome death babbling insanely about the imminent annihilation of the aristocracy. What rings untrue about their portraiture is that they are as much propagandist material as the virulent slum descriptions, and it was largely for this reason that the one called forth the admiration of Mrs Harrison as the other did that of her husband.

In creating the debased characters that are treated with so much repulsion in *Workers in the Dawn*, Gissing was consciously rebelling against the methods employed by his idol, Dickens. Although always eager to insist that 'had the word been in use [Dickens] must necessarily have called himself a Realist',[46] he disagreed strongly with Dickens's presentation of lower-class characters. Gissing could not subscribe to what he regarded as one of Dickens's leading principles, 'that the decent poor aret he salt of the earth';[47] nor could he follow the Master in striving 'to make the common and the unclean most forcibly picturesque'.[48] It is a commonplace of criticism that Gissing sadly lacked a sense of humour, but here, like so many other late-Victorian novelists, he felt that in earlier fiction humour had been misused, and that Dickens had glossed over painful subjects in order to maintain the intimate author-reader relationship prevalent in the mid-Victorian period. Furthermore, unlike most twentieth-century critics, Gissing did not draw too sharp a distinction between Dickens's early and later work. He recognized Dickens's increased concern with the structure and symbolism of his novels, and also his growing disillusionment with society, but he did not believe that this represented a basic change in attitude towards the

working classes. Like many of his contemporaries Gissing regarded *David Copperfield* as Dickens's finest achievement, and the
spontaneous humour of the earlier novels as his most characteristic
work. When Gissing criticized the 'realism' of Dickens's working-
class characters it was primarily the great comic creations that he
used as a standard for comparison. Thus Gissing yielded to no
one in his admiration of Sam Weller, but:

> In the flesh, we know, he never walked the streets of London;
> the man most nearly resembling him was deformed with no
> little coarseness, and made but an imperfect response to the
> appeals of humanity or honour.[49]

With Mrs Gamp the same distinction has to be made:

> In plain words, then, we are speaking of a very loathsome
> creature; a sluttish, drunken, avaricious, dishonest woman.
> Meeting her in the flesh, we should shrink disgusted, so well
> does the foulness of her person correspond with the baseness
> of her mind. Hearing her speak, we should turn away in
> half-amused contempt. Yet, when we encounter her in the
> pages of Dickens, we cannot have too much of Mrs. Gamp's
> company.[50]

But if, in the presentation of characters like Sam Weller and Mrs
Gamp, Gissing was unwilling to dispense with Dickens's humour
in exchange for photographic realism, he was less impressed by
Dickens's more serious working-class portraits. Referring to Alice
Marwood he wrote: 'It is doubtful whether one could pick out
a single sentence, a single phrase, such as the real Alice Marwood
could conceivably have used.'[51] Lizzie Hexam he criticized in a
similar manner, and dismissed Betty Higden as 'one of the least
valuable of [Dickens's] pictures of poor life'.[52] It was in this
respect that he hailed Hogarth as the true English forerunner of
the late-Victorian realistic novelists who 'desire above everything
to be recognized as sincere in their picturing of life'.[53] In his own
working-class novels he was determined to reject the idealism of
Dickens and present the unvarnished horror of it all. The debased
poor in *Workers in the Dawn* represent Gissing's attempt to show
Sam Weller and Mrs Gamp without the transforming quality of
humour.

The Blatherwicks, Pettindunds and Carrie Mitchell's cronies

are shown as beasts feeding with glee on the foulness of slum life, who enjoy nothing better than attempting to corrupt those in possession of finer sensibilities than themselves. Bill Blatherwick who earns a living by skilfully acting the part of a deformed beggar carries a piece of cardboard reading:

CHRISTIEN FRIENDS!

Pray concider a widood Father
The victim of a Explogion
And may God bless you.[54]

When Arthur Golding returns to Whitecross Street he lives with Bill Blatherwick and his mother because he knows no other home. There he is trained to sing hymns as a pathetic companion to the phoney street beggar. In drunken fits the Blatherwicks starve and torture him until he is rescued by Ned Quirk. Drunkenness and sadism are shown to be accepted features of the Blatherwicks' way of life. They have no streak of humanity in them. They are what Gissing must have felt Sam Weller and Mrs Gamp to have been in reality; yet, ironically, they most clearly testify to the strong influence of Dickens upon Gissing, recalling as they do the black portraits of the workhouse crones in *Oliver Twist*.

Nowhere in Gissing is the conscious attempt to contrast his own view of working-class life with that of Dickens more pronounced than in his description of the Pettindunds' Christmas festivities. All the trappings associated with the Victorian image of Dickens are there: the time of happiness even for the poor, the flaming pudding and the succulent bird, the music and dancing. What has changed is the author's good will. The feast becomes an orgy, the merry-making insensate drunkenness, and the warm feeling of humanity towards others a begrudging selfishness. Christmas in the Pettindund household cannot possibly be a time when the better side of human nature comes to the fore because here there is only bestiality and that becomes flagrant and repellently open.

The expectation and preparation which in Dickens are important and happy aspects of the Christmas scene become public manifestations of fearful greed. For weeks before Christmas all efforts are concentrated on this one great feast of the year. Gissing explains the intricate social customs. The Pettindunds enrol in the 'goose' and 'grocer's' clubs, manage to save a pound a week out of the meagre family income, gradually pawn every inessential, and even procure a loan on the security of their house and furniture. The preliminaries completed the family rests: 'It was like the diver taking a long breath before he springs into the water, like the athlete reposing his sinews for a moment before he tries an enormous effort of strength.'[55] On Christmas Eve the orgy begins, with the Pettindunds and their guests pausing only to sleep off the effects of their continuous eating, drinking, dancing and fighting, and finally to turn with righteous indignation upon Carrie Mitchell and her illegitimate baby. It is Arthur Golding who points the moral: 'Do not such blackguards as these give good cause to the upper classes to speak of us working men with contempt? I warrant they waste as much money today in guzzling and swilling as would give twenty or thirty poor starving wretches a good dinner for a week to come.'[56]

In *The Unclassed* there is almost no attempt to present working-class characters, yet a sense of shameful poverty pervades the novel. This is achieved partly by the amoral behaviour of Casti's wife, Harriet, and her friend Mrs Sprowls, and partly by the frequent discussions on Art and social questions among the unclassed characters. But most of all the reader is made aware of the evils of slum life through the occasional appearances of a symbolic slum inhabitant called Slimy. Until the climax of the novel he is hardly presented as human at all. He stands as a substitute for the virulent slum descriptions of Gissing's first novel:

> Leaning on the counter, in one of the compartments, was something which a philanthropist might perhaps have had the courage to claim as a human being; a very tall creature, with bent shoulders, and head seeming to grow straight out of its chest; thick grizzled hair hiding almost every vestige of feature, with the exception of one dreadful red eye, its fellow being dead and sightless.[57]

He first appears scrounging drinks in the pub. When the rent collector calls he is lying on a bare bedstead in his filthy room, surrounded by the junk he has collected; and later he is shown standing on his head in the gutter singing songs for pennies, and being tormented by street urchins who hurl mud into his open mouth. Suddenly he comes to life. When Waymark calls to collect the rent, Slimy attacks him, takes the money and goes out to drink himself to death.

Slimy's role in *The Unclassed* is almost identical with that of Tom-All-Alone's in *Bleak House*. He symbolizes all the uncertainty, ignorance, distress and latent violence of an unknown world. Just as he is transformed into an animal so the slum is humanized. When Abraham Woodstock, the rack-renter, pays his one sympathetic visit to his property, he catches smallpox and dies. In *The Unclassed* the slum is a power that cannot be neglected. Like Slimy it can reach out and suddenly strike at society, and is at its most dangerous when ignored.

With *Demos* Gissing returned to a more direct portrayal of working-class life. In artistic terms it is a considerable advance on *Workers in the Dawn* and *The Unclassed*, but, excepting Richard Mutimer, the presentation of working-class characters in *Demos* is less interesting than in any other Gissing novel. We have already seen that *Demos* was Gissing's first attempt at placing a genuine working man at the heart of a working-class novel, and that Richard Mutimer's betrayal of his Socialist principles is symbolic of the misguided and ultimately hopeless revolutionary aspirations of the people. In a very real sense Richard Mutimer is the essence of 'Demos'. He may appear to be superior to his working-class environment but when put to the test, when placed under pressure, he fails. At such moments the very worst aspects of his personality (the working-class aspects) come to the fore, and the upper-class life he covets is seen to be totally unattainable The main point Gissing is making about Mutimer is that he is an incomplete human being, he is tainted by his class background to such a degree that the positive qualities he possesses are destroyed by the negative qualities he is incapable of correcting.

Demos is the most didactic and the most snobbish of Gissing's novels. The central message is that the working classes are incapable of any meaningful kind of material or intellectual development. This idea is fully realized so long as the action centres upon the symbolic figure of Mutimer, but breaks down when minor working-class characters are introduced. Lacking Mutimer's complexity they are presented merely as types who epitomize specific working-class qualities. Mutimer's brother 'Arry (the very name comes from a cartoon character) is described as representing 'a very large section of Demos'.[58] He is by name and nature a street layabout, a wastrel, for whom the inherited money can do nothing but harm. The same is true of Alice Mutimer, the pretty working-class snob to whom money will bring only discontent. Another type is represented by Daniel Dabbs, 'the proletarian pure and simple':

> A man of immense strength, but bull-necked and altogether ungainly – his heavy fist, with its black veins and terrific knuckles, suggested primitive methods of settling disputes; the stumpy fingers, engrimed hopelessly, and the filthy broken nails, showed how he wrought for a living. His face, if you examined it without prejudice, was not ill to look upon; there was much good humour about the mouth, and the eyes, shrewd enough, could glimmer a kindly light. His laughter was roof-shaking – always a good sign in a man.[59]

In this one paragraph everything is said about Daniel Dabbs that needs to be. His type has been noted and fixed; he is ready to play his representative part in the novel.

The family group consisting of Emma Vine, Kate Clay and the dying child Jane, serves a similar representative function. The surnames used to differentiate the two sisters are clearly symbolic. Emma Vine is the idealized, ignorant girl who 'clings' to Mutimer in spite of his cruelty; and Kate Clay represents the slatternly, mean-minded side of working-class womanhood. The sentimentalized dying child who makes up this family group is a figure taken from working-class romance, the sole concession to the suffering poor made in the novel. Only with the portrait of old Mrs Mutimer does Gissing escape from working-class types. Her rejection of the new way of life offered by her wealthy son is treated with considerable psychological understanding and no sentimentality. She is the first of Gissing's working-class characters to come over to the reader as a human being, and in this sense anticipates the profounder working-class characters in *Thyrza* and *The Nether World*.

Towards the close of *Demos* there is one point of view advanced that stands in complete contradiction to the central theme of the novel. It comes from Mr Wyvern, the country priest:

> It is a mistake due to mere thoughtlessness, or ignorance, to imagine the labouring or even the destitute, population as ceaselessly groaning beneath the burden of their existence. Go

along the poorest street in the East End of London and you will hear as much laughter, witness as much gaiety, as in any thoroughfare of the West. Laughter and gaiety of a miserable kind? I speak of it as relative to the habits and capabilities of the people. A being of superior intelligence regarding humanity with an eye of perfect understanding would discover that life was enjoyed every bit as much in the slum as in the palace.[60]

In *Demos*, Gissing (the 'being of superior intelligence') had not regarded working-class humanity with 'perfect understanding'. He is now coming to believe that the novelist can only present the truth about the working classes by regarding their behaviour as relative to their habits and capabilities. This realization signifies a crucial stage in the history of working-class fiction, and a turning point in Gissing's artistic development.

There are no Blatherwicks, Pettindunds, Slimys or even 'Arrys in *Thyrza*. From their window the two sisters see some beggar children 'visaged like debased monkeys',[61] but they only pass across the scene; just one grotesque image amongst a mass of normal street sounds and smells. All the inhabitants of Paradise Street belong to the working class but no longer does this automatically equate them financially with the beggar or culturally with the beast. In *Workers in the Dawn* there were no important characters who came between the extremes of a Blatherwick and a Will Noble. In *Thyrza*, every working-class character, excluding the exceptional heroine, is skilfully placed in a social hierarchy. At the top stands the slightly better-off, mean-minded factory foreman Mr Bower, and at the base the rather sentimentalized Mr Boddy, whose death from starvation and pride recalls Betty Higden in *Our Mutual Friend*.

Within this group the most significant advance is in the presentation of Luke Ackroyd and Totty Nancarrow, the former an artisan friend of Gilbert Grail, the latter a factory girl. Both are presented as sharper witted than their companions, showing a response to events that has nothing to do with the superior potential of Thyrza Trent or Gilbert Grail, but is firmly based on a love of independence for its own sake:

'Have you heard any talk,' he asked presently, 'about lectures by a Mr. Egremont? He's a son of Bower's old governor.'
'No, what lectures?'

'Bower tells me he's a young fellow just come from Oxford or Cambridge, and he's going to give some free lectures here in Lambeth.'

'Political?'

'No. Something to do with literature.'

Ackroyd broke into another laugh – louder this time and contemptuous.

'Sops to the dog that's beginning to show his teeth!' he exclaimed. 'It shows you what's coming. The capitalists are beginning to look about and ask what they can do to keep the people quiet. Lectures on Literature! Fools! As if that wasn't just the way to remind us of what we've missed in the way of education. It's the best joke you could hit on. Let him lecture away; he'll do more than he thinks.'[62]

This sounds very much like Kingsley, but if we compare the presentation of Ackroyd with that of Crossthwaite or Jemmy Downes, we can see how Gissing has transformed Kingsley's simple moral attitude into an objectively observed reality. For Kingsley the man who sneers at upper-class attempts to educate the workers is guilty of subversion and such a person either goes on to advocate class violence, is justly punished, repents and emigrates (which is what happens to Crossthwaite); or he loses all power of self-control and sinks into the slums, like Jemmy Downes. In *Alton Locke* everything is directed towards proving the rightness of the hero's final conversion.

Ackroyd, however, neither turns to active politics, dies a gruesome death, nor repents. He rejects Egremont's idealism because he regards it as pointless; the political terminology he uses is merely his way of expressing a determination to remain free. When he first appears he has just spent eighteenpence on an electrical handbook which is something, unlike imaginative literature or upper-class educational schemes, that helps him to define his position in life. In *Demos* Richard Mutimer had incurred Gissing's wrath for a similar attitude, but in the later novel, Ackroyd, while seen as lacking character, is treated with a sympathy that shows a growing understanding of the true nature of the exceptional working man, for Ackroyd's ability has no spiritual outlet as has Gilbert's or Thyrza's. He is bound by his slum environment, not by intellectual frustration:

Ackroyd had his idea of a social revolution and, though it seemed doubtful whether he was exactly the man to claim a larger sphere for the energies of his class, his thought often had a genuine nobleness, clearly recognisable by Gilbert.[63]

When Gilbert Grail is depressed it is because of his lack of knowledge; when Ackroyd is depressed it is for reasons which can find expression solely in vague, revolutionary clichés, and going deliberately to get drunk. His aimlessness and lack of purpose owe little to his rejection by Thyrza (that is merely one further disappointment) but grow out of his realization that, through no fault of his own, he is incarcerated in a social ghetto. The diffident courtship of Totty Nancarrow, the refusal to respond to Egremont's lectures, the street fight he picks for no apparent reason, and his occasional absences from work to go drinking, are details which have considerable meaning within the total pattern of the novel. When Gilbert Grail takes a message from Egremont, Ackroyd's answer is typical:

I liked his lectures well enough, as far as they went, but they're not the kind of thing to suit me nowadays. If I go and talk to him I'm bound to go to the lectures. What's the good? What's the good of anything?[64]

And certainly, what is the good of Egremont's approach? Only Grail truly responds to the lectures on Elizabethan dramatists. Ackroyd, like the rest of the class, is incapable of, or uninterested in, doing so. In *The Nether World* the hero was to be much nearer Ackroyd than Grail; the movement towards placing a working man at the heart of a working-class novel takes an important step nearer with *Thyrza*.

If Ackroyd anticipates Sidney Kirkwood, then Totty Nancarrow leads to Clem Peckover. A little of Ackroyd's roughness is smoothed out, and Totty's carefree vivacity is transformed into brutal selfishness, but in spite of this, the essential spirit of Ackroyd and Totty was later to be transferred from cheerful Lambeth to bleak Clerkenwell.

Just as Ackroyd is employed as a contrast to the exceptional Gilbert Grail so is Totty employed as a foil to Thyrza. In terms of grace and deportment Thyrza belongs with the upper class; not so Totty who is shown to be typical of her social group:

Ackroyd smoked a cigar, and Totty walked with her usual
independence, with that swaying of the haunches and swing
of the hands with palm turned outwards which is characteristic
of the London work-girl. Her laugh now and then rose to a
high note; her companion threw back his head and joined in
the mirth.[65]

None of Gissing's heroes could laugh like Ackroyd any more than
his heroines could walk like Totty. They are minor personages
whose ordinary class characteristics are employed to thrust into
prominence the superiority of Gilbert and Thyrza. Like Ackroyd,
Totty values above everything else her independence, and her total
acceptance of a working-class environment is expressed in a blunt,
common-sense manner which offers an ironic, and probably
unintentional, contrast to the sufferings of Grail and Thyrza.
Unfortunately the presentation of Totty required a lightness of
touch which Gissing did not possess, and although he managed to
avoid condescension, there is a feeling of self-consciousness about
the scenes in which she figures:

> 'Don't be a fool and waste your money!' was Totty's
> uncompromising advice. 'It's only sillies believes things like
> that.'
> 'Totty ain't no need of charms!' piped Tilly with sweets in
> her mouth. 'She knows who *she*'s going to marry.'
> 'Do I, miss?' Totty exclaimed scornfully. 'Do you know as
> much for yourself, I wonder?'
> 'Oh, Tilly's a-going to marry the p'liceman with red hair
> as stands on the Embankment!' came from Mrs. Allchin;
> whereupon followed inextinguishable laughter.[66]

Yet in spite of this the portraits of Ackroyd and Totty represent
a significant advance in that Gissing attempts to explore in some
depth the character of a working-class man and woman who are
neither exceptional nor debased. A small example shows this
change of attitude. When Totty's uncle dies and leaves her £250
she acts characteristically, offering the money and herself to Joe
Bunce, one of Gissing's eccentrics, so that he can set up shop and
attain his own independence. A vociferous atheist, a widower with
two children, consolidation within the only way of life she knows –
thus is money employed by Totty Nancarrow. The Pettindunds

would have drunk themselves to death, and Gilbert Grail would have rushed off to Athens or Rome. Gissing obviously was beginning to feel that there were other alternatives to choose from.

V

The Nether World (1889) is Gissing's most sustained study of slum life. It is the culminating achievement of the stages of development we have been tracing, yet, in a curious way, it is the most pessimistic of his working-class novels, standing in complete contrast to the gentle *Thyrza*. Most notably there is a return to the imagery of disease and death that dominated his early novels, indicating a resurgence of Gissing's bitter personal involvement with working-class life. But the early hysteria is now artistically controlled; and the novel, instilled with a fatalistic philosophy of stoical acceptance, gives class suffering tragic power.

There are several aspects of *The Nether World* that distinguish it both from Gissing's earlier work and also from any previous English novel. Every important character belongs by birth to the working class, and although one of the themes of the book is the urgent need to escape from the slums, no one is given those special qualities which by their very nature allow the working man to transcend the stultifying environment within which he is born and by which he is nurtured. Sidney Kirkwood and Jane Snowdon, although superior in both morality and intellect to the other characters, are totally unlike earlier Gissing heroes. They no longer stand aside from the working-class section of the book, acting out a separate, even a central drama, but are as much a part of the total pattern as the very lowest slum inhabitant. Even the stock romantic idea of the working man returning from the Colonies, wealthy and with a plan to employ his fortune in philanthropic schemes, contributes fully to the dominant theme – that there is no escape from the slums, there is only self-preservation.

This view of working-class life prohibits the use of substitute heroes. For the slum is a trap from which there is no truly satisfying form of escape. To reach the upper world would be to undertake a journey the route of which all the inhabitants of the nether world are ignorant. Gissing's usual answer that high culture provides a way out of the slums is here shown as merely an incipient yearning that can never mature: 'To select for one's chamber a woodcut after Constable or Gainsborough is at all events to give proof of a capacity for civilisation.'[67] But capacity alone is useless because it is beset on all sides by snares: 'In the upper world a youth may "sow his wild oats" and have done with it; in the nether, "to have your fling" is almost necessarily to fall among criminals.'[68] Gissing now fully accepts that merely to transplant upper-class qualities on to a lower-class girl is to ignore the totally different family structures that exist in the two worlds:

> We're working people, we are; we're the lower orders; our girls have to go out and get their livings. We teach them the best we can, and the devil knows they've got examples enough of misery and ruin before their eyes to help them to keep straight. Rich people can take care of their daughters as much as they like; they can treat them like children till they're married; people of our kind can't do that, and it has to be faced.[69]

Thus, for Sidney Kirkwood to have even an inkling of a better world outside, can at best lead only to frustration; for Bob Hewett to act, for instance, like Arthur Pendennis, is to be seized by the police; for Clara Hewett to move away from her father's control is to come in contact with forces which she has neither the experience nor the will to combat.

The nether world is one of ironic contrasts. It exists because of work and is a social problem because of that same work:

> Here every alley is thronged with small industries; all but every door and window exhibits the advertisement of a craft that is carried on within. Here you may see how men have multiplied toil for toil's sake, have wrought to devise work superfluous, have worn their lives away in imagining new forms of weariness.[70]

The streets no longer have the gaiety and friendly activity of Thyrza's Lambeth. Everywhere a passive ugliness prevails:

> On all the doorsteps sat little girls, themselves only just out of infancy, nursing or neglecting bald, red-eyed, doughy-limbed abortions in every stage of babyhood, hapless spawn of diseased humanity, born to embitter and brutalise yet further the lot of those who unwillingly gave them life.[71]

Even the brief, photographic slum descriptions that Gissing had so painstakingly learnt how to handle, are here rejected as pointless:

> Needless to burden description with further detail; the slum was like any other slum; filth, rottenness, evil odours, possessed these dens of superfluous mankind and made them gruesome to the peering imagination.[72]

As the central characters are now themselves working class they can be allowed to define actively their own world. The slum setting serves to evoke an atmosphere of universality. When Sidney Kirkwood takes a train into the country he looks down over 'the pest-stricken regions of East London . . . across miles of a city of the damned . . . above streets swarming with a nameless population'.[73]

Throughout the novel the idea of the slum as a human trap is relentlessly pursued, and the actions of every character are circumscribed by it. Sidney Kirkwood struggles in vain to persuade the Hewett family to move to more comfortable lodgings but 'it was like contending with some hostile force of nature'.[74] Clara rejects self-control completely: 'It was not her own doing; something impelled her, and the same force – call it chance or destiny – would direct the issue once more.'[75] Even her father gives up as useless the struggle to prevent her leaving home:

> What a vile, cursed world this is, where you may see men and women perish before your eyes, and no more chance of saving them than if they were going down in mid-ocean![76]

He fails to save his daughter because social frustration forces her to adopt the only philosophy open to her: 'We have to fight, to fight for everything, and the weak get beaten. That's what life has taught me.'[77] Ironically the girl on the receiving end of this advice follows the same code when she hurls acid into Clara's face.

That Clara's view of life is not the only possible choice open to the working classes is clear from the presentation of Sidney Kirkwood. If he does not escape from the slums, he does discover the means of both staying alive and establishing a humane code of values. Clara chooses a path of weakness but she is no more to blame for her actions than most of the others. At one point Gissing directly states the economic reality underlying his thesis:

Genuine respect for law is the result of possessing something which the law exerts itself to guard. Should it happen that you possess nothing, and that your education in metaphysics has been grievously neglected, the strong probability is, that your mind will reduce the principle of society to its naked formula: Get, by whatever means, so long as with impunity.[78]

In *The Nether World* those who act according to this formula (Clara, Clem Peckover, Bob Hewett, Joseph Snowdon), eventually discover that they are playing into the hands of fate, that they are further limiting the possibility of life by their own selfishness. But even some who try to resist the temptation to act selfishly, such as John Hewett and Pennyloaf Candy, are crushed, simply because passivity in the nether world is as self-defeating as vigorous opposition. Only those who strive to replace the 'naked formula' by a positive moral code win a semblance of self-respect; only the iron-willed can combat, although never really defeat, the inexorable power of the slum, for 'poverty makes a crime of every indulgence'.[79]

One of the most remarkable aspects of this novel is the manner in which Gissing presents working-class women of such diverse types as Pennyloaf Candy and Clem Peckover. The two women are completely opposite products of the slums. Both rivals for the affections of Bob Hewett, they are fated to be defeated by forces they are incapable of comprehending. It is the defenceless and passive Pennyloaf who actually wins Bob:

She was a meagre, hollow-eyed, bloodless girl of seventeen, yet her features had a certain charm, that dolorous kind of prettiness which is often enough seen in the London needle-slave.[80]

First introduced on the way to the pawnbroker (the most potent reminder of the impermanence of property in working-class life), she marries Bob only after she has been savagely mauled by Clem. Even though, with a brutal father and a drunken mother, she is accustomed to violence, Clem Peckover terrifies her. Spurned by Bob's parents because he had 'married beneath him', they spend their wedding day at the Crystal Palace, described in the often quoted chapter 'Io Saturnalia'. Gissing had tried to write such scenes before but had never managed to objectify his personal feelings. Here he succeeds in presenting a panoramic picture of the working classes at play, using indirect speech both to describe and comment ironically. It is a remarkable *tour de force* – the milling crowd, the coarse banter, the evident animal enjoyment, the dancing and music, all bound together by the voice of the commentator. These people are no longer the vile harpies of *Workers in the Dawn* but a vast mass of discontented human beings, seizing upon the final Bank Holiday before the winter sets in as the only excuse for a communal orgy until the spring. If Gissing can hardly be considered sympathetic, at least the pity of earlier days now becomes sadness:

> A great review of the People. Since man came into being, did the world ever exhibit a sadder spectacle?[81]

Although she knows it must end in violence Pennyloaf accepts the treat. For her it has a special significance, an opportunity to shine which she must not forgo:

> How proud she was of her ring! How she turned it round and round when nobody was looking! Gold, Pennyloaf, real gold! The pawnbroker would lend her seven-and-sixpence on it, any time.[82]

When they return to their single room, Pennyloaf with her wedding clothes torn, Bob drunk and bloody from a fight of Clem Peckover's arranging, they hear from outside their window the sounds of a drunken woman:

> 'That's mother,' sobbed Pennyloaf. 'I knew she wouldn't get over to-day. She never did get over a Bank-holiday.'[83]

The pattern of her life is immediately established. Already it is possible to foresee the breakdown of the first hours' tenderness, the quiet acceptance of a dying child, the beating from her husband, and the struggle to find sufficient money for food when he returns to the more exciting life of the streets. While Bob sleeps drunkenly beside her, Pennyloaf lies awake: 'She was thinking all the time that on the morrow it would be necessary to pawn her wedding-ring.'[84]

No husband will ever beat Clem Peckover. In many respects she is the triumph of the book. Nowhere in earlier English fiction had such a portrait of a working-class woman appeared. She has no qualities which could take her into any other society save that of the slums, nor does she desire any. Her particular brand of power, portrayed frequently in novels of upper-class life, has here a new force:

> One would have compared her, not to some piece of exuberant normal vegetation, but rather to a rank, evilly-fostered growth. The putrid soil of that nether world yields other forms besides the obviously blighted and sapless. [85]

She is described as 'an embodiment of fierce life, independent of morality', and at sixteen her 'charms' were 'of the coarsely magnificent order'. [86] As we have already seen, Gissing had earlier avoided presenting working-class girls as sexually attractive by endowing them with upper-class qualities of bearing, grace and spiritual beauty; other working-class girls had not been considered in sexual terms at all. Now, however, he is willing to face the fact that 'the soil of [the] nether world yields other forms besides the obviously blighted and sapless'. Clem Peckover is this world's equivalent of the *demi-mondaine*.

The problem of presenting her in a frank, 'realistic' manner was considerable. At this time there were several precedents in French fiction but none in English. Furthermore, in 1889 the opposition to Zolaism was at its height, and Gissing had never really forgotten the rough handling he had earlier received from *Punch* for daring to suggest that Thackeray's famous preface to *Pendennis*, in which he said that no writer since Fielding had 'been permitted to depict to his utmost power a MAN', referred to Arthur's sex life. [87] Although Gissing often delighted in seeing himself as a social outcast he was unwilling to become a martyr for the cause of realism, and the portrait of Clem is approached obliquely. Yet, by skilful placing and the accumulation of psychological detail, the true nature of Clem's power is conveyed.

In the chapter that introduces her, Gissing imbues her every action with a slothful sensuality. The detailed description of the greasy plate of food she gloatingly devours, together with her manner of spending a day off work lolling in front of a blazing fire, and taking her exercise in the form of a fearful assault on the young Jane Snowden, conveys faithfully a vivid picture of all-consuming animality. She is also always associated with men. Women are all enemies or potential enemies. Even the relationship with her mother is one of mutual selfishness. Her sadistic love of violence combined with her crude sensuality gives her a control over the men of the district which she ruthlessly employs. She sets Jack Bartley on to Bob Hewett during the Crystal Palace bacchanal because he has dared to marry Pennyloaf; urged on by her mother she traps Joseph Snowden into marrying her; and later when this marriage does not bring the hoped-for financial gain, she returns to Bob Hewett, urging him to help murder her husband, and to 'starve [Pennyloaf] and her brats half to death'.[88] Women she can deal with in her own manner:

> Pennyloaf flew with erected nails at Clem Peckover. It was just what the latter desired; in an instant she had rent half Pennyloaf's garments off her back, and was tearing her face till the blood streamed.[89]

Like Clara Hewett she believes that the law of the jungle alone has meaning in the slums. Violence is part of her natural expression: 'I'll have a kitchen-knife near by when I tell him,' she remarked with decision. 'If he lays a hand on me I'll cut his face open, an' chance it!'[90]

The violence of Clem, the bitterness of Clara, the passivity of Pennyloaf; all are self-defeating and merely emphasize the encircling trap, a movement which reaches its symbolic climax with the police hunt for Bob Hewett. It is the renewed contact with Clem that finally destroys him: 'Corruption was eating to his heart; from every interview with Clem he came away a feebler and baser being.'[91] His crime, making 'queer', detested by even the poor, "cause how can you tell who gets the bad coin',[92] is discovered only when a friend informs on him. Seriously wounded while trying to escape, he seeks refuge in Shooter's Gardens:

> The room contained no article of furniture. In one corner lay some rags, and on the mantle-piece stood a tin teapot, two cups, and a plate. There was no fire, but a few pieces of wood lay near the hearth, and at the bottom of the open cupboard remained a very small supply of coals. A candle made fast in the neck of a bottle was the source of light.[93]

Mrs Candy lies drunk on the floor, her half-idiot son watches blankly, the dying Bob sits propped against a wall. Outside Mad Jack can be heard shouting his bizarre sermon in French, and the trap finally closes in on Bob Hewett when Pennyloaf unwittingly leads the police to him.

Bob's death symbolizes the plight of every working-class character in the novel. Crushed and helpless, surrounded by drunkenness, idiocy and poverty, he dies with only the sound of meaningless religious exhortations in his ears. Gissing's technique here is considerably different from the straightforward realism of *Thyrza*. The simple tragic structure he employs is very similar to that of Hardy, whom Gissing greatly admired; and his use of grotesque images and extreme human situations in order to symbolize a corrupt social structure, shows the influence of Dickens's later novels. Like novelists before and after him Gissing had learnt that it was easier to write of the sensational than the normal aspects of working-class life; to concentrate upon the outcast and the derelict as though their behaviour signified the norm. In *The Nether World* he seriously attempted to strike a balance, but the most memorable sections of the novel are those which deal with Bob Hewett and Clem Peckover. Against this powerfully conceived treatment of amorality and violence, the qualities of moral strength and personal honesty that Gissing tries to set up as working-class positives, seem pale and insipid.

The most humanly tragic figure is John Hewett who watches bewildered as, through no fault of his own, the sense of independence born of regular employment as a skilled artisan is slowly eaten away. With his hair dyed black to make him look younger he walks the streets seeking work. When Clara returns home she finds that a vast slum-clearance plan has been put into effect and that her father now lives in the prison-like building that is society's answer to the working-class problem:

> What terrible barracks, those Farringdon Road Buildings!
> Vast, sheer walls, unbroken by even an attempt at ornament;
> row above row of windows in the mud-coloured surface,
> upwards, upwards, lifeless eyes, mirky openings that tell of
> bareness, disorder, comfortlessness within. One is tempted to
> say that Shooter's Gardens are a preferable abode.[94]

Slum clearance is no answer because it merely disrupts the basic structure of working-class life without offering any worthwhile compensation. The key phrase in this description is 'unbroken by even an attempt at ornament'. Shooter's Gardens had possessed a communal sense that helped palliate individual suffering, but the Farringdon Road flats serve both to destroy the community and further isolate the individual. Once again Gissing's powerful symbolism gives an ironic thrust to his central theme, for it is Bob Hewett, the criminal, who avoids the police by dying in Shooter's Gardens, while his father, the respectable working man, is sent to the Farringdon Road 'prison'.

The most bitter stroke of irony is the failure of Michael Snowdon's idealism. The money that was to help the poor goes, almost by accident, to Joseph. It has already made a marriage between Sidney Kirkwood and Jane impossible, and now, although the money enables Joseph to escape from Clem, it is soon lost in a business speculation. Idealism or philanthropy, slum clearance, attempts to live quietly, all are without hope in the nether world.

Although *The Nether World* presents a bleak picture of working-class life, in the response of Sidney Kirkwood there is established a sense of dignity which prevents pessimism from becoming despair or hysteria. Jane Snowdon is far less of a success. She is, as Mabel Donnelly has pointed out, 'Helen Norman off the pedestal',[95] but she is a pale and insignificant heroine besides Pennyloaf Candy and Clem Peckover, possessing goodness but not the will to survive. Her love for Sidney Kirkwood is destroyed by Michael's idealism, and in an attempt to pull together what remains of the Hewett family, Sidney marries Clara. All of the slum-dwellers live according to the law of the survival of the fittest and in *The Nether World*, the fittest are those who are true to self, those who nurture the finest qualities of which they are capable. Those who actively encourage the evil inherent in their natures are destroyed. Gissing points the moral at the close of the book:

> In each life little for congratulation. He with the ambitions
> of his youth frustrated; neither an artist, nor a leader of men
> in the battle for justice. She, no saviour of society by the
> force of a superb example; no daughter of the people, holding
> wealth in trust for the people's needs. Yet to both was their
> work given. Unmarked, unencouraged save by their love of
> uprightness and mercy, they stood by the side of those more
> hapless, brought some comfort to hearts less courageous than
> their own. Where they abode it was not all dark.[96]

These words signify Gissing's farewell to working-class fiction.

After *The Nether World* he felt that he could not trust himself to write further on the subject. Unlike Dickens, he had not shrunk from criticizing the poor, but with his new-found conviction that working-class life was a trap from which no one could really escape, he realized the hollowness of his particular brand of criticism. Occasionally, at the request of an editor, Gissing did write short stories on working-class themes.[97] But these belong to the different atmosphere of the nineties and represent no important change in his personal or artistic attitudes. Gissing now began to write his most characteristic work – studies of the classless intellectual helpless in the face of hostile social forces, whose only chance of survival is to 'make a world within the world'.[98] In the novels discussed here this subject is already beginning to emerge, for Gissing in *The Nether World* had finally dispensed with the view that such a hero must necessarily be connected, in one way or another, with working-class life. He was no longer confusing the classless intellectual with the working-class intellectual. It is one of his later heroes, Godwin Peake, who gives Gissing's reason for completely dissociating himself from the working classes. He explains that he has never gone among the very poor 'because a sight of their vileness would only have moved me to unjust hatred'.[99]

4

Walter Besant and the 'discovery' of the East End

I

Like Gissing, Walter Besant came to write about the working classes through his personal contact with the London slums. His response, however, was totally different:

> In 1880 and in 1881 I spent a great deal of time walking about the mean monotony of the East End of London. It was not a new field to me. That is to say, I had already seen some of it . . . but I had never before realised the vast extent of the eastern city, its wonderful collection of human creatures; its possibilities; the romance that lies beneath its monotony; the tragedies and the comedies, the dramas that are always playing themselves out in this huge hive of working bees.[1]

In *All Sorts and Conditions of Men* (1882) and *Children of Gibeon* (1886) Besant attempted to express something of the romantic feelings the East End inspired in him. His aims were frankly propagandist; his goal was the middle-class conscience:

> [*Children of Gibeon*] was the most truthful of anything that I have ever written . . . it offered the daily life and the manners – so far as they can be offered without offensive and useless realism – of the girls who do the rougher and coarser work of sewing in their lodgings.[2]

Late in his life he could justify the writing of *Children of Gibeon* on three grounds. First, it was accurately observed. Secondly, it drew people's attention to social problems, and even directly influenced the way that one Hoxton firm treated its work girls. Thirdly, the intense personal research it entailed took its author into philanthropic work.[3] It is interesting to note how close these three points seem to be to Gissing's early view of the working-class novel, and how at the same time he would have abruptly rejected the attitudes behind them. Although for a short while Gissing advocated the use of the novel as a platform for social-reform programmes, he never believed that there was little difference between a work of fiction and a sociological document. He was always a conscious, frequently self-conscious, artist, rather than a social reformer. Besant, on the other hand, was always more the reformer than artist. He evaluated his working-class novels according to the public interest they aroused in social problems, pressed home his advantage by lecture tours and sociological studies, and willingly participated in the administration of philanthropic schemes; whereas Gissing bitterly rejected the public that showed little interest in his work and retreated into a private, intensely introspective, world.

Yet the two novelists shared many qualities, notably an intimate knowledge and love of London, sympathy with the suffering of the poor, and determination to write only of those areas of life which they had personally examined. Where they differed was in their attitude towards 'offensive and useless realism'. To Besant such detail was offensive and therefore useless; to Gissing it was offensive and therefore true. As we have already seen it was on this very point that Gissing criticized Dickens, and in this respect Besant certainly belonged to the older school of thought. His belief that a girl who does the 'rougher and coarser work of sewing' should not herself be shown to be rough or coarse, was not merely a matter of literary prudery, but an essential part of his social philosophy.

What Besant preached was a simple theme of inter-class co-operation based on 'joy' or 'delight', qualities which, if certain social ills could be remedied, all men might share in common. The language of class war Besant loathed and in these two novels his aim is to bring together the rich and the poor in order that each can come to better understand the other. By using their money to help lighten the monotonous grind of the poor, the rich discover a meaningful role in life and, at the same time, strike at the very root of class discontent. The middle classes would fit uneasily into this scheme and are ignored, though the general tone of the novels ensured that the middle-class reader would find such a view of life attractive. For while Gissing's portraits of slum life confirmed his readers' worst fears, Besant assured his readers that those fears could be removed, simply and painlessly:

It is not by setting poor against rich, or by hardening the heart of rich against poor, that you will succeed: it is by independence and by knowledge. All sorts and conditions of men are alike. As are the vices of the rich, so are your own; as are your virtues, so are theirs. But, hitherto, the rich have had things which you could not get. Now all that is altered: in the Palace of Delight we are equal to the richest: there is nothing which we, too, cannot have: what they desire we desire; what they have we shall have: we can all love; we can all laugh; we can all feel the power of music; we can dance and sing; or we can sit in peace and meditate.[4]

Such feelings taken by themselves are certainly not to be mocked. The stress on cultural attainment as a means of transforming the life of the poor is a recurrent Victorian theme, and in slightly varying forms has affinities with the thought of Arnold, Ruskin and Morris; with the increasingly non-doctrinal approach to philanthropy by the various religious groups during this period; and, perhaps most of all, with the University Settlement movement.

But when Besant tried to express these theories in the form of a novel he was unable to breathe life into them. His refusal to struggle with the problems of realism that obsessed Gissing would have mattered less if he had openly acknowledged the utopian nature of his propaganda, as, for instance, Edward Bellamy and William Morris did in *Looking Backward* (1888) and *News from Nowhere* (1891), both of which are about the resolution of class war. But Besant insisted on presenting his world as a carefully documented actuality. He wished to describe not some future utopian state, but late-Victorian England, and in order to do so he drew upon the considerable knowledge of London he had gained in his twin public roles as antiquarian and amateur sociologist. To this knowledge he added all the clichés of the melodramatic love story, welding the two elements together in a search for 'the romance that lies beneath the monotony'. In his mind the one was no less real than the other: 'I have been told by certain friendly advisers that this story is impossible. I have, therefore, stated the fact on the title-page, so that no one may complain of being taken in or deceived. But I have never been able to understand why it is impossible.'[5]

Within five years of writing these words about *All Sorts and Conditions of Men*, Besant seemed to have won a spectacular victory over his 'certain friendly advisers', when the People's Palace was built in Whitechapel. It looked very much like a fantastic dream come true, for if Besant's novel did not actually inspire the idea, the publicity arising from it brought the necessary money pouring in. In May 1887 the Queen travelled to the Mile End Road to declare the Palace officially open and Sir Edmund Hay Currie, with a distinguished career in philanthropic work already behind him, was placed in charge of administration. Besant was appointed editor of the *Palace Journal* and eagerly awaited his chance to stir into life the dormant literary talent of the East End. Many years later he wrote of the bitter disappointment he experienced:

> Everything did not go on quite well. At the billiard tables, which were very popular, the young men took to betting, and it was thought best to stop billiards altogether. The literary club proved a dead failure; not a soul while I was connected with the Palace, showed the least literary ability or ambition.[6]

Within a few years Besant's Palace of Delight ran into financial difficulties and, under the aegis of the Drapers' Company, became 'a polytechnic and nothing else'.[7] The story of the People's Palace must be looked at again a little later; here it can serve as a rather sad real-life example of the utopian-realistic imbalance that typifies Besant's working-class novels.

II

All Sorts and Conditions of Men and *Children of Gibeon* are extremely crude variations on the substitute working-class approach that has been noted as typical of the romantic novel. The plots of both novels are based upon cases of mistaken identity in which wealthy men and women disguise themselves as workers and go to live in the slums. In *All Sorts and Conditions of Men*, Angela Messenger, the wealthiest heiress in England, whose money comes from a great brewery in the East End, goes straight from Newnham to Whitechapel where she sets up a model dressmaker's shop. She is helped by a young man, Harry Goslett, who has also turned his back on an upper-class life, and returned to the slums disguised as a cabinet maker with the intention of discovering his working-class ancestors. Struck by the terrible monotony of the slums, they plan a vast Palace of Delight, which is secretly built by Angela. The novel ends with a ritualistic marriage in the Palace which is attended by all the poor people with whom the two aristocrats have come in contact.

In *Children of Gibeon*, a wealthy aristocrat, Lady Mildred Eldridge, brings up the child of a washerwoman with her own daughter. The two girls are so alike that it is impossible to tell them apart, although everyone knows that one is a wealthy heiress and the other is penniless. Even the two girls, Valentine and Violet, do not know the answer to the riddle. Valentine, sure that she is the child of the washerwoman, goes to live with her poor 'sisters' in Hoxton. There she shows the poverty-stricken seamstresses how they can brighten their lives. She organizes them, dresses them in pretty clothes, prepares them dainty food and tidies their rooms. When the secret is revealed it is Valentine who is the heiress and Violet, whose one visit to the East End had disgusted her, who is the daughter of the washerwoman. This novel also ends ritualistically. Valentine marries her cousin Claude, who has been her constant companion in the slums and for most of the novel has been regarded as her brother. The classes are thus united, although Claude, the working-class representative who has been the object of Lady Mildred's philanthropy, now possesses a first-class Cambridge degree and an assured future as a lawyer.

A close look at the ludicrous plots of these two novels is worthwhile for several reasons. First, certain aspects of them – especially the new image of the East End – were taken up and used by many later, and often more important, writers than Besant. Secondly, their popular success gives some indication of the attitudes which readers of the eighties regarded as appropriate to the subject. And thirdly, as laughable as the bare outline of these plots may seem, when clothed with more detail they provide classic examples of that process of avoidance which has already been noted as characteristic of working-class romance. Besant's avoidance of central issues is extreme, but similar tendencies are observable in many greater novelists, both earlier and later.

It has already been sufficiently stressed that Besant places at the heart of his novels substitute working-class heroes and heroines, employing the wealthy aristocrat in a manner not far removed from Gissing's use of the classless intellectual. But whereas Gissing established a recognizably true working-class environment, Besant takes the process of avoidance one crucial step further. The men and women who inhabit his world have nothing whatsoever to do with any kind of slum life. His poor characters can be divided into two distinct groups – those who while poor are defined in terms of individual eccentricities, and those who are poor but have access to charity from wealthy patrons.

When Angela Messenger goes to live in Bormalack's lodging house on Stepney Green, her fellow boarders are an American husband and wife, in England to pursue their misguided claim to an English peerage, a crazy Australian Hebrew scholar, a clerk from the brewery who many years earlier had been falsely accused of stealing a vast sum of money, and Harry Goslett, the aristocratic cabinet maker. Of course Besant never actually advances these people as representatives of the East End slums, but their 'poverty' and the working out of their various problems are central to the theme of individual charity that runs through the book. There is clearly no difference between those for whom slum conditions are the normal way of life and those who have fallen from a higher social position and are obliged to live temporarily in the slums. It is all part of the romance that lies beneath the monotony:

> There is nothing at all beautiful or picturesque or romantic in it. There is only the romance of every life in it – there are sixty thousand lives in Hoxton, and every one has its own story to tell. [8]

The more genuine group of working-class people is that which Angela Messenger gathers about her to work in the dressmaker's shop. Every girl is shown to possess sufficient qualities to fall naturally, after the initial shock, into a way of life which includes playing tennis during a tea-break, eating a cooked lunch provided by Angela, and spending the evenings reading, singing and listening to music in the daintily decorated parlour. The benefits conferred upon this select group are merely a rehearsal for the full scale transformation of the East End to be effected by the Palace of Delight.

In *Children of Gibeon* the same two types of poor characters predominate, although here Besant does show the social evils he is trying to reform. The three sewing girls – Mclenda, who for most of the novel holds out against the charity offered to her; Lotty, who is dying and both unwilling to accept and unable to refuse the bribes offered her; and Lizzie, who at the last moment is saved from becoming the mistress of a profligate artist – do, for all their melodramatic and tiresomely moral treatment, represent genuine slum dilemmas. The scene in which Melenda is 'drilled' by her employer represents Besant at his best. He is able to lecture the reader on the process of drilling, display an intimate knowledge of his subject, and use the fiercely independent girl as a humbled, pathetic victim. But in this instance revolt against social injustice comes not from Melenda, but from Valentine, who by exerting her aristocratic influence succeeds only in getting Melenda the sack, thus making her more willing to accept charity.

This small example shows clearly what is most pernicious in Besant's philosophy. He continually preaches the theme of self-help, encouraged at first by charity from the wealthy, but the attitude that comes through expresses exactly the opposite view – that the working classes are not fit to rule themselves and can achieve success only if led by substitute heroes. To hold out against patronage is held to be foolish, but it is impossible to see how the eventual surrender is anything but a humiliation:

> She threw her arms around poor Melenda's neck, and kissed her a dozen times. 'I told you when I came,' she said, 'that perhaps I was your sister Polly. Perhaps I am not after all. Polly or not, we are sisters, you and I, always sisters. Shall we promise?'
>
> 'If-if you like,' said Melenda, with such sobs and tears as become the vanquished; 'if you like.'
>
> 'Then, my dear, sisters must do everything they are told

to do by each other. You will order me and I will order you.
First I am going to dress you.'

Melenda was conquered.

Valentine ran into her own room, and came back with a
bundle of things.

'Do you think I am going to have my own sister go about
in such shocking rags as these any longer? Take off your
frock this minute, and – oh, the ragged petticoat! Here is one
of mine, and a frock, and a pair of my own stockings.
Everything has got to be changed.'[9]

This sense of, on the one hand, heralding the misunderstood
virtues of the working man and on the other taking away the genuine
expression of those virtues, is apparent throughout. Those men
who support radical politics receive from Besant nothing but
scorn. They are shown as empty-minded, loud-mouthed fools,
completely lacking in knowledge or understanding of the social
structure. All that is needed to put them on the right road is
for Harry Goslett, a real leader of men, to address the Radical
Club:

But you get nothing in the long run, and you never will:
because, promise what they may, it is not laws or measures
that will improve our lot: it is by our own resolution that it
shall be improved. Hold out your hands and take the things
that are offered you. Everything is yours if you like to have
it. You are in a beautiful garden filled with fruits, if you care
to pick them, but you do not, you lie grubbing in the mud
and crying out for what will do you no good.[10]

Upon hearing this the Radicals cheer him to the ceiling, recognizing the inherent superiority of such views over those of the earlier
speakers who had demanded the abolition of the House of Lords
and payment of Members of Parliament.

Besant's frequent outbursts against people who hold static,
stereotyped images of the working man were needed at this time,
but he himself fails completely to provide a genuine picture. The
'portrait' of Joe Monument could have been written by someone
who had remained in his West End club reading *Punch*:

He carried a bag of tools in one hand; on his arm he slung
his jacket because it was hot, and he preferred to work in his

shirt-sleeves; and he really had that loose red handkerchief which the girls expected to find about their brother's neck. There was also a pipe in his mouth. Quite the working-man. And perhaps in order to make it perfectly clear that he was not play-acting, whatever his sisters might be, his hands were grimed with dirt and oil.[11]

Even the vices of the working man are allowed to be only a form of cultural deficiency:

You will find yourself in a work-shop full of disagreeable people, who pick out unpleasant adjectives and tack them on to everything, and whose views of life and habits are – well, not your own. You will have to smoke pipes at a street corner on Sundays; your tobacco will be bad; you will drink bad beer – Harry! the contemplation of the thing is too painful.[12]

But hardly a character who fits even this mild description appears in Besant's pages, and if he does appear he is easily reformed, for all that is needed is a simple lesson in taste and manners. Besant's eccentrics, because they have fallen from a higher social stratum, already possess the necessary qualities, while the second group needs only a little encouragement to develop them:

She stopped him and offered him her hand. He did not take it, but he made as if he would take off his hat. This habit, as has already been remarked, is an indestructible proof of good breeding. Another sign is the handling of the knife and fork. A third is the pronunciation of the English language.[13]

Here, sounding very similar to Gissing at his worst, is the explanation of Besant's curious, muddled, simple-hearted philosophy. The disguised aristocrats enacting their bizarre slum pastoral are essential because they alone possess the way of life that can be transferred to the poor. Poverty and wealth are really unimportant. All that matters is happiness, and no one can be happy if he cannot at the very least profess acquaintance with the outward trappings of an upper-class culture.

It is not difficult to account for the enormous popularity of Besant's novels. In an age shaken by dangerously new democratic ideas, he created a fictional formula which offered an easy solution to the problem of class conflict by denying that any such problem

existed. Earlier romantic novelists had concentrated, to the virtual
exclusion of all else, on working-class life as something ugly and
debased. Besant ignores even the elements of truth in this point of
view and stresses instead the universality of human nature.
Society, he argues, does not consist of warring classes but of 'all
sorts and conditions of men'. In such a scheme of things the aristocrat and the workman can, and indeed do, change places quite
easily because there is really no difference between them. William
Empson has written that:

> The essential trick of the old pastoral, which was felt to imply
> a beautiful relation between rich and poor, was to make
> simple people express strong feelings (felt as the most
> universal subject, something fundamentally true about
> everybody) in learned and fashionable language (so that you
> wrote about the best subject in the best way). From seeing
> the two sorts of people combined like this you thought better
> of both; the best parts of both were used. The effect was in
> some degree to combine in the reader or author the merits of
> the two sorts; he was made to mirror in himself more
> completely the effective elements of the society he lived in.[14]

This describes exactly what Besant was trying to do. But once we
understand the 'trick' and can look behind it to the plot mechanism,
then we see that there is a considerable difference between Besant's
ostensible views and those unconsciously expressed within the
pastoral framework of his novels. Unlike earlier romantic novelists,
Besant accepts, without qualification, that there is an urban working *class*, whose interests are totally opposed to those of a ruling-
class group. This group (for Besant, the aristocracy) possesses
money but no real power. The working class, on the other hand,
has power but no money. In *The Nether World* Gissing was to
describe the same situation, and show the workers trying to
redress the balance by acting according to the 'naked formula' –
'Get, by whatever means, so long as with impunity.' Besant,
however, makes his active agents the aristocrats, who, disguised
as the enemy, set out to disseminate their own particular brand of
cultural propaganda. So long as they only meet with potential
link heroes and substitute working-class eccentrics (and Besant
makes sure that these are the only people they do meet), then their
position in society is safe. The type of working-class romance

established by Besant is one peculiar to the new democratic age. It represents a fresh stage in the process of avoidance, in that the traditional street and low-life characters, stark and firm in outline, and socially harmless by virtue of their eccentric qualities, are replaced by a class mass which is dull, steady, undemanding and vaguely defined.

By the close of the eighties we can see two distinct images of working-class life beginning to emerge in the novel. From Gissing comes the view that working-class life is ugly and squalid, a human trap from which no one can escape. The highest example of slum life is provided by Sidney Kirkwood and Jane Snowdon who, in spite of their suffering, manage to survive in this working-class hell without being morally corrupted. For the problem of working-class life as a whole there is, and can be in the foreseeable future, no social solution. From Besant comes the view that working-class life is dreary, dull, eminently respectable, and completely lacking in any means of genuine cultural expression. In order to write a novel about the working class it is therefore necessary to deal with 'the romance that lies beneath its monotony'. To Besant's mind the problem of working-class life can be easily solved by means of the proper kind of patronage. What is required most of all is public support for philanthropic schemes. The schemes themselves need to be put into effect by practical men and the money to finance them can come from Besant's symbolic aristocrats, but all such plans will achieve little if they are not accompanied by a change of heart in the public as a whole. The popular novelist is a man peculiarly fitted to bring about this change. By crystallizing the complex issues involved into one clearly defined idea or image he is often able to arouse public enthusiasm in a cause more effectively than the most scrupulously exact sociological document, or indeed, more than the finest work of art. George Gissing was one of the best working-class novelists of the nineteenth century, Walter Besant one of the worst; but it was Besant who came to be regarded as an authority on working-class life and who, by means of a strikingly simplified image of the East End, helped mould public opinion, encouraged philanthropic schemes and, ironically, exercised a considerable indirect influence on many later novelists. It is this public aspect of Besant, his connection with social reform movements of the eighties, that needs to be examined more closely.

H

III

'English people,' Gissing wrote in 1898, 'are distinguished among nationalities by the profound mutual ignorance which separates their social ranks.'[15] At this late date such an observation had become commonplace. Throughout the Victorian age social critics, novelists, political reformers and foreign visitors had frequently noted the same peculiarity and prophesied dire social consequences if steps were not taken to redress the balance. But it was not until after 1880 that systematic attempts to set class relationships on a new footing were seriously supported by a significant number of the middle and upper classes. This change of attitude can be seen in the public response to the most important political development of the period – Socialism; and to the dominant social reform issue – urban poverty.

Late-Victorian novelists concentrated almost exclusively on the problem of urban poverty. Although this period saw riots in London, serious strikes in several industries, an unprecedented growth of Trade Union membership and the emergence of an independent Labour party, there were very few worthwhile novels written on these subjects. This is not to say that novelists ignored the basic issue of potentially explosive class relationships; merely that they stressed just one manifestation of it; that, like Besant, they were concerned more with reform than revolution. Socialism in the late-Victorian working-class novel plays a part similar to that of Chartism in the industrial novels, in that while the fear of class war is never really faced, it is also never far from the surface.

Furthermore, just as the fear of Chartism helped bring about important social legislation, so the late-Victorian urban-reform movement, comprising a number of groups diverse in aims and methods, was given special impetus by the desire (sometimes consciously expressed, sometimes unconsciously), to seize the initiative from the Socialists; to lessen the problem of class divisions by non-political action. Henry Nevinson, an early Socialist who finding the policies of the S.D.F. 'too abstract and doctrinal' turned instead to slum work, neatly captures the ambiguous mood of the eighties: 'One was carried along by a tide setting strongly towards "social reform," "social economics," and all the various forms of "Socialism" then emerging as rather startling apparitions.

There was some talk of a revolution, more of "the workers' rights," most of "Outcast London."'[16] As the decade progressed, this tendency on the part of novelists and social reformers to concentrate upon class relationships in London, to the exclusion of larger political or social issues, increased and attained its most striking aspect in the sudden realization that the different classes in London were divided from each other not merely economically or spiritually but topographically as well. Awareness of this fact provides, as Asa Briggs has pointed out, 'the great contrast of the 1880s and the 1890s'.[17]

Journalists, sociologists and novelists vied with each other in producing images and metaphors sufficiently bizarre to indicate the outcast state of the East London poor. T. H. Huxley compared them unfavourably with the 'Polynesian savage', William Booth chose the 'African pigmy', and Jane Addams the 'salt miners of Austria'. For William Barry the East End slums were like a 'slave ship', and George Sims, employing a more traditional comparison, 'saw a vision of hell more terrible than the immortal Florentine's'.[18] This late-Victorian use of the language and imagery of exploration is distinguished from that of earlier writers by the almost total stress placed upon the *East End* slums and the *East End* workers. When Besant addressed a Birmingham audience on the subject of 'Art and the People' in 1884, he was obliged to make what at any time earlier in the century would have seemed an audacious confession:

> As regards Birmingham, Manchester, Sheffield, Glasgow, and any other place where there is a great industrial population, I know nothing. If, therefore, exception be taken to any expressions of mine as applied to some other city, I beg it to be remembered that East London alone is in my mind.[19]

But at this time his narrow approach was perfectly well understood, for by the mid-eighties the East End had become as potent a symbol of late-Victorian urban poverty as Manchester had been of industrial conditions in the 1840s. The imagery of discovery and adventure, of distant tribes and unknown regions, is little different in kind from that used by earlier writers, but the point of emphasis is totally new. It was not the contrast between wealth and poverty in close proximity that shocked late-Victorian writers (as, for instance, it horrified and fascinated Dickens) but the complete lack of wealth; the sprawling, seemingly never-ending streets of poor houses and people, similar in area and density, as it was frequently claimed, to the jungles of equatorial Africa. The East End was not just a part of a city. It was a complete city in itself.

Historians usually consider that the starting point for this upsurge of interest in the East End was the publication of George Sims's newspaper articles collectively called *How the Poor Live* (1883), and the appearance of the immensely influential *Bitter Cry of Outcast London* in the same year. But a distinction must be made between the awakening of the public conscience to the problem of urban poverty as a whole, and the almost immediate acceptance of the East End as a symbol of that poverty. For although these two books do refer to the East End they are by no means primarily concerned with it. *The Bitter Cry* concentrates mainly on South London slums, while Sims moves from area to area (the Mint, Borough and Drury Lane as well as the East End) in much the same way as Dickens and Greenwood had done in their sketches of London life. Furthermore, neither the tone of the books nor the information contained in them represented anything new. The mixture of religious emotion, dramatized characterization, graphic descriptions of poverty and rather hazy statistics, can be found, in like proportion, in many earlier works. The success they achieved was largely due to their being published at just the right time. They coincided with the final stage of a process of change in Victorian England which Beatrice Webb described as: 'A new consciousness of sin among men of intellect and men of property; a consciousness at first philanthropic and practical . . . then literary and artistic . . . and finally analytic, historical and explanatory.'[20]

Of much more importance than *How the Poor Live* and *The Bitter Cry* in establishing the late-Victorian image of the East End was Besant's *All Sorts and Conditions of Men*, although in the wider issue of publicizing slum conditions the three books should be considered as reacting upon each other. We have already seen that Besant's working-class characters in *All Sorts and Conditions of Men* are fairy-tale figures, but it is worth considering the image of the East End he advances separately because it was his most original and influential contribution to working-class fiction. What Besant stresses is not individual poverty and hardship presented

as pathetic case studies, but a generalized total picture in which
the essence of East End life is defined entirely in negative terms.
He concentrates almost exclusively on creating an atmosphere
of 'meanness' and 'monotony'; a portrait of a huge cultureless
void:

> Two millions of people, or thereabouts, live in the East End
> of London. That seems a good-sized population for an utterly
> unknown town. They have no institutions of their own to
> speak of, no public buildings of any importance, no
> municipality, no gentry, no carriages, no soldiers, no
> picture-galleries, no theatres, no opera – they have nothing.
> It is the fashion to believe that they are all paupers, which is a
> foolish and mischievous belief, as we shall presently see.
> Probably there is no such spectacle in the whole world as that
> of this immense, neglected, forgotten great city of East
> London . . . Nobody goes east, no one wants to see the
> place; no one is curious about the way of life in the east.
> Books on London pass it over; it has little or no history;
> great men are not buried in its churchyards; which are not
> even ancient, and crowded by citizens as obscure as those
> who now breathe the upper airs about them. If anything
> happens in the east, people at the other end have to stop and
> think before they can remember where the place may be.[21]

In this novel, his many articles and lectures, and finally in his
study *East London* (1901), the message Besant repeatedly presses
home is that the most urgent problem of the East End is not
poverty or crime but meanness. What the East Ender needs, he
argues, is leadership, contact with the upper classes, and an
awareness of art, books and music; and all of these things can be
achieved through vocational education. In *All Sorts and Conditions
of Men* Besant captured, just as it was emerging, a dominant mood
of late-Victorian England and conveyed it to a vast audience in
three graphic images – the East End, the Palace of Delight and
the upper-class slum worker. In each case Besant was drawing
upon ideas currently circulating among social reformers. His
fundamental faith in education and cultural consciousness had its
roots (as, indeed, had the whole of the Settlement movement) in
the Christian Socialism of Maurice and Kingsley, and in the
social theories of Ruskin. The idea of a Palace of Delight had been

conceived, in a less romantic form, by John Barber Beaumont forty years earlier, and plans for its construction were being made at the very time Besant was writing his novel.[22] And most important of all, the image of the East End publicized by Besant came from Edward Denison ('The pioneer of a great invasion')[23] whose strange and tragic life haunted the minds of many East End social workers in the eighties and nineties.

Edward Denison was born in 1840 and educated at Oxford. For four years after leaving university he toured the Continent and on his return to England took a post as almoner of the Society for the Relief of the Distressed in Stepney. This, his first contact with the poor, deeply shocked him, and in 1867 he moved to Philpot Street in Stepney, where he lived among the poor doing what he could to help educate them. After a period of eight months he could no longer bear the loneliness and accepted an offer to become M.P. for Newark. He died of tuberculosis in 1870. The letters he wrote to his West End friends while living in Philpot Street were published in 1872, and these, together with his practical example, profoundly influenced Besant and many others. At times Denison directly anticipates Besant: 'I imagine that the evil condition of the population is rather owing to the total absence of residents of a better class – to the dead level of labour which prevails over that wide region, than to anything else. There is I fancy less absolute destitution and less crime than in the Newport Market region; but there is no one to give a push to struggling energy, to guide aspiring intelligence, or to break the fall of unavoidable misfortune.' Poverty and suffering were not seen by Denison as the most evil aspects of East End life but rather 'its uniform mean level, the absence of anything more civilizing than a grinding organ to raise the ideas beyond the daily bread and beer, the utter want of education, the complete indifference of religion'. Open-handed charity and well-meaning philanthropy were useless because 'the lever has to be applied from a distance, and sympathy is not strong enough to bear the strain'. The answer to the problem was, as Denison demonstrated, to go and live in the East End, to work in the same manner, although he himself does not use the image, as an African missionary. Finally Denison saw the East End as a complete city, cut off from the rest of London: 'Stepney is on the Whitechapel Road, and the Whitechapel Road is at the east end of Leadenhall Street, and Leadenhall is east of Cornhill, so it is a good way from fashionable, and even from business London.'[24]

Twenty-five years after Denison wrote these words they reappeared in Arthur Morrison's *Tales of Mean Streets* (1894): 'The East End is a vast city, as famous in its way as any the hand of man has made. But who knows the East End? It is down through Cornhill and out beyond Leadenhall Street and Aldgate Pump, one will say: a shocking place, where he once went with a curate.'[25] The line of influence that stretches from Denison (the isolated saint-like figure whose letters were widely read in the seventies), through Besant (who publicizes a new image of the East End in the eighties), to Arthur Morrison (whose short stories and novels establish the tone of slum fiction in the nineties), is an important one. Morrison himself belongs to a second generation of East End explorers, and is open to the influence of a whole range of social and literary forces which Denison and Besant, as pioneers, helped to formulate. The most potent of these forces was the exploration of the East End, and the sociological examination of the working man.

IV

'It seems incredible now,' James Adderley wrote in 1910, 'that it should have been thought something very extraordinary to propose to live in the East End, if you were not obliged to do so, but it certainly was twenty five years ago when I went to live there as a layman.'[26] The approximate date fixed by Adderley, 1885, is the crucial one in the 'discovery' of the East End. In that year Toynbee Hall had been officially opened, an event which was a personal triumph for Samuel Barnett, who, when he accepted the living of St Judes, Whitechapel, in 1873, had been warned by his Bishop that 'it is the worst parish in my diocese, inhabited mainly by a criminal population'.[27] It was also largely due to Barnett's influence that one year earlier the Universities' Settlement Association had been registered and the breakaway settlement Oxford House established. In 1886 Charles Booth began work on his great survey of East End life, and in the following year the Queen officially opened the People's Palace. In 1887 the Salvation Army, which had originally been founded by William Booth after a visit to the East End in 1865, announced a change of policy which included social reform as an essential prerequisite to the saving of souls. In the wake of this three-pronged invasion (the Settlements, Salvation Army and social analysts), came religious missions, philanthropic laymen, university graduates, fashionable slummers and journalists, in such numbers that by 1896 an international survey of urban poverty reached the conclusion: 'Awakening is not needed. Every thinking man has thoughts upon this matter. And along with this realization has come practical experiment, in many places and on an immense scale, towards a solution.'[28]

From the early eighties onwards it became customary to talk of the East End as somewhere heathen, outcast and totally neglected by religious leaders and social reformers. In relative terms such a view was true, but there was also a considerable amount of rather empty rhetoric involved, rhetoric which was employed to arouse public interest in various causes. When, for instance, Walsham How was appointed to the East London Bishopric in 1879 he declared: 'The Church is *nowhere* in East London',[29] and his cry was taken up by many other clergymen during the next twenty years. How's statement, however, was by no means absolutely true. It has already been noted that an exception was usually made of the layman Edward Denison who was himself much influenced by the famous historian J. R. Green who had settled in the East End in 1860 and taken charge of a derelict parish in Hoxton three years later. Even then he was not alone as Father Lowder had opened a dockside mission in 1856, and other priests in the East End at this time included E. C. Hawkins of Hackney and Brooke Lambert of Whitechapel.[30] Furthermore, although the Salvation Army is often thought of as belonging to the final decades of the nineteenth century, William Booth had first preached in the East End in 1865 at the invitation of the East London Special Services Committee, and the first paper he launched was called *The East London Evangelist* which anticipated the *War Cry* by many years.

Many of the great mid-Victorian social critics also had connections with the East End. T. H. Huxley had served his medical apprenticeship there in 1842 and 'used to wonder sometimes why these people did not sally forth in mass and get a few hours' eating and drinking and plunder to their hearts' content, before the police could stop and hang a few of them'.[31] Ruskin chose the

East End, together with the Houses of Parliament and the National Gallery, as one of the places he would like to destroy and rebuild;[32] and Matthew Arnold in his public role as school inspector had frequently visited the East End, and in 1867 published a sonnet on the subject. Nor was it entirely neglected by early- and mid-Victorian urban explorers. The Bible-women and tract distributors visited Stepney and Whitechapel as well as St Giles's and Covent Garden, but only Hector Gavin in his house-by-house study of Bethnal Green, *Sanitary Ramblings* (1848), and Henry Mayhew in those sections of *London Labour* which deal with the docks and riverside, gave special prominence to East London.

Public interest was aroused during the cholera epidemic of 1866, and the involvement of many priests and social workers in East End life began at this time. It was, however, only after 1880 that the East End attained the symbolic importance it still possesses. The few laymen, parish priests, and religious missionaries already there, found themselves swamped by a vast number of visitors and institutions all eager to help or study the working man. Viewed retrospectively it is easy enough to see the work of settlers and salvationists, university graduates and upper-class slum teachers, as superficial, condescending or even laughable. There can, for example, have been few more uncomfortable philanthropic occasions than the East-West tea parties organized by Henrietta Barnett. The compilation of a guest list containing an equal number of the different classes must have been daunting enough. But even with this delicate task completed, the hostess still suffered agonies of conscience trying to decide whether having her servants pass the cakes round would upset the social equilibrium.[33] This intense example of class consciousness seems to epitomize the very worst aspects of late-Victorian philanthropy. And there were doubtless many people like the girl recorded by Henry Nevinson who on being warned of the complexity of different 'cases' submitted to her care replied: 'Character presents no difficulty to me; I took a First in Moral Philosophy at Cambridge.'[34] It is also no doubt true, as George Lansbury complained, that young men on the make used their brief experience as settlers to obtain influential jobs as authorities on questions of social reform.[35]

But at best the social workers genuinely attempted to break down class barriers, to bring East and West closer together; and the great virtue of their efforts was the firm belief that both sides had something to contribute. All the various groups were determined to stamp out casual dole-giving, but were unwilling to adopt the methods of the Charity Organziation Society, which was widely criticized at this time for heartlessness and lack of understanding. True sympathy, it was felt, could only be achieved by helping the working classes to develop the best qualities they were capable of. The poor were now regarded as rather deprived than debased. Barnett's advice to would-be settlers clearly expresses this:

> There must be no affectation of asceticism, and no
> consciousness of superiority. They must show forth the taste,
> the mind, and the faith that is in them. They have not come
> as 'missioners', they have come to settle, that is, to learn as
> much as to teach, to receive as much as to give.[36]

Thus no single religious or political viewpoint was adopted. The aim of Toynbee Hall was not to convert or quieten the working classes but to help them relieve their state of cultural monotony:

> While other systems aimed at enabling people to *possess* more
> of the good things of life, our system aimed at enabling
> people to *enjoy* more of such good things; other systems
> aimed at enabling people to *get*, our system aimed at enabling
> people to *give*. The subjects chosen were those which deepen
> the mind, which open the eye of the mind.[37]

Barnett firmly believed that Toynbee Hall was laying the foundations for a university of the East End, and the natural comparison was with Oxford and Cambridge in the Middle Ages, when the poor scholars had 'crowded in thousands round the feet of the great scholastic teachers';[38] and by appealing mainly to the more respectable elements of East End life Toynbee Hall did achieve some success in setting up scholarships to send its best students to university. But the most important single aspect of Barnett's leadership was his insistence that 'exact knowledge of the true needs of an area must be gained before anything else can be done'.[39] Settlers were encouraged to conduct scientifically organized research and to employ the knowledge obtained to play a full part in the life of the community. There were few reform movements of this period in which the Toynbee residents did not play a large part. They helped found Whitechapel Public Library in 1892, and conducted publicity campaigns in the 'phossy jaw', dock and busmen strikes. In the mid-nineties they actively participated in local-government reform, urban development and the systematic analysis of the causes and extent of poverty in London. J. A. R. Pimlott's description of Toynbee Hall as 'one of the sociological laboratories on the patient work of which legislators and administrators so largely depend',[40] is by no means exaggerated.

The People's Palace was both more idealistic and less successful than Toynbee Hall. It was perhaps inevitable that Besant's fairy-tale Palace which was to cure the evils of the East End overnight should have become a dull, steady, eminently practical Technical School. Yet during its brief existence as a cultural catalyst the Palace did attempt to bring a whole new range of experiences (art shows, public debates, literary study groups, cheap holidays at home and abroad, and sports facilities), within the reach of the working man. At times, Besant, who remained a guiding light of the Palace if not a principal administrator, talks in a way similar to Barnett:

> Whatever be the future of the Palace as regards the recreation of the people, one thing is quite clear – that its educational capacities are almost boundless, and that there will be founded here a University for the people of a kind hitherto unknown and undreamed of.[41]

Besant's enthusiasm is a little misleading, for, unlike Toynbee Hall, the People's Palace did not see university education as an essential working-class goal, but rather strove to help the working man express himself within his own environment. One of Besant's deepest hopes was that the Palace would inspire a large and vital working-class artistic movement taking as subject matter not scholarship and learning but life in the East End. When talking of this he sounds more like William Morris than Samuel Barnett:

> Let us . . . never be content until our own bands play our own music; our own journal prints our own literature; our own novelists lie upon our tables; our own critics pronounce our judgments; our own artists paint the pictures for our exhibitions.[42]

A few weeks after these words were written, Arthur Morrison was appointed sub-editor of the *Palace Journal*. It is ironic that while he was the only person connected with the People's Palace to take Besant's advice, no one seems to have been aware of his East End working-class background.

The Salvation Army approached the working classes from the opposite direction to the settlers. In the early days of the Army it was the spiritual rather than the cultural lack in working-class life that disturbed William Booth. Evangelical fervour discountenanced all issues save that of individual salvation. As late as 1881 Catherine Booth could write: 'What does it matter if a man dies . . . on a doorstep covered with wounds, like Lazarus – what does it matter if his soul is saved?'[43] But such an attitude was already inconsistent with the methods being employed by the Army to reach the poor. In 1878 the newly named Salvation Army received its first volume of *Orders and Regulations*, which directed the officers always to live in the very worst areas of cities, and as far as possible to exist on the same financial sum as their working-class neighbours. Furthermore, they were urged to convert the lowest sections of the community; to make contact with the unbelievers, drunkards, prostitutes and social outcasts. The relative success of these drastic methods, coupled with the failure of the purely emotional religious campaign, led William Booth to a radical change of policy. In 1887 he announced that if the Army were to succeed in reaching the lowest segments of society then it could not afford to stand aside from social-reform issues. Lazarus's physical condition was no longer to be regarded indifferently; he was to be sheltered and fed before being saved. The publication of *In Darkest England and the Way Out* (1890) with its carefully documented case studies, its praise of Charles Booth's survey and the final great plan for dealing with the 'submerged tenth', brought the Salvation Army much nearer to the views of settlers and missionaries. Where it continued to stand alone was in its publicity methods, for as K. S. Inglis has noted, 'with minor exceptions they were the only group of Christian evangelists of their time who approached working-class non-worshippers at their own cultural level'.[44] The use of brass bands, slick advertising, smart repartee, jingles and catch phrases, turned the Salvationist into a performer, competing for the attention of the worker with the music-hall artist and street singer. Unique among social-reform groups in late-Victorian England, the Salvation Army supported a policy of like speaking to like. William Pett Ridge tells how he once heard a group of working men in Finsbury Park gleefully shouting the refrain to a Salvation Army verse:

There may be some on me and you
But there ain't no flies on Jesus.[45]

It was in this way that the Army tried to resolve the East-West conflict – by smothering West End values and addressing the 'submerged tenth' in what the Army considered was its own accent.

In the late eighties the attempts by the various religious and social-reform groups to publicize the life and labour of the people in East London received unexpected help from three spectacular events. The first was the strike by Bryant and May match girls led by Annie Besant. In 1888 they tried to create public sympathy for their cause by personally delivering a petition to the Houses of Parliament. Dressed in their ragged working clothes they marched through the West End, indicating in the most graphic manner the gulf that separated the two areas of London. Later in the same year five Whitechapel prostitutes were savagely murdered by Jack the Ripper and the press of the whole world temporarily directed its attention on the East End. Among others, George Bernard Shaw seized the opportunity to goad upper-class consciences:

The riots of 1886 brought £78,000 and a People's Palace . . . it remains to be seen how much these murders may prove to be worth to the East End in *panem et circenses*. Indeed, if the habits of duchesses only admitted of their being decoyed into Whitechapel backyards, a single experiment in slaughterhouse anatomy on an aristocratic vicitim might fetch in a round half million and save the necessity of sacrificing four women of the people.[46]

For many months the newspapers were obsessed with Jack the Ripper; suggesting bizarre methods by which he might be apprehended, giving intimate details of the lives and deaths of his victims, upbraiding society for allowing the East End to exist and the police for their incompetence. One of the most recent of the many writers who have tried to solve the mystery of Jack the

Ripper has claimed that 'the case points to the use of murder as a means of social protest', and further that many of the social reforms of the nineties proceeded directly from the publicity gained by the murders.[47] So long as this type of publicity is considered only as part of a much wider and more inclusive interest in the East End, there may be some truth in the contention. But more relevant here is that coming at a time when social reformers were slowly building up a less sensational picture of East End life, the gruesome activities of Jack the Ripper thrust into the public mind an image of East London as somewhere violent and outcast, rather than monotonous and outcast. It is a temporary movement away from the East End of Denison, Besant and Booth, and back to the Ratcliffe Highway of the early-nineteenth century.

Only a few months after Jack the Ripper had claimed his fifth and final victim, the London dock strike showed a more progressive aspect of East End life to set against the retrograde image of the Whitechapel murders. Like the match girls, the dockers drew attention to their cause by daily debates on Tower Hill and by marching on the City and West End:

> There were forty-one banners, some no more than red rags on poles, but some stranger. There were stinking onions, old fish-heads, and indescribable pieces of meat stuck on spikes, to show the City magnates what the dockers had to live on. Each day the processions were repeated, growing larger and larger, and commonly ending in Hyde Park.[48]

The dock strike also tested the faith of settlers and Salvationists, who responded with sympathy, enthusiasm and practical aid. Support from institution representatives such as Canon Barnett, Stewart Headlam, William Booth and Cardinal Manning served both to give a sense of direction to public sympathy, and to consolidate the position of the institutions in the East End.

The social-reform groups impelled by different motives and meeting with varying degrees of success, all approached the working classes with old theories in new wrappings, but on a scale much greater than ever before. It was inevitable, taking into account the institutional nature of their organizations, that attempts to solve working-class problems were still largely paternal and individualistic. The lesson learnt from events such as the strikes by match girls and dockers, and the Whitechapel murders, was that despite the opportunities offered by settlements and missions, the East End as a whole was still misunderstood and neglected. What was required was further detailed knowledge of the East End workers as a class. Hitherto the institutions had only managed to reach the individual within the mass; now there was a serious attempt made to understand the mass within the individual.

The publication of *East London* (1889), the first volume of Charles Booth's *Life and Labour of the People*, marks a culminating point in the 'discovery' of the East End. Whereas earlier writers had relied on emotional arguments to make their case, Charles Booth, for the first time in the nineteenth century, set out to study not the poor but poverty. Unlike the settlers, Salvationists, journalists and missionaries, Booth was not concerned with advancing panaceas but with showing 'the numerical relation which poverty, misery, and depravity bear to regular earnings and comparative comfort, and to describe the general conditions under which each class lives'.[49] Although he eventually allowed himself to make certain suggestions for reform he did so 'with much hesitation', believing that his task should be to help others solve problems. He too, however, was faced with the difficulty of combating widely held public images:

> East London lay hidden from view behind a curtain on
> which were painted terrible pictures: – Starving children,
> suffering women, overworked men; horrors of drunkenness
> and vice; monsters and demons of inhumanity; giants of
> disease and despair. Did these pictures truly represent what
> lay behind, or did they bear to the facts a relation similar to
> that which the pictures outside a booth at some country fair
> bear to the performance or show within? This curtain we have
> tried to lift.[50]

Out of a total population of 908,959 Booth estimated that only 1.2 per cent could be classified under section A ('the lowest class of occasional labourers, loafers and semi-criminals'); while the largest single group, E, consisting of those workers living above the line of poverty, who drew a regular wage, comprised 42.3 per cent of the total. The upper-middle class, H, accounted for only 5.0 per cent, and more than two-thirds of this group lived in Hackney. The most disturbing of Booth's statistics showed that 35.2 per cent (groups A–D inclusive) lived in conditions of poverty. Taken as a whole Booth concluded that the proportion of those who lived in 'comfort' to those who lived in poverty was approximately 65/35 per cent.[51] Separate areas, however, showed enormous variations. Hackney stood completely apart with its 'well-to-do suburban population'; and while the poverty level in Mile End Old Town dropped to 24.6 per cent, it rose to 49.1 per cent in Whitechapel and to 58.7 per cent in Bethnal Green.[52]

We can see from these statistics that the image of the East End set out by Denison and Besant (predominantly an area of monotonous and bleak respectability, interspersed with sections of terrible suffering, a relatively small but vicious criminal element, and virtually no upper-middle-class members to provide a lead or contrast) is in the main vindicated by Booth's survey, although Besant, of course, deliberately exaggerated the lack of cultural expression in the East End and underestimated its degree of poverty. The total portrait is graphically illustrated by Booth's maps, on which the East End is represented by various shades of blue and grey varied only by streaks of black, while the black patches of the West End are swamped by a brilliant orange.

But the cold statistics give little indication of the importance of a book which is concerned with the 'life' as well as the 'labour' of the people. Booth observed that the different districts were distinguished from each other not only by relative levels of poverty, but by indefinable, characteristic, 'flavours':

> One seems to be conscious of it in the streets. It may be in the faces of the people, or in what they carry – perhaps a reflection is thrown in this way from the prevailing trades – or it may lie in the sounds one hears, or in the character of the buildings.[53]

This goes some way to recognizing a meaning of 'culture' far beyond that accepted unthinkingly by most of the settlers and missionaries. Booth's keen sense of observation together with the confidence which his statistical framework provided, encouraged him to refrain from offering the standard moral condemnations. He noted the happiness as well as the poverty; the singing and dancing; the public support that kept three legitimate theatres and many music halls running in the East End; the enthusiastically attended Sunday debates in Victoria Park and the political clubs; as well as discussing, often with sharp perception, the role being

played by missions and settlements.[54] Booth's sympathy occasionally leads him to make maudlin judgements, as when he begins to
see 'nothing improbable in the general view that the simple
natural lives of working-class people tend to their own and their
children's happiness more than the artificial complicated existence
of the rich'.[55] But this is merely a fleeting conjecture and does
not intrude upon his largely impersonal analysis. Sometimes his
extreme objectivity comes as a surprise, as when he refuses to
condemn outright public houses which 'play a larger part in the
lives of the people than clubs or friendly societies, churches or
missions, or perhaps than all put together'.[56]

Booth's study, while painting a general picture of poverty in
London even worse than he himself had believed possible, found
in certain aspects of working-class life degrees of cultural compensation of which he had also not been aware. Perhaps his greatest
single achievement was that once and for all he destroyed the view
that the working classes were 'debased'. We have seen that his
basic analysis showed that only 1.2 per cent of the East End
population could be classified as such, and that 35.2 per cent lived
in conditions of poverty. These figures are horrifying enough, but
if we add to them the small proportion of middle-class inhabitants,
we are still left with approximately 60 per cent of the East End
population who presumably led decent, respectable lives. Booth's
findings highlight in the strongest possible manner the rigorous
process of selection exercised by early- and mid-Victorian novelists
in commonly choosing the suffering poor and debased as representatives of working-class life.

His study of the causes of poverty further weakened the
position of those who argued that the working classes were poor
because of character weakness or innate idleness. In groups A and
B only 4 per cent were described as loafers, while 55 per cent
suffered from 'questions of employment', 27 per cent from
'questions of circumstance' (e.g. illness), and 14 per cent from
'questions of habits' (e.g. drunkenness). In groups C and D the
loafers disappear entirely, and 'questions of employment' are
shown to cause the poverty of 68 per cent, circumstance 19 per
cent, and habits 13 per cent.[57]

One of the findings that most surprised Booth himself was the
extent of poverty in areas of London other than the East End.
Compared with the average East End poverty level of 35.2 per

cent, that of London as a whole was 30.7 per cent. With regard to individual districts, three were even worse than Bethnal Green (58.7 per cent). They were certain areas of Southwark (67.9 per cent), Greenwich (65.2 per cent), and Goswell Road (60.9 per cent), while many other areas were not much worse than the East End.[58] This point was taken up by Arthur Sherwell who, in his study *Life in West London* (1897), which he saw as a complement to Booth's work, claimed that Soho was the 'terra incognita' of London and supported his argument with an impressive collection of statistics.[59] Many of Sherwell's contemporaries pointed out the same peculiarity – that while the East End received all the attention, there were more deprived areas of London being neglected. But this kind of criticism merely serves to emphasize the symbolic importance of the East End in this period. When Robert A. Woods tried to draw attention to poverty in other areas of London he admitted that 'East London will still continue to be thought of in a special way as the nether London'.[60]

It has been stressed that the most pervasive aspect of this new image of the East End was the contrast it provided with the West – a city of poverty on the one hand, and a city of wealth on the other. This comparison was not new, as Renton Nicholson's jingle shows:

From East-End to West-End
From worst end to best end.[61]

The important difference is, however, that here, as in many early- and mid-Victorian writers, stress is placed upon the bizarre and violent aspects of East End life. Apart from the few priests and missionaries in the East End during the middle years of the century, slummers in the main followed the example of Pierce Egan. They went East to wonder at the sailors, prostitutes, drunken fights, rat and cock fighting. Many writers have left accounts of the young 'Corinthians', often accompanied by professional 'minders', seeking out the violent night life of the Ratcliffe Highway.[62] In the later period some slummers did visit the East End in the eager expectation of being shocked, but they now came to look rather than participate. Furthermore, the sensation-seekers were outnumbered by others determined to set up schools, read Milton to a working-class audience, show sympathy for the dock strikers, or help found a university. Most important of all, these new-style visitors noted the ordinary and decent as well as the gruesome and grotesque, and significantly struggled to understand the relationship between the two:

> Go to docks early in the morning. Permanent men respectable, sober, clean. Casuals low-looking, bestial, content with their own condition. Watch brutal fight and struggle; the sudden dissolution of the crowd with coarse jokes and loud laugh. Look of utter indifference on their faces: among them the one or two who have fallen from better things – their abject misery.[63]

This is Beatrice Webb in the mid-eighties, and her approach is typical of a whole new school of thinkers and writers. In a matter of two decades the pleasure seeking of the mid-Victorian Corinthian is transformed into the earnest, devoted attention of the late-Victorian sociologist. The 'discovery' in this sense is very much a change of heart and feeling – that awareness of upper-class sin and guilty conscience that Ruskin, Arnold Toynbee, Samuel Barnett and Beatrice Webb all noted.

V

The changing attitude of novelists towards the East End can be seen by glancing at the topography of Dickens's novels. While it is true that 'Dickens always seems out of his bearings West of King Charles's Statue',[64] it is further true that, in his novels, he rarely deals extensively with any district east of Aldgate Pump, the traditional entrance to the East End. Indeed, a circle drawn with these two points as the diameter would enclose the greater part of Dickens's London. That he was as familiar with the East End as with all other areas of London can be seen from *The Uncommercial Traveller* (1861), where he describes some of his walks in Wapping and Shadwell, but in his novels the East End appears only briefly and then usually in connection with criminals or crime. In *Oliver Twist* Nancy is murdered at Bill Sikes's house in Whitechapel, and she herself came originally from 'the remote but genteel suburb of Ratcliffe',[65] but most of the novel's slum scenes centre on Clerkenwell. In *Edwin Drood* (1870) the East End is employed as the natural setting for an opium den, and in *Great*

Expectations (1861), which features the eastern reaches of the Thames, Magwitch is moved to a house 'between Limehouse and Greenwich' where he prepares for his escape. Even in *Our Mutual Friend* (1864), where the East End plays a larger role than in any other of his novels, Limehouse is primarily employed as the home of Gaffer Hexam and Rogue Riderhood. There are, however, certain aspects of this late novel that interestingly anticipate the slum fiction of the nineties; for example, the opening East/West contrast between Gaffer Hexam and the Veneerings, and the portrait of Mr Milvey, the slum priest of Brentford. Whitechapel appears briefly in several of Dickens's early novels for the practical reason that the Bull Inn was then the City terminus for coaches travelling to the north of England.

In *Sketches by Boz* Dickens wrote: 'The gin-shops in and near Drury-Lane, Holborn, St. Giles's, Covent-Garden, and Clare-market, are the handsomest in London. There is more of filth and squalid misery near those great thoroughfares than in any part of this mighty city.'[66] If we add Southwark and Clerkenwell to Dickens's own list, then these are the principal slum areas in his novels. Tom-All-Alone's was probably in Holborn where Mrs Gamp also lived; Bleeding Heart Yard was in Hatton Garden; the Nubbles family lived in the Seven Dials; Betty Higden lived in Brentford, and Bill Sikes died in Jacob's Island, Bermondsey. Staggs's Gardens were in Camden Town and 'Little Britain' in Smithfield. Only Captain Cuttle, Gaffer Hexam and Rogue Riderhood really lived in the East End.

Dickens's choice of slum areas is interestingly echoed by James Greenwood. Pointing out to an ignorant public the prevalence of slums in London he gives examples from all over the metropolis, noting that 'in the East you might take your pick from a hundred examples; but I should recommend a neighbourhood between Rosemary Lane and Limehouse Hole . . . But it would be fairest, perhaps, to take a slice out of the centre of the city. It is rotten to the core'.[67] Gissing was little influenced by the developing public concern with the East End, though he was aware of East London as a gathering ground for working-class material, and the slum settings of his novels follow much the same pattern as those of Dickens. As has been shown it was Besant who broke with tradition and drew the attention of novelists to the East End as a special case. There is, however, one qualification to be made.

Besant's view of upper-class slum workers was essentially secular and non-intellectual. The novel which played a large part in bringing to public attention the changing attitude of priests and intellectuals towards social-reform work was Mrs Humphry Ward's *Robert Elsmere* (1888). The working classes play only an incidental role in this novel, and the East End does not figure prominently. But it is in the East End that the hero recovers his lost faith:

> He had spent a Sunday or two wandering among the East End churches. There, rather than among the streets and courts outside, as it had seemed to him, lay the tragedy of the city. Such emptiness, such desertion, such a hopeless breach between the great craving need outside and the boon offered it within.[68]

The overall image – even, it seems, some of the phrases – comes from Besant, but the theme of spiritual redemption is alien to him. In the nineties a very popular formula for working-class romance was a combination of *All Sorts and Conditions of Men* and *Robert Elsemere*. In novel after novel upper-class heroes and heroines find personal salvation, and usually love, in the monotonous, irreligious, waste-land of East London. The interest of this kind of fiction is in its relationship to the work produced by more independently minded working-class novelists.

Not all of the working-class novels written in the nineties dealt with the East End. Somerset Maugham's *Liza of Lambeth* (1897) is an obvious exception, as is Richard Whiteing's *No. 5 John Street* (1899), which employed the Dickensian contrast of a West End slum surrounded by wealth. Most novelists did, however, choose the East End as their slum setting, and all were profoundly influenced by its discovery and exploration. Some of the writers were involved in social work during this period and translated their experiences into fiction (e.g. Margaret Harkness, Henry Nevinson, G. T. Kimmins and Somerset Maugham); some were themselves from working-class backgrounds who got caught up in the general movement (e.g. Arthur Morrison and Edwin Pugh); others combined a Dickensian love of London with a different kind of awareness fostered by the changed conditions (e.g. Arthur St John Adcock and William Pett Ridge). But of much more importance than these direct, personal influences, was the widespread assault on old attitudes and values. The various social and religious movements discussed here all challenged, in their different ways, romantic images of the working man whereby he was invariably seen in relation to a code of behaviour unnatural to his normal way of life. The perennial problem of how a writer who was not himself working class could deal intimately and knowingly with the details of working-class life seemed to have found one kind of solution with the new link heroes (settlers, salvationists and missionaries), all of whom figure prominently in the slum fiction of the nineties. It was pointed out in Ch. 1 that it is only during moments of social crisis that any significant number of English novelists have attempted to write fiction centred upon working-class life. The crisis provides a ready-made framework, a way into working-class life. In the 1840s and 50s it was industrial conflct; looking forward to the 1920s and 30s it was mass unemployment and the general strike. In the period 1880–1900 this framework was provided by the 'discovery' of the East End.

5

French naturalism and English working-class fiction

During the last twenty years of the nineteenth century English novelists and critics were convinced that the art of fiction was at a critical stage of its development, and that French naturalism, as publicized and practised by Émile Zola, was mainly responsible for the crisis. In spite of the serious moral and aesthetic doubts raised by French naturalism, many people believed that under its influence a new era of the English novel was about to begin. Edmund Gosse wrote that naturalism 'has cleared the air of a thousand follies, has pricked a whole fleet of oratorical bubbles . . . the public has eaten of the apple of knowledge, and will not be satisfied with mere marionettes'.[1] Havelock Ellis made a similar point – that while Zola's own work was limited in scope, his courageous example had paved the way for others to follow:

> It has henceforth become possible for other novelists to find
> inspiration where before they could never have turned, to
> touch life with a vigour and audacity of phrase which, without
> Zola's example, they would have trembled to use, while they
> still remain free to bring to their work the simplicity,
> precision, and inner experience which he has never possessed.
> Zola has enlarged the field of the novel.[2]

Hubert Crackanthorpe took the same point a step further, arguing that a change had taken place not only in the attitudes of novelists and critics but in the reading public as well:

Heroism is at a discount; Mrs. Grundy is becoming mythological; a crowd of unsuspected supporters collect from all sides, and the deadly conflict of which we had been warned becomes but an interesting skirmish. Books are published, stories are printed, in old established reviews, which would never have been tolerated a few years ago.[3]

These quotations all come from articles written in the early nineties when the critical hostility that had first greeted the appearance of Zola's novels in England was rapidly disappearing. The recognizably exultant tone sounded by these critics was the result of release from tension, relief that the persecution of the eighties was not to be extended into the succeeding decade. But if the public debate on naturalism was brief it was also extremely bitter. The principal events are well known and can be quickly outlined.

The first serious attack came in 1879 from Swinburne whose denunciation of the French edition of *L'Assommoir* (1877) set the tone of hysterical indignation that was to dominate critical discussion of Zola's work throughout the eighties. The basic objection voiced by Swinburne and later by W. T. Stead and the National Vigilance Association was entirely moral. They argued that Zola's frank presentation of sex, violence, human cruelty, slang and swearing was indecent, liable to injure public morals and that therefore his novels should be banned from England. Until 1883 only the French editions of Zola's novels were available in England, but in that year the first translation appeared and in the following year Henry Vizatelly began systematically to publish English translations, beginning with *Nana*, *L'Assommoir*, *Germinal* and *Thérèse Raquin*. In 1886 further Zola translations were added to Vizatelly's list together with works by Flaubert and Edmond de Goncourt. Two years later Vizatelly was summonsed for having published three obscene books (*Nana*, *La Terre* and *Pot Bouille*), fined, and placed on probation for twelve months, only to be re-arrested in 1889 and charged with the same offence. This time the 'obscene' books mentioned, apart from those by Zola, included Bourget's *Un Crime d'Amour* and Maupassant's *Bel Ami*. Vizatelly was sent to prison for three months, a sentence which seems to have satisfied the retributive demands of the National Vigilance Association, as the public attack immediately began to fade away.

In 1893 Zola was invited to London to address the Institute of Journalists. On this occasion and on his later visits to England, he was received with acclaim, there being hardly a dissenting voice. W. C. Frierson and Clarence R. Decker, in their detailed studies of the reception of French naturalism in England, agree that the controversy reached its climax with the jailing of Vizatelly in 1889, that from 1890 onwards the purely moral criticism of Zola's work was replaced 'in some quarters by tolerance, in others by curiosity, and in others by sympathetic understanding', and that by 1893 open hostility had almost disappeared.[4]

Taken in its widest aspect, a discussion of the controversy over naturalism or 'realism' in late-nineteenth-century England should concern itself with issues such as the critical reception of Ibsen, the influence of French novelists other than Zola, the reading of Russian novels in England (at this time mainly in French translations), and the English conflict between the realist and the romantic schools. The relevance, however, of these various issues to the presentation of the working classes in English fiction is slight. Gissing had read Turgenev, Dostoyevsky and Tolstoy with great enthusiasm and in this respect seems to have been unique among the late-Victorian working-class novelists, but no specifically 'Russian' influence is discernible in his work. The influence of French novelists other than Zola also appears to be negligible. The short stories of Maupassant are very influential in the nineties (for both their form and content) but the urban working classes play only an incidental part in them. Huysman's early naturalistic novels written under the direct influence of Zola seem to have made no impact in England, though the novels of his later symbolist phase play an important part in the 'yellow' side of the nineties. Perhaps most surprising of all is Clarence R. Decker's finding that 'the literary reputation of the Goncourt Brothers in England was not, at this time, widespread, and had little connection with the naturalist controversy'.[5] In discussing the influence of French naturalism on English working-class fiction one always returns to Zola.

There are two main questions of special interest here. First, what part did the urban working classes play in French naturalistic novels? And secondly, to what extent were English working-class novelists influenced by the theory and practice of naturalism?

II

Both the urban and industrial traditions begin at a much later date in French than in English fiction. Balzac was fully aware of 'l'ouvrier, le prolétaire qui remue ses pieds, ses mains, sa langue, son dos, son seul bras, ces cinq doigts pour vivre',[6] but such a man is entirely absent from *La Comédie humaine*. During the 1840s and 50s the romances of Eugène Sue, in which the Parisian workers play a significant role, were extremely popular both in France and England, but the first serious attempt to present the urban working classes in French fiction was made by the Goncourt brothers. In their preface to *Germinie Lacerteux* (1864) they claimed that the working classes had been unjustly ignored by French writers: a situation they were determined to put right:

> Vivant au dix-neuvième siècle, dans un temps de suffrage
> universel, de démocratie, de libéralisme, nous nous sommes
> demandé si ce qu'on appelle 'les basses-classes' n'avait pas
> droit au Roman; si ce monde sous un monde, le peuple,
> devait rester sous le coup de l'interdit littéraire et des dédains
> d'auteurs qui ont fait jusqu'ici le silence sur l'âme et le coeur
> qu'il peut avoir.

In the event their great claims were not really justified, for although there are several fine working-class scenes in the novel, it is primarily concerned with a maidservant's decline from respectability and neither the psychological nor the sexual analysis deals with a specifically working-class situation. Zola, however, was much struck by *Germinie Lacerteux* and in a long article on the Goncourt brothers praised them for having introduced a new social class into serious fiction.[7] Even at this time Zola was planning to include in the *Rougon-Macquart* 'un roman qui aura pour cadre le monde ouvrier',[8] but it was a task he continually postponed. When he did finally write *L'Assommoir* (1877) he seems to have temporarily forgotten his earlier remarks on *Germinie Lacerteux* and claimed his own work as 'une oeuvre de vérité, le premier roman sur le peuple, qui ne mente pas et qui ait l'odeur du peuple'.[9] *L'Assommoir* became immediately, both in France and in England, the archetypal late-nineteenth-century slum novel. The various artistic problems that, as we have already seen,

English working-class novelists were struggling with, are triumphantly solved in *L'Assommoir*. The direct influence of Zola upon the English slum novelists must be looked at a little later, here it can be said that *L'Assommoir* was the kind of novel that most of them were trying to integrate into the English tradition, although they were never to attain anything like Zola's degree of success. It is not necessary to discuss *L'Assommoir* in detail, but merely to indicate certain important aspects of it.

In the *ébauche* for *L'Assommoir* Zola wrote that 'le roman de Gervaise n'est pas le roman politique, mais le roman des moeurs du peuple',[10] and his success in maintaining this distinction between two essentially different kinds of novel was something that had been achieved by no earlier English novelist. The rise and fall of Gervaise, unlike the decline of Germinie Lacerteux, is presented entirely within a working-class framework. By standing aside from the central action of the book, the author allows everything to be defined in terms of 'les moeurs du peuple', while he himself refuses to offer political, social or even humanitarian comment. Zola certainly possessed personal views on the Parisian working classes but these views are subordinated to the artistic demands of the novel:

> J'ai voulu peindre la déchéance fatale d'une famille ouvrière, dans le milieu empesté de nos faubourgs. Au bout de l'ivrognerie et de la fainéantise, il y a le relâchement des liens de la famille, les ordures de la promiscuité, l'oubli progressif des sentiments honnêtes, puis comme dénoûment la honte et la mort. C'est de la morale en action, simplement.[11]

It is true, as has often been pointed out, that Zola's use of symbolism amounts to an implied comment by the author, but in *L'Assommoir* symbolism is employed to advance 'la morale en action', and rarely to superimpose a moral upon the action.

As a natural corollary of presenting everything through the minds of his characters, Zola felt it was essential not merely to show a familiarity with working-class speech patterns but to evolve a uniform colloquial tone so that there could be no discrepancy between the workers' and the author's response to any given situation. In answer to a critic of this method Zola wrote:

Vous me concédez que je puis donner à mes personnages leur langue accoutumée. Faites encore un effort, comprenez que des raisons d'équilibre et d'harmonie générale m'ont seules décidé à adopter un style uniforme.[12]

The early French criticism of *L'Assommoir* as a work vulgar in both style and subject was very similar to that which had greeted the appearance of *Oliver Twist* in England,[13] and further recalled the claim made by the Goncourt brothers that the working classes were 'sous le coup de l'interdit littéraire et des dédains d'auteurs'. Zola answered such critics in the preface to *L'Assommoir*: 'Mon crime est d'avoir eu la curiosité littéraire de ramasser et de couler dans un moule très travaillé la langue du peuple'.

Zola's use of a central environmental symbol around which all the action of the novel revolves was a further important innovation in working-class fiction. In *L'Assommoir* he traces the history of the individual members of a particular family but constantly expands the significance of their story by a skilful, symbolic use of the dram shop itself, the tenement block and the wash-house. These environmental symbols are employed in such a way that the major characters are always seen in relation to a working-class community rather than to society as a whole. This technique is very different from that of Dickens and other earlier English novelists. In Dickens, for instance, Tom-All-Alone's in *Bleak House* and the river in *Our Mutual Friend* are used symbolically to link different sections of society; to point the moral of social responsibility. The view of society presented in all English novels of working-class life before Gissing's *The Nether World* (1889) is vertical; Zola's cuts into society were horizontal.

By these means Zola was able to explore aspects of working-class life hitherto ignored by novelists, and furthermore he could do this without passing moral judgement on the life he described. He demanded the authorial right of amorality and it was for this reason that English critics, accustomed to a policy of retribution and class comparison in fiction, denounced him as immoral. Viewed retrospectively the anger is understandable, for no previous author had so successfully demonstrated the way that a working-class environment breeds a culture of its own, the fictional presentation of which renders middle-class value judgements futile:

Et il ne faut point conclure que le peuple tout entier est mauvais, car mes personnages ne sont pas mauvais, il ne sont qu'ignorants et gâtés par le milieu de rude besogne et de misère où ils vivent.[14]

Thus Gervaise's fight in the wash-house, her sexual relations with Lantier and Coupeau, Bijard's sadistic treatment of his daughter, the working-class wedding feast and the eventual moral and physical disintegration of the Coupeau family, are seen merely as manifestations of one particular way of life. It is the total picture rather than the individual scene with which Zola is concerned; his eyes are set upon the 'mould' into which he pours the material he has gathered.

Three years after the publication of *L'Assommoir* Zola advanced the famous rationalization of his artistic theories in *Le Roman Expérimental* (1880), in which he drew a series of analogies between his own attitude to the world around him and that of Claude Bernard. Many of Bernard's observations, Zola points out, required only the substitution of the word 'novelist' for 'doctor' to be applicable to the aims of the naturalist:

From the moment that the result of the experiment is manifest, the experimenter confronts a true observation which he has induced, one which he must set down without preconceived ideas like any other observation.

(Bernard)

The naturalistic novelists observe and experiment, and . . . their whole task begins in the doubt which they hold concerning obscure traits, inexplicable phenomena, until an expcrimental idea suddenly arouses their genius and impels them to make an experiment, in order to analyze the facts and become master of them.

(Zola)

For Zola, as scientist-novelist, the phenomena are people whose behaviour can be understood by analysing the twin forces of heredity and environment. Naturalism, he writes, is the 'literature of our scientific age', and the role of the scientist is to 'show the mechanism of the useful or the harmful; we disengage the determinism of human and social phenomena so that we may one day control and direct those phenomena'.[15]

It is extremely important to note that what attracted English working-class novelists to naturalism was not Zola's scientific theories but the practical results of those theories. Today the scientific claims made for naturalism arouse little interest or enthusiasm. One of the most sympathetic of Zola's admirers can write: 'It had better be acknowledged at the outset that the concept of the "experimental novel", with most of what this concept involves, is infantile, and the manner of its presentation unbelievably naïve.'[16] In the nineties English critics were often equally distrustful of scientific naturalism, and were quick to point out the long 'realistic' tradition in the English novel, invoking primarily the work of Defoe, Jane Austen, Dickens and George Eliot as examples of accurate and detailed observation of human behaviour. Edmund Gosse was by no means alone in arguing that if an Académie des Goncourts was to be built, then a statue of Jane Austen should be placed in the vestibule.[17]

The continuing working-class tradition in English fiction has already been sufficiently stressed to show that Zola's work did not bring life to an unknown world, but show that with artistic courage that world could be faithfully presented in fiction.

Before looking at the attitudes of English working-class novelists towards naturalism, there is one further point that must be made. The scandalous success that surrounded *L'Assommoir* naturally associated naturalism with the portrayal of the working classes. Zola was annoyed that this should be so and pointed out that naturalism was merely an aesthetic theory, a literary method, applicable to all walks of life, and that the greater part of the *Rougon-Macquart* did not deal with the working classes.[18] The only three novels of the series which did were *L'Assommoir*, *Germinal* (1885) which dealt with the industrial worker, and *La Terre* (1887), in which Zola portrayed the French peasantry; although urban workers do appear in other novels in the series. The whole emphasis of naturalism being upon the forces of heredity and environment, novelists were often attracted to 'sordid' or 'low life' aspects of society, in particular prostitution, drunkenness and marital incompatibility. These subjects are not necessarily connected with the working classes, and it should be remembered when we consider the limited impact French naturalism made upon the English working-class novel, that its influence was widespread in other areas of late-Victorian and Edwardian fiction.

III

George Moore, ever on the look-out for new artistic experiences, has recorded the profound impact that French naturalism had upon him:

> The idea of a new art based upon science, in opposition to the art of the old world that was based on imagination, an art that should explain all things and embrace modern life in its entirety, in its endless ramifications, be, as it were, a new creed in a new civilization, filled me with wonder, and I stood dumb before the vastness of the conception, and the towering height of the ambition.[19]

If we place beside this statement Morrison's defence of his 'realistic' position, we can clearly see the two critical poles within which late-Victorian working-class novelists moved:

> It seems to me that the man who is called a 'realist' is one who, seeing things with his own eyes, discards the conventions of the schools, and presents his matter in individual terms of art . . .
> If I had been a rich man I might have attempted to discharge my peculiar responsibility in one way; if I had been a statesman I might have tried another. Being neither of these things, but a simple writer of fiction, I endeavoured to do my duty by writing a tale wherein I hoped to bring the condition of this place within the comprehension of others.[20]

This second statement might have been made by Defoe, or indeed by many other English novelists writing at any time during the previous century and a half. The former statement could only have been made by someone writing in the later years of the nineteenth century. So far as English working-class fiction is concerned, Moore's attitude is extremely rare, and Morrison's commonplace.

What excited Moore about naturalism was that it seemed to be an all-embracing philosophy of art. He was able to recognize not merely the isolated aspects of Zola's work which could be used to serve his own non-naturalistic purpose, but the imaginative genius of the total plan. The simple reason why most slum novelists of the nineties did not follow Zola more closely was that they did not possess the necessary imagination or technical ability. In their novels, and in Gissing's working-class novels of the eighties, 'realism' or 'naturalism' is employed to describe the more sordid or violent aspects of life, rather than to create an harmonious artistic pattern. Moore, on the other hand, had written several naturalistic novels before *Esther Waters* (his only working-class novel), the most successful of which was *A Mummer's Wife* (1885). In this novel every aspect of Zola's work is faithfully translated into English. The minutely detailed studies of the Potteries, seduction of a lower-middle-class provincial wife, careful analysis of marital incompatibility, as well as the naturalistic set pieces of Kate Eade's descent into drunkenness and her meticulously described death, show that Moore had completely absorbed the wider sweep of French naturalism from Flaubert, through the Goncourt brothers, to Zola. By the time he came to write *Esther Waters* Moore's early enthusiasm for Zola was on the wane and other influences are apparent. We thus have the odd situation that the only English working-class novel of this period that can be said to be profoundly influenced by French naturalism belongs in many ways to a purely English tradition. The conclusion that Ian Gregor reaches in his exhaustive study of *Esther Waters* is perfectly sound:

> Moore's example reminds us that, though the English novel learnt much from the French in terms of technical rigour and impersonality, their paths never really converged. Though he described his literary evolution in terms of allegiance to various French writers his very waverings of taste suggest a dissatisfaction, prompted in its turn by the weight of a completely different tradition.[21]

Just as this is true of George Moore, so it is, to an even greater degree, true of the other working-class novelists in this period. The central fault of *Esther Waters* lies, as Ian Gregor has so convincingly illustrated, in the character of the heroine. On the one hand Moore presents her as the victim of forces she is unable to combat (the naturalistic tradition), and on the other, he allows her qualities of moral strength that enable her eventually to survive (the English tradition). The symbolic structure of *Esther Waters* owes everything to Zola. It centres upon the social disease

5 'Selling Him a Pennyworth'
Philanthropist: 'There's a penny for you, my lad. What will you do
with it?'
Sweeper: 'What all this at once! I'll toss yer for it, double or quits.'
Charles Keen, *Punch*, 7 October 1876

6 'Street Arab', *c.* 1900

of gambling which reaches out and strikes at all those who, for reasons of either character weakness or social expediency, cannot resist its temptations until, at the close of the novel, both masters and servants are ruined. Esther's personal story is determined by her contact with gambling. From the moment at the beginning of the novel when she innocently accepts a ticket for the sweep-stake, her happiness ebbs away and reaches its lowest point when she fleetingly considers turning to prostitution as a way out of her troubles. Then she finds a post with Miss Rice and her fortunes begin to revive, reaching a climax with the prosperity of her husband's pub (the prosperity being founded on gambling) and the great dinner party that follows a joyous Derby Day at Epsom. From this moment her fortunes begin to decline once again until the final scene when she sits with Mrs Barfield in the now ruined Sussex mansion waiting for her soldier son to return home. This chart of Esther's fortunes is very similar to that of Gervaise, and the symbolic high spots of her life (the Latches' pub and the Derby Day scene) are taken directly from *L'Assommoir*. But there are other aspects of *Esther Waters*, apart from the incongruous psychology of the heroine, that rest uneasily within the naturalis-tic framework. Esther being saved at the last moment from prostitution by the appearance of Miss Rice and later being sheltered by the deeply religious Mrs Barfield, are Victorian solu-tions; the working-class issue is not resolved but merely postponed by Moore's recourse to the literary convention of middle-class paternalism. Moore, the reader feels, was always aware that *he* knew what was best for his characters. In spite of the supposedly inexorable forces at work upon her, Esther is finally rewarded for her 'virtue', and we are left wondering if this is to be the case then why should she be shown to suffer such terrible experiences. The answer is that she belongs to the working classes and such experi-ences are endemic in working-class life. Her family, consisting of a brutal stepfather, a gentle mother with religious leanings, and selfish sisters, is a classic example of the fictional working-class household as we find it throughout the Victorian period. It is not at all like the Coupeau family in *L'Assommoir* where all members of it (father, mother and daughter) are subject to the same effects brought about by heredity and environment. Esther is allowed to escape because of the qualities of moral strength, religious prin-ciples and maternal love she exhibits in moments of adversity; or

K

to quote Ian Gregor once again, 'Esther is innocent because with two strings to her bow she has never been in a position to be guilty'.[22] We can see from this that, in *Esther Waters*, Moore is in some respects as close to George Eliot, Mrs Gaskell or Dickens as to Zola. For all his claims of scientific objectivity Moore's only working-class novel is very much a work of class propaganda.

Enough has perhaps already been said about George Gissing to show that he was no mere disciple of Zola's, although his attitude towards French naturalism was always equivocal. When Frederick Harrison complained that *Workers in the Dawn* reminded him of the 'so called realism of Zola', Gissing could reply that he had never read anything by Zola.[23] The discussions that take place on the art of fiction in *The Unclassed*, and especially the way that Waymark is praised for having written a novel that is 'hideous and revolting' yet absolutely true,[24] show that Gissing had soon rectified this deficiency in his reading. What most attracted Gissing in French naturalism was the greater freedom it gave the novelist to deal with certain subjects (especially sex in this case) normally avoided or approached obliquely in English fiction. Unlike Moore, Gissing was not at all impressed by the scientific theories of naturalism which he dismissed quite contemptuously; nor did he ever speak of Zola with unqualified praise.[25] Furthermore, his working-class novels show little formal influence that might have come from Zola. He maintains at all times the omniscient-author convention, and alternates between realism (for the working classes) and idealism (for the upper-class or classless characters) in a way that is nearer Kingsley than Zola. In Gissing's case this dichotomy epitomized his own persistent belief in the natural superiority of one code of behaviour above another. For Gissing the man who possessed a highly developed aesthetic sensibility, immaculate table manners and a standard English accent, was inevitably 'better' than other men. This belief was not merely a private quirk, but was frequently expressed in his novels, and rendered impossible the social impartiality theoretically essential to naturalism.

The case of the slum novelists is different from that of either Moore or Gissing. In the nineties one finds Zola's name everywhere, but at this time it was invoked whenever anything horrific or sordid required description. This metaphorical use of the words Zola, Zolaism or Zolaesque, does not, of course, necessarily signify even the faintest familiarity with the theory or practice of naturalism. The slum novelists did not make ambitious claims for their work, and there is little evidence that it was produced under the influence of any specific literary theory. Certainly the common critical view, expressed most definitely by W. C. Frierson, that the slum novelists were writing under the dual influence of admiration for Zola and reaction against Dickens is a gross over-simplification.[26] This judgement can only be defended by looking closely at the slum novels, but several points can be made in the present context.

First, the most important single benefit the slum novelists derived from French naturalism was the change it brought about in the attitude of the English reading public towards realism in fiction. Dates are important here. As we have seen, the activities of the National Vigilance Association declined after the jailing of Vizetelly in 1889, and four years later Zola was being hailed in England as a great artist. This change of atmosphere was by no means absolute as the examples of Wilde and Hardy indicate, but in 1893–4 when slum life began to emerge as a popular fictional subject it no longer received the hostile press reception that Gissing, for example, writing just a few years earlier, expected as a matter of course. The special nature of this change has been noted by Kenneth Graham: 'When a novel is attacked for not observing the moral code, the critic now takes it for granted that it could have been written *better*, instead of deducing that the whole genre is inferior.'[27] Critics and reading public were now more willing to accept that the novelist should be allowed to explore subjects hitherto ignored in English fiction, so long as those subjects were treated with due artistic sincerity. The slum novelists, if they were big enough to rise to the occasion, were given advantages possessed by no earlier English working-class novelist.

Secondly, although it is easy enough to find theoretical statements by the slum novelists that appear to refer to lessons learnt from the French, they did not hail naturalism as a great liberating force, and what is most striking about their novels is their essential Englishness. They firmly believed in the novel as a vehicle for social propaganda, in the main expressed admiration for Dickens, referred slightingly to Zola, and often used contrived plot patterns. Furthermore, they called themselves 'realists' rather than 'naturalists', and in their interpretation of the term they once again showed greater affinity with the mid-Victorian novelists than with the French. Kenneth Graham has written that: 'Detailed verisimilitude is demanded, and any offences against it are considered fatal to the work: reviews abound with triumphant discoveries of minute inaccuracies'[28] and Richard Stang has pointed out that the words 'copy' 'transcript' 'photograph' and 'daguerreotype' were the words most commonly used by both defenders and attackers of English realism.[29] These two critics are both referring to mid-Victorian fiction; to Dickens, Thackeray and George Eliot and not to Morrison, Pugh or Pett Ridge; but they might well have been, for the same is true of both periods. The slum novelists, involved as they were with the 'discovery' of the East End, were concerned more with sociological than artistic truth.

There are two aspects of their work which they did share with the French naturalists, rather than their English predecessors; two qualities that firmly stamp them as *late*-Victorian writers – first, the widespread belief in and attempt to adhere to the doctrine of authorial objectivity; and secondly, the determination to present the working classes entirely within a working-class environment, to make horizontal rather than vertical cuts into society. Yet once again qualifications must be made, for given this adherence to two of the most important naturalistic tenets, it becomes all the more surprising that the work of the slum novelists should have been both firmly rooted in the English tradition and yet markedly different from the working-class fiction of the eighties. The answer to this problem lies in the remarkable work of the young Rudyard Kipling.

6
Rudyard Kipling and cockney archetypes

I

Rudyard Kipling wrote only one slum story, 'The Record of Badalia Herodsfoot', which first appeared in *Harper's Weekly* (November 1890) and later in *Many Inventions* (1893). The historical importance of this story has not been neglected by critics. William C. Frierson argued that it was 'responsible for establishing the tone of a new kind of fiction'; and much earlier Jane Findlater claimed that with its publication the 'school of pity was fairly ushered in'.[1] While these observations are sound it is extremely misleading to discuss 'Badalia Herodsfoot' as though it is isolated, in subject matter, treatment and attitude, from Kipling's other work at this time. To do so is seriously to underestimate Kipling's own achievement and his influence on the presentation of the working classes in fiction.

We have already seen that by 1890 the sociological investigation of the East End had brought the London working classes to public attention as never before, and that the debate on French naturalism was gradually creating in England an intellectual climate favourable to the frank portrayal of working-class life. The slum novelists of the nineties were influenced by both of these movements. The discovery of the East End provided a sociological framework for their novels, and French naturalism supplied the objective method they attempted to follow. French naturalism, however, could obviously not offer a realistic model of a London working man, and, excepting the little-read work of George Gissing, English literature was still dominated by old-fashioned, stereos typed images of the cockney. It is Rudyard Kipling who bring-about a complete break with convention and provides English fiction with a new cockney archetype.

During the nineteenth century two fictional characters came to symbolize, for the reading public, the qualities of the cockney: Dickens's Sam Weller (1836) and E. J. Milliken's 'Arry (1877). Both characters gave their names to certain types of speech and attitude; both names were used as synonyms for cockney man-nerisms; both inspired a host of imitators; and the personality projected was in each case a crystallization of cockney character-istics current in popular literature of the time. Of the two, Sam Weller can be most readily described as working class. He is a completely urban type, though he is also firmly rooted in a literary tradition of the devoted servant-valet. Flashily dressed, sharp witted, cheekily humorous, physically courageous, yet appreciative of the right kind of middle-class paternalism, he is the most famous cockney in literature. Although his portrait was extremely idealized, he immediately came to be regarded as typical of his class. In the dangerous years of the 1830s and 40s it was no doubt convenient to imagine the urban working man as being like Sam Weller. Certainly the portrait did not go unchallenged. As early as 1855 one anonymous critic pointed out that Dickens had succeeded in creating a 'thoroughly genuine man' only by removing from him 'all the lower and coarser features' of his class.[2] Gissing, as we have seen, criticized Dickens on the same grounds, but in attempting to redress the balance merely produced a different kind of working-class stereotype, the debased Bill Blatherwick.

'Arry shares some of Sam Weller's characteristics, especially his colourful dress and quick tongue, but differs from him in certain important respects. He is lower class by virtue of his 'caddishness' – the principal defining characteristic – but is not necessarily working class; he has plenty of money; he is self-opinionated and vulgar. Whereas it is possible to see the 'thoroughly genuine man' in Sam Weller, 'Arry is always the butt of Milliken's social satire:

My real subject indeed, is 'Arryism rather than 'Arry. And 'Arryism is not confined to the streets. Its spirit pervades only too plentifully the Race Course, the Betting Ring, the Sporting Club, the Music Hall, many spheres of fashion, and some sections of the press.[3]

Milliken's 'Cockney Cad' belongs to the mainstream of *Punch*'s comedy of manners, and shows the influence of such diverse types as Thackeray's Snobs, Albert Smith's Gents, and the music hall's Heavy Swells and Lion Comiques. M. H. Spielmann, the early historian of *Punch*, described him as being:

> Self-sufficient, brazen, and unblushing in his irrepressible vulgarity, blatant and unashamed, he is distinguished by a sort of good-humour that is as rampant and as offensive as his swaggering selfishness, his arrogant familiarity and effrontery, and his sensuous sentiment.[4]

In spite of Milliken's protests his cockney character became associated almost entirely with working-class life. 'Arry (with his girl friend 'Arriette) provided journalists and novelists of the late seventies and eighties with an easy label for the young cockney out on the spree; and Phil May, bringing the Charles Keene cartoon tradition up-to-date, interpreted him for the nineties. Even Gissing came under the spell. When he wanted a name for the young working-class rake in *Demos*, it was natural that he should choose 'Arry.

The two cockney archetypes represent changing social patterns in the Victorian period. Sam Weller belongs to an age of turmoil. In social terms he is the working man who is harmless so long as he is well treated; in literary terms he links the age-old stable tradition of master and servant with the era of mid-Victorian realism. 'Arry is the product of an age grown wealthy and pompous, a society absolutely sure of what kinds of manners can and cannot be tolerated. Neither type could suitably represent the mood of the sociologically realistic nineties. Both Sam Weller and 'Arry (as conceived by Milliken) would have been very much out of place in Charles Booth's East End.

It is this problem that Kipling solves, and he does it not by studying behaviour patterns in 'outcast' London, but by becoming acquainted with the English working classes in India. There are three distinct, though closely related, stages in Kipling's early development. First, the stories about private soldiers written in

India during the late eighties; secondly, Kipling's disillusionment with England as expressed in the stories written in the years 1890 and 1891; and thirdly, the composition of the *Barrack Room Ballads* (1892) which were inspired by Kipling's association with the London working classes, and which established a new 'realistic' cockney archetype – Tommy Atkins.

II

On 25 March 1890 *The Times* welcomed Kipling to England with a eulogistic article in which he was hailed as 'the discoverer, as far as India is concerned, of "Tommy Atkins" as a hero of realistic romance'.[5] Andrew Lang, Kipling's most fervid admirer at this time, expressed the same sentiment: 'Among Mr. Kipling's discoveries of new kinds of characters probably the most popular is his invention of the British soldier in India.'[6] The use of words such as 'discoverer' and 'inventor' is significant, for nothing quite like Kipling's soldier stories had ever appeared in English literature before. Henry James, writing an appreciation of Kipling's tales, decided that 'the most brilliant group is devoted wholly to the common soldier, and of this series it appears to me that too much good is hardly to be said'. James went on to describe 'The Courting of Dinah Shadd' as a 'masterpiece' and picked out for especially high praise 'The Madness of Private Ortheris' and 'The Drums of the Fore and Aft'.[7] Judgements such as these were very common in the early nineties for in spite of the serious reservations that Lang, James and others had to make about Kipling's work as a whole, the 'freshness' (a favourite term of praise) of the soldier tales was undisputed. The reason for this has been given by Charles Carrington: 'Search English Literature and you will find no treatment of the English soldier on any adequate scale between Shakespeare and Kipling.' Unlike the sailor, who had received considerable attention from writers and collectors of songs, and who had long been a romantic, sentimentalized national hero, the soldier was regarded as a social outcast 'drawn from the unemployed or unemployable, so that "going for a soldier" was, in the respectable working-class regarded as the last degradation, analogous with "going to the bad".'[8]

This was the unpromising material that Kipling chose for his remarkable group of short stories. The three principal soldiers, Mulvaney (an Irishman), Learoyd (a Yorkshireman) and Ortheris (a Cockney), represent a select cross-section of British working-class life. Isolated from their home environments; their actions circumscribed by the twin forces of army discipline and hostile climate, they are driven into a complex relationship in which each soldier is dependent upon the other two for his physical and mental survival. Although they come from different parts of Britain and speak different dialects, they share working-class attitudes, amusements and emotions. Most of all they are united by their unrelenting opposition to authority (the upper or Army Officer class), and by the environment they inhabit (Indian barracks or English slums). Their memories of civilian life serve rather to reinforce than alleviate their outcast state, for in the social structure of Anglo-India they occupy very much the same position as they did at home in England. They are firmly rooted in the lowest, downtrodden stratum of society, with, in India at least, only the native soldier below them. The exotic country they now inhabit provides them with the possibility of romantic adventures, but the part they play in those adventures is determined by attitudes formed in working-class Britain.

This theme of the individual split by the conflicting claims of two different environments is most clearly seen in Ortheris and Learoyd. Mulvaney, the central and more fully rounded character, is someone who belongs so completely to barrack life that it is impossible to believe he has ever experienced any other kind of existence. He attains, as Andrew Lang was first to point out, 'mythical' status.[9] His social background is never exactly pinpointed; it is a cornucopia of memories and adventures from which he can draw fabulous tales as and when the occasion demands. It is notable that when he does temporarily leave the army, as described in 'The Big Drunk Draf' (1888), he returns to India as a civilian. But if Ortheris and Learoyd do not possess the mythical quality of Mulvaney, they are more human, more realistic, more conscious of the ineradicable ties they have with their pre-army lives. This places upon them an intolerable strain that Mulvaney can understand even though he does not experience it himself.

The moment when Kipling came to realize the importance of this is described in 'The Madness of Private Ortheris' (1888). Mulvaney knows that the cockney's bout of homesickness must be allowed to run its course. He has seen it all too often before: 'I've belted him, an' I've bruk his head, an' I've talked to him, but 'tis no manner av me whin the fit's on him'; but Kipling, the friendly and involved observer, stands by horrified as Ortheris pours out his yearning for the slums of home:

> I'm sick for London again; sick for the sounds of 'er, and the sights of 'er, an' the stinks of 'er; orange-peel and hasphalte an' gas comin' in over Vaux'all Bridge. Sick for the rail goin' down to Box 'ill, with your gal on your knee an' a new clay pipe in your face.

The patriotic images customarily employed to weld India and England together as one country in the soldier's mind, merely make Ortheris further loathe his outcast state: 'There's the Widder sittin' at 'Ome with a gold crowned on 'er 'ead; and 'ere am Hi, Stanley Orth'ris, the Widder's property, a rottin' FOOL!' Eventually he can be tricked into calmness, but Kipling is unable to forget that he has witnessed the disintegration of a person he felt he knew:

> I left, and on my way home thought a good deal over Ortheris, in particular, and my friend Private Thomas Atkins whom I love, in general.
> But I could not come to any conclusion of any kind whatever.[10]

As J. H. Fenwick has noted, this story 'shows significant changes in the narrator's relationship with the three men, and in his attitude to military life in general. From being a writer who buys their stories with drinks and claims them (rather over-insistently) as friends, he has become a humble listener aware of his own ignorance, his lack of experience or real understanding'.[11] Kipling's 'love' of Thomas Atkins, on the one hand, and his inability to come to any conclusions about him, on the other, encouraged him to observe closely, to stand aside and to attempt to reach a sympathetic understanding of his subject by objective analysis. It represents an important stage in the development of Kipling's technique which Noel Annan has seen as bearing a strong resemblance to that of European sociologists such as Weber and Durkheim, in that it gives the impression of 'a man who sees human beings moving in a definable network of social relationships, which impose upon them a code of behaviour appropriate to their environment' – a technique, it should be remarked, little different from that of Zola.[12]

In the stories immediately following 'The Madness of Private Ortheris', Kipling frequently stressed the strain imposed upon the individual by memories or dreams of England. A discussion of future civilian plans provides the starting point of 'Private Learoyd's Story' (1888), and 'In the Matter of a Private' (1888), which traces a similar but more tragic 'madness' than Ortheris's, the framework of the story is established by a comparison between the potentially explosive listlessness of soldiers in a stifling hot barracks, with a class of giggling English schoolgirls. Sometimes Kipling directly links working-class England and India, as in the description of Jakin in 'The Drums of the Fore and Aft' (1888) who 'had sprung from some London gutter and may or may not have passed through Dr. Barnardo's hands ere he arrived at the dignity of drummer-boy'.[13] Usually, however, in these early stories, the comparison is made indirectly. The barracks, it has already been noted, corresponds to an English slum; and the married quarters, as presented in a story such as 'The Solid Muldoon' (1888), stand in relation to the holiday resort of Simla as the East of London stands to the West. As in England these two separate worlds, with their dissimilar attitudes and values, are brought into contact with each other only by way of upper-class authority or paternalism. While sociologists and writers were discovering these class differences in London, Kipling was observing exactly the same phenomena in India.

The private soldier especially haunted his imagination. He was determined to reach the conclusions that had eluded him about Private Ortheris's madness. At times he appears to distrust the objective presentation of character, and, as though trying to get things straight in his own mind, sets out in a few rather glib generalizations the essential qualities of Thomas Atkins:

He has, let us say, been in the service of the Empress for, perhaps, four years. He will leave in another two years. He has no inherited morals, and four years are not sufficient to drive toughness into his fibre, or to teach him how holy a thing is his Regiment. He wants to drink, he wants to enjoy himself – in India he wants to save money – and he does not in the least like getting hurt. He has received just sufficient education to make him understand half the purport of the orders he receives, and to speculate on the nature of clean, incised, and shattering wounds.[14]

This debate Kipling was having with himself could not be resolved until, with his Indian experiences fresh in his mind, he returned to England. After having spent almost a year in London, he returned to the theme of Private Ortheris's madness and produced one of his most successful stories, 'On Greenhow Hill' (1890). No longer is the soldier's complaint voiced in a simple longing for the smells, sights and sounds of his home town; Kipling now employs the actual structure of the story, the contrasting moods and actions of the soldiers, their reasons for being where they are, to make his point. The story opens with the desertion of a native soldier who hovers above the camp sniping at the sleeping soldiers. When an order is given that he must be shot, Ortheris takes the task upon himself – a personal mission of death. While the three friends lie in the sun awaiting their chance, the conversation turns to women, and Learoyd tells of the unhappy love affair that drove him into the army. Like the soldiers in India the Yorkshire people whom Learoyd remembers led lives dominated by the climate and environment:

> You could tell Greenhow Hill folk by the red-apple colour o' their cheeks an' nose tips, and their blue eyes, driven into pinpoints by the wind. Miners mostly, burrowin' for lead i' th' hillsides, followin' the trail of th'ore vein same as a field rat.

Learoyd's own position in this community is symbolic of his role and status in the Indian army:

> I didn't belong to that country-side by rights. I went there because of a little difference at home, an' at fust I took up wi' a rough lot. One night we'd been drinkin', an' I must ha hed more than I could stand, or happen th'ale was none so good. Though i'them days, By for God, I never seed bad ale.

When he falls in love he comes face to face with an enemy he had never before been aware of – the 'cast-iron pride o' respectability' among 'poor chapel-folk'. His memory stirred he begins to draw some of the conclusions himself:

> And now I come to think on it, one at strangest things I know is 'at they couldn't abide th' thought o' soldiering. There's a vast o' fightin' i' th' Bible, and there's a deal of Methodists i' th' army; but to hear chapel folk talk yo'd think that soldierin' were next door, an' t'other side, to hangin'. I' their meetin's all their talk is o'fightin'.

The moment he learns his girl is dying Learoyd rebels against the respectability he had begun to cultivate, and takes 'the Devil's colours'. While he says good-bye to her the recruiting sergeant sits waiting for him in the corner pub. Learoyd understands little of the powerful social forces and contrasts Kipling is exploring; only the image of the dying girl stays constant in his mind.

Throughout Learoyd's narrative Ortheris has concentrated steadfastly on the immediate task in hand. When the camp had been disturbed in the night he had amused his comrades by calling out to the sniper, 'as a 'bus conductor calls in a block, 'Igher up, there! 'Igher up!' Now the 'blood-thirsty little mosquito' is determined to end all such disturbances. As Learoyd's tale closes Ortheris shoots the deserter:

> Learoyd thoughtfully watched the smoke clear away.
> 'Happen there was a lass tewed up wi' him, too,' said he.
> Ortheris did not reply. He was staring across the valley, with the smile of the artist who looks on the completed work.[15]

This is the type of scene that often brings down charges of sadism or brutality upon Kipling, but to think in these terms is to ignore the powerful ironic tone of the story. Ortheris and Learoyd are products of precisely the same social forces. They have been deliberately created to think and act as they do. This has been a relatively easy process because the lives they led in England and the lives they are taken to in India, amount to virtually the same thing. The hypocritical English public does not understand this, and closes its eyes both to conditions in the slums and in the army. The final image of the artist is ambiguous. It refers to Ortheris – who is the 'completed' product of one class of English society, and it refers to Kipling himself who has finally come to understand the 'madness' that so puzzled him two years earlier.

III

When Kipling arrived in England in October 1889 his name was already known to London literary circles, and editors of periodicals were eager to publish his poems and short stories. With the publication of *Soldiers Three* (1890), which reprinted the Indian stories for his new English market, the second phase of his remarkable success story began. Yet from the beginning he was discontented. The description of Dick Heldar's arrival in England expressed Kipling's own ambiguous feelings: 'A thin gray fog hung over the city, and the streets were very cold; for summer was in England.'[16] It was not merely 'homesickness' for India, the exchange of the sun for the fog; it was rather that he, like his soldier characters, was now faced with the problem of how to reconcile in his own mind the claims of two entirely different environments. One of the first poems he wrote in England began with the famous line, 'Oh, East is East, and West is West, and never the twain shall meet'. Disillusioned and miserable, Kipling became obsessed with the need to discover the links between East and West which he felt sure existed, and he found them by contemplating 'the Three Musketeers' whom he described as the 'dearest of all my children to me'.[17]

The first expression of his discontent was a hatred of London in general and of 'literary' London in particular:

> London is a vile place, and Anstey and Haggard and Lang and Co. are pressing on me the wisdom of identifying myself with some set, while the long-haired literati of the Savile Club are swearing that I 'invented' my soldier talk in *Soldiers Three*. Seeing that not one of these critters has been within earshot of a barrack, I am naturally wrath.[18]

Only two months after arriving in England he published in the *Civil and Military Gazette* (which remained for him an important link with India and an outlet for his unhappiness), a poem clearly stating what it was he so disliked about England:

> The sky, a greasy soup-toureen,
> Shuts down atop my brow.
> Yes, I have sighed for London town,
> And I have got it now:

And half of it is fog and filth,
   And half is fog and row.
But I consort with long-haired things
   In velvet collar-rolls,
Who talk about the Aims of Art,
   And 'theories' and 'goals,'
And moo and coo with women-folk
   About their blessed souls.[19]

The aesthetes and the fog had not existed in India and he was
shocked by their strange unreality, but the filth (by which he
means both dirty cities and vice) and the 'row' had existed in
India, and he was struck by the hypocritical double standard that
Imperial England adopted towards them. While in India Kipling
'came to realise the bare horrors of the private's life, and the
unnecessary torments he endured on account of the Christian
doctrine which lays down that "the wages of sin is death"'.[20] In
his early stories he had frequently attacked this ruling-class hypocrisy, but now he learned that exactly the same was true of society
in England, and to express his disgust he wrote one of his most
bitter sketches in which an Indian visits and describes London, as
Kipling had visited and described India:

> I see clearly that this town, London, which is as large as all
> Jagesur, is accursed, being dark and unclean, devoid of sun,
> and full of low-born, who are perpetually drunk, and howl in
> the streets like jackals, men and women together. At nightfall
> it is the custom of countless thousands of women to descend
> into the streets and sweep them, roaring, making jests, and
> demanding liquor. At the hour of this attack it is the custom
> of the householders to take their wives and children to the
> playhouses and the places of entertainment; evil and good
> thus returning home together as do kine from the pools at
> sundown.[21]

In this story, written in 1890, with its images of Hell and the idea
of lower-class London as somewhere outcast and spiritually lost,
Kipling ceases to be an outsider and enters the mainstream of
social criticism in the nineties. As in India he had constantly
compared life in the bazaars and barrack rooms with the upper-
class holiday town of Simla, and found more to his liking in the

former, so, in London, he turned away from 'the long-haired literati' and towards the working classes.

From his quarters in Villiers Street which he described at this time as 'primitive and passionate in its habits and population',[22] he set out to study the English half of Ortheris:

> The Private Soldier in India I thought I knew fairly well. His English brother (in the Guards mostly) sat and sang at my elbow any night I chose; and, for Greek chorus, I had the comments of my barmaid – deeply and dispassionately versed in all knowledge of evil as she had watched it across the zinc she was always swabbing off.[23]

In the land of fog and filth Kipling observed two aspects of working-class life that helped him to understand the private soldier – the slums and the music halls.

'The Record of Badalia Herodsfoot' (1890), traces the life and death of a costermonger's girl, in a style that mingles Biblical cadence with almost frigid personal unconcern:

> Those were her days of fatness and they did not last long, for her husband after two years took to himself another woman, and passed out of Badalia's life, over Badalia's senseless body; for he stifled protest with blows.

Kipling's Gunnison Street, like Gissing's nether world, is a place where ordinary values and attitudes are meaningless: a working-class ghetto in which the forces of law and the aims of philanthropists are powerless to change the amoral behaviour of the inhabitants. What good there is in Gunnison Street is to be found in Badalia, whose practical common sense and sympathy for those worse off than herself arise not out of religious conversion or revolutionary politics, but a simple personal conviction that those who are suffering should be helped. The Reverend Eustace Hanna also feels this, but as an outsider he lacks the local knowledge that alone can prevent the funds he is in charge of from going to the undeserving. Badalia gives him a lesson in the charitable dispensation of goods:

> 'You give Lascar Loo custids,' said she, without the formality of introduction; 'give her pork-wine. Garn! Give 'er blankits. Garn 'ome! 'Er mother, she eats 'em all, and

SOLDIERS THREE

BY

Rudyard Kipling

ONE RUPEE.

A.H. WHEELER & Co's
No. 1.
INDIAN RAILWAY LIBRARY.

7 'Soldiers Three', Allahabad, 1888

8 "Arry introducing 'Arriet to Bill'
'Arry (shouting across the street to his Pal): 'Hi! Bill! This is 'er!'
Phil May, *Punch*, 27 October 1894

drinks the blankits. Gits 'em back from the shop, she does, before you come visiting again, so as to 'ave 'em all handy an' proper.'

The philanthropist's faith in Badalia is rewarded by her extravagant honesty (epitomized by the meticulous accounts she keeps), which is based on the understanding that charity, in such a place as Gunnison Street, has no chance of transforming character and should not attempt to do so. At best it can only prevent disaster:

Mrs. Hikkey, very ill brandy 3d. Cab for hospital, she had to go, 1s. Mrs. Poone confined. In money for tea (she took it I know, sir) 6d. Met her husband out looking for work.

Badalia's skill at keeping the accounts is a throw-back to her 'days of fatness' when she and her husband ran a barrow, and her success where trained philanthropists had failed is a device which Kipling employs to show that working-class life, even in its most debased aspect, possesses values of its own which the onlooker can never really understand. Yet Kipling himself does not always manage to achieve total objectivity, for although he refrains from overt comment on the actions of his characters, the narrator's tone of voice and choice of certain deprecatory words sometimes serve to establish a vicarious kind of judgement. A good example of this is Badalia's death scene:

It was impossible for a self-respecting man to refrain from kicking her: so Tom kicked with the deadly intelligence born of whiskey. The head drooped to the floor, and Tom kicked at that till the crisp tingle of hair striking through the nailed boot with the chill of cold water, warned him that it might be as well to desist.[24]

The sentimental ending, when Badalia refuses to denounce her brutal husband, also weakens the genuine power the story possesses, and recalls one of Gissing's complaints against Dickens: 'The drunkard's wives who bend meekly to a blow, the streetwalkers who readily burst into tears, are merely conventional figures.'[25]

In spite of these strictures the importance of Kipling's only slum story is clear. He had shown that it was possible to write about working-class characters in a working-class environment without presenting their words and actions in middle-class terms.

L

In subject matter and mood, 'Badalia Herodsfoot' is little different from Gissing's *The Nether World*; but in terms of technique it represents a crucial step forward. Many novelists of the nineties, and especially Arthur Morrison, were to learn much from it.

What is most disheartening about 'Badalia Herodsfoot' is the tone of total despair that pervades it. In his Indian-soldier stories Kipling had managed to write sympathetically of the 'weaknesses' or 'vices' of the soldier because he recognized that in such an unnatural setting life was cheap, and that to expect people to adopt absolutely pure moral standards would be to act the hyprocrite. Now, in England, he learned that the same was true of the working-class soldier's home environment. His temporary bewilderment found relief in 'Badalia Herodsfoot'. Badalia, representing the best qualities that Gunnison Street is capable of, is kicked to death by her husband. The philanthropists are completely helpless, and with Badalia out of the way, the forces of evil which she had striven to keep at bay have the field to themselves. The story ends with 'the wail of the dying prostitute who could not die'. Even Gissing never struck a note of such total disillusionment.

Although he was horrified by the slums, Kipling realized that they represented only one, and that not perhaps the most important, part of the working-class life. In the music halls he found the strength and vitality that he had searched for in vain in other areas of English life. It would be difficult to over-estimate the influence of the music hall on Kipling's mind and work at this time. Its emotional impact he described in 'My Great and Only' (1890) where the narrator is a song composer whose first ballad is to be performed in a music hall. The song 'was made up of four elementary truths, some humour, and, though I say it who should leave it to the press, pathos deep and genuine'.[26] Sitting unknown among an audience that rises to cheer his song, the composer recognizes that he has played a principal part in helping to establish a profound and moving relationship between the entertainer and the entertained. Elated by his success and humbled by the emotional power he has aroused, he sadly realizes that he can never repeat this success. For the first time Kipling had made contact with the workers as a *class*:

But it needs a more mighty intellect to write the Songs of the People. Some day a man will rise up from Bermondsey,

Battersea or Bow, and he will be coarse, but clear-sighted, hard but infinitely and tenderly humorous, speaking the people's tongue, steeped in their lives and telling them in swinging, urging, clinging verse what it is their inarticulate lips would express. He will make them songs. Such songs![27]

Kipling was not discovering the music hall for the first time. As we shall see there is considerable evidence to support Charles Carrington's contention that he had been fascinated by it since childhood.[28] Now, however, he could clearly see the important role it played in working-class lives, and further realized that his own style and taste were nearer to the 'songs of the people' than to the mooing and cooing of the aesthetes. In 'The Courting of Dinah Shadd' (1890) Ortheris had sung 'in the raucous voice of the Ratcliffe Highway';[29] Kipling was determined to learn how to do the same. The Barrack Room Ballads and poems such as 'Mary, Pity Women' were, as Kipling himself later acknowledged, the direct result of his apprenticeship to the music hall.[30] Many critics have commented on this debt of Kipling's, especially Charles Carrington and T. S. Eliot, but what is not usually considered is the particular kind of song or artist that might have influenced him. Yet this point is of some importance, for the final, and crucial, stage in the development of Tommy Atkins's character coincides almost exactly with the rise of a new type of cockney entertainer.

The final twenty years of the nineteenth century is the 'great period' of English music hall. Following the example set by Charles Morton's Canterbury (founded 1848), the music halls had completely shed the rather shady reputation which the Song and Supper Rooms had bequeathed to them, and with increasing popularity and respectability there arose the narrow specialization that has ever since dominated the variety stage. The music hall, standing midway between legitimate theatre and the later depersonalized gramophone, encouraged the development of dramatized character sketches, the successful presentation of which depended as much upon the artist's ability to act a part as to sing the lyric or melody. Although many music-hall stars continued to try to vary their acts, they became associated in the public mind with just one kind of character. The most popular of these new 'types' were the costers.

In the early days of music hall the cockney had usually appeared in eccentric or melodramatic roles. One of the earliest, and most popular, was W. G. Ross, who, acting the part of 'Sam Hall', a chimney sweep condemned to death, sang his infamous song 'Damn Their Eyes' (c. 1840).[31] Other cockney singers in the same melodramatic tradition were Frederick Robson ('Villikins and his Dinah') and Sam Cowell ('The Ratcatcher's Daughter'). These singers seem to have been primarily influenced by Thomas Hood's poetry of social conscience, and exhibited both his sense of social message and taste for gruesome punning on serious subjects.[32] Their conventional costume has been significantly described as 'a cross between that of Sam Weller and Bill Sikes'.[33] In the sixties and seventies the cockney was presented as a working-class equivalent of the 'Heavy Swell', a precursor of Milliken's 'Arry. The most famous of these singers were Alfred Vance ('Chickaleary Cove'), Arthur Lloyd ('The Shoreditch Toff'), and George Leybourne, who rang the changes (the gap is not so great as is often supposed) between coster songs and his famous 'Champagne Charlie'. From the late seventies onwards the eccentric and melodramatic stereotypes were largely superseded by a more realistic, although often very sentimentalized, cockney act. The change was not completely revolutionary and it is possible to instance early singers who anticipated some of the qualities of the late-Victorian costers.[34] But they are isolated examples and did not establish a universal type. The singers who really form a link between, say, Alfred Vance and Albert Chevalier, are Jenny Hill and Bessie Bellwood, both of whom were very popular in the late seventies and early eighties. It is these songs, sung by working-class cockneys, which need to be looked at a little more closely. In Jenny Hill's most famous song ''Arry' (c. 1882) much of the 'Heavy Swell' slang remains but the tone is raucous and the theme realistic satire:

> Oh, 'Arry, what, 'Arry!
> There you are then 'Arry!
>   I say, 'Arry,
>   By Jove! you are a don.
> Oh, 'Arry! 'Arry!
> There you are then 'Arry.
> Where are you going on Sunday, 'Arry,
> Now you've got 'em on.[35]

As with almost all music-hall songs the words by themselves are banal to the point of nullity. Presentation (gesture, tonal inflection, innuendo and dress) was everything. 'For Kipling,' wrote T. S. Eliot, 'the poem is something which is intended to *act* – and for the most part his poems are intended to elicit the same response from all readers, and only the response which they can make in common.'[36] This was one of the techniques he learnt from music hall.

Not all of Jenny Hill's songs were like ''Arry'. She would move from this mocking treatment of a working-class swell, to the more traditionally melodramatic 'The City Waif', and then to a simple realistic portrayal of working-class life:

> I've been a good woman to you,
> And the neighbours all know that it's true,
> You go to the pub
> and you 'blue' the kid's grub,
> But I've been a good woman to you.[37]

But this represents only one facet of working-class life, and Jenny Hill was capable of expressing excitement as well as pathos, as in 'Good Old London Bill':

> If you hear a fellow singing late at night –
>   That's Bill!
> Who, when his wish he's got,
> And up three p'licemen trot
> He downs the blessed lot –
> That's Bill – that's Bill!
> That's good old London Bill.[38]

Bessie Bellwood's best-known song, 'Wot Cher, Ria' (1885), is similar to Jenny Hill's ''Arry' in that it mocks those members of the working classes who try to put on airs:

> I am a gal what's doing very well
> In the vegitible line,
> And as I've saved a bob or two
> I thought I'd cut a shine.
> So I goes into a music 'all
> Where I'd often been afore;
> I didn't go in the galler-y
> But on the bottom floor.

I sit me down quite comfy like
An' calls for a pot of stout.
My pals in the gallery spotted me
An' all commenced to shout:

Chorus: Wot Cher, Ria.[39]

In the late eighties and early nineties many of the greatest cockney singers ever to appear on the variety stage made their débuts. Kate Carney, Alec Hurley, Tom Costello, Albert Chevalier, Gus Elen, Marie Lloyd and Alf Chester, are merely the most famous. The songs they sang followed the tradition of music hall in that they dealt predominantly with urban themes, but these cockney singers placed a new emphasis on the ordinary aspects of life – domesticity, street courtship, work and play – an almost total concern with the simple details of working-class life, expressed with that wry sense of humour for which the cockney had been renowned throughout the Victorian age. The change that came over music-hall songs at this time can be best indicated briefly by looking at two treatments of a perennial music-hall theme – the joys of Paris. The first, 'Oh the Continong', popular in the seventies:

We've 'done' the Continong
And they've 'done' our 'larjong';
Of course, it's all very nice, you know,
Those foreigners tickle your fancy so.
And there's the gay Paree
For those who like a spree,
But after all, old England's
Good enough for me![40]

The working-class expression here is in the tradition of 'Arry, with its 'heavy' slang, air of vulgarity, and the final simple nationalistic statement. We can compare with this the chorus of Marie Lloyd's song 'I'd Like to Live in Paris all the Time,' which probably dates from the late eighties:

Still, I'd like to go again, to Paris on the Seine,
For Paris is a proper pantomime,
An' if they'd only shift the 'Ackney Road, and
                                    plant it over there,
I'd like to live in Paris all the time.[41]

Here the heavy slang and vulgarity disappear and the simple-minded nationalism is replaced by a specific working-class joke which is directed at both the audience and the singer herself. This sense of presenting unvarnished working-class values in terms of a double-hinged joke has always been a mainstay of cockney humour (Dickens employs it with Sam Weller), but never had it been so realistically conveyed as in the songs of this late-Victorian period. Charles Coborn's ''E's All right When you Know 'Im' also dates from the late eighties:

> Bill Sloggins is a party you don't meet with every day,
> 'E's always bluff an' 'earty – free and easy in 'is way,
> You wouldn't call 'im 'ansome but that isn't 'is disgrace
> 'E looks as though a regiment 'as marched across 'is face.
> Oh, 'e's all right when you know 'im though 'e 'atcs it when
> 'e's wexed,
> 'E'll black your eye one minute
> And 'e'll stand a pint the next.
> 'E wouldn't hurt a baby 'e's a pal as you can trust
> 'E's all right when you know 'im
> But you 'ave to know 'im fust.[42]

In historical terms, although not perhaps artistic, the most important late-Victorian music-hall cockney is Albert Chevalier, who was dubbed 'The Coster's Laureate' by Arthur Symmons.[43] Chevalier, a straight actor, came from a solid middle-class home and for many years refused to appear on the music-hall stage, although in the late eighties some of his songs became well known through his own semi-public appearances and the performances of them by his friend Charles Coborn. He finally made his music-hall début in February 1891, and was an immediate sensation. Chevalier employed his acting skill to create the tradition of the 'pearly' coster which still lingers on today. He was more senti-mental than the singers already discussed, but his sentiment was genuinely and unashamedly cockney. His best-known sentimental number is 'My Old Dutch'; a similar, less famous song, is 'The Coster's Serenade':

> You ain't forgotten yet that night in May,
> Down at the Welsh 'Arp which is 'Endon way,

You fancied winkles and a pot of tea,
'Four 'alf' I murmured "'s good enough for me.'
'Give me a word of 'ope that I may win' –
You prods me gently with the winkle pin –
We was as 'appy as could be that day
Down at the *Welsh* 'Arp which is 'Endon way.[44]

Another of Chevalier's sentimental numbers was 'The Rose of Our Alley':

Lor! Wot a funny fing love is,
　An' don't it change a man;
The *gals* may understand it, I
　Don't fink a *bloke* 'e can!
When I meets little Rosie, well,
　I know it sounds absurd.
I've allus lots to tell 'er, but
　I 'ardly sez a word.'[45]

Chevalier's best-known rowdy number 'Wot Cher! or Knock'd 'Em in the Old Kent Road', like Jenny Hill's ''Arry' and Bessie Bellwood's 'Wot Cher, Ria', mocks the working-class upstart, and clearly shows the domestic nature of the new songs:

Last week down our alley come a toff,
Nice old geezer, with a nasty cough,
Sees my Missus, takes 'is topper off
In a very gentlemanly way!
'Ma'am,' says he, 'I 'ave some news to tell,
Your rich Uncle Tom of Camberwell,
Popped off recent, which it ain't a sell,
Leaving you 'is little Donkey Shay.'
　'Wot cher!' all the neighbours cried,
　'Who're yer goin' to meet, Bill?
　Have yer bought the street, Bill?'
　Laugh! I thought I should 'ave died,
　Knock'd 'em in the Old Kent Road![46]

The cockney singers who were contemporaries of Chevalier, or who closely followed him, produced songs such as 'Never Introduce Your Donah to a Pal', 'At Trinity Church I Met Me Doom', 'Why Did I Leave My Little Back Room In Bloomsbury?',

'Wink the Other Eye', 'Are We To Part Like This Bill?', and countless others. When Kipling speaks of Ortheris's English brother
sitting and singing at his elbow, it was songs such as these he heard.
It is no coincidence that the title of the song the music hall composer writes in 'My Great and Only' is 'That's what the Girl told
the Soldier', which strikes just the same cheeky tone as the cockney
songs of the eighties and nineties.

It would not be sensible to try to estimate which of these songs
or singers Kipling might have taken special notice of, but it is
worth mentioning that critics in the nineties did not fail to remark
the similarities between his work and that of Albert Chevalier.
One admirer described Chevalier's stage performance in the
following terms: 'It is all very ugly, very quaint – and very interesting. For you at once feel yourself in the presence of one of M.
Zola's "human documents". It is a genuine type; the East-end
costermonger in his habit as he lives.'[47] Another hailed Chevalier
as 'the Kipling of the music hall',[48] while Richard Le Gallienne,
himself a music-hall enthusiast, significantly changed this emphasis, saying that the Barrack Room Ballads were 'perfect things of
their kind like a song by Mr. Albert Chevalier'.[49] But it is hardly
necessary to pursue this comparison, as even apart from the evidence provided by the short stories written in the late eighties and
early nineties, there is good reason to believe that Kipling had long
been attracted by music hall, and was almost certainly familiar
with the work of most of the artists mentioned here. In his first
published book, *Schoolboy Lyrics* (1881), which was written mainly
under the spell of Swinburne and Browning, there is one poem
strikingly different from the rest. It is a perfect example of an
early, sentimental cockney music-hall ballad:

I wanted them walks so bad
With you, and missus is mad
'Cos she says I gad out at night,
No doubt but what she's quite right.
Well, I can't stay long, but see,
Promise to 'old to me,
    An' I'll 'old to you for hever!
Them people may *court* a bit,
    They don't love like we two!
    O George! I've got no one but you.

'Old by me! Promise it?
And I'll never leave you, never.[50]

Much later in his life Kipling entered into a correspondence with
James Benion Booth, whose many volumes of late-Victorian
memoirs included studies of the music hall. Kipling expressed his
gratitude for Booth's work saying that 'Those old music-hall
ditties . . . supply a gap in the national history, and people haven't
yet realized how much they had to do with the national life.'
Kipling begged Booth to undertake a comprehensive study of
music-hall songs in order to establish an exact chronology before
it was too late. In the course of the correspondence, Kipling
frequently refers to songs and artists he had admired in his youth.
The artists he remembered with most affection were Nellie Farren
and 'Jemmy' Fawn. He also praises Fred Leslie and mentions
some old songs: 'Cerulea' (which was sung by Harry Rickards),
'I wish I was with Nancy' (usually associated with E. W. Mackney,
a black-faced comedian who was performing before Kipling was
born), and writes: 'Personally I date from "Kafoozelum" – which
by the way is a work of art.'[51]

These various references would place Kipling's first experiences
of the music hall in the early eighties, when he was aged fifteen
or sixteen. At this time the kind of interest he showed can be seen
from the *Schoolboy Lyrics* poem, but when he returned to England
in 1889 and was living opposite Gatti's he found a new depth and
vitality in the songs he heard:

> I listened to the observed and compelling songs of the Lion
> and Mammoth Comiques, and the shriller strains – but
> equally 'observed' – of the Bessies and Bellas, whom I could
> hear arguing beneath my window with their cab-drivers, as
> they sped from Hall to Hall.

Kipling's reference here to the 'Bessies and Bellas' is interesting
as he possibly has in mind Bessie Bellwood, and the distinction
he draws between the 'Lion and Mammoth Comiques' and the
'Bessies and Bellas' shows he was fully aware that one music-hall
tradition was being replaced by another, but the key word is
'observed'.[52] Arriving in England at a time when new music-hall
artists were challenging old, stale views of the cockney, Kipling
was able to approach an important facet of working-class culture

from a unique angle, and he employed this new experience to resolve some of the doubts he had about his presentation of the private soldier. On the one hand Kipling benefited from the 'observed' detail of the cockney songs, while on the other he seized upon the very essence of music hall – its no-nonsense approach to life, its colour, dry humour, lilting melodies, easy catch phrases, and most of all its secret of how to draw the genuinely sentimental and emotional feelings from an audience.[53]

IV

Barrack Room Ballads (1892) was dedicated to the man whose adventures it celebrated – Tommy Atkins. He immediately replaced Sam Weller and 'Arry as *the* working-class cockney archetype, and reigned supreme for at least a quarter of a century. What is really new about him is that he is totally of the working class; he is representative in a way that Sam Weller (with his roots in a literary convention of the devoted servant-valet) and 'Arry (in all his flashy, pretentious 'moneyed' vulgarity) are not. Although the ballads deal mainly with military situations, the soldier hero is no longer someone like Ortheris who is linked with home by sentimental memories, his personality divided because of Kipling's own narrow experience. He is a much more complete character who combines all of the qualities that Kipling – under the four-fold influence of love of India, disillusionment with England, horror at slum conditions, and fascination with the music hall – felt symbolized the English working classes. He is a synthesis of Ortheris, whose madness Kipling did not understand, and his English brother who sat and drank at Kipling's elbow in Gatti's.

The most influential single aspect of Tommy Atkins's presentation was Kipling's use of phonetics to indicate the sound of a cockney voice. This will be dealt with separately, but what can be noted here is the way that speech rhythms, aided by a music-hall song beat, are used to create that perky sense of all-knowing self-sufficiency which had long been an important part of the cockney's personality:

You may talk o' gin and beer
When you're quartered safe out 'ere.

> An' you're sent to penny-fights an' Aldershot it;
> But when it comes to slaughter
> You will do your work on water,
> An' you'll lick the bloomin' boots of 'im that's got it.

'Gunga Din'

This has the same ring of working-class truth that, for instance, Sam Weller's detailed London street directions possess, and which 'Arry's discourses on the political situation of the day, do not. What distinguishes Tommy Atkins from Sam Weller is not the hard life he leads (Dickens allows Sam Weller, for one superb moment, to tell the truth about life in pre-Pickwick days),[54] but the frank, casual way that the soldier's own values are accepted as the norm:

> Yes, it's pack-drill for me and a fortnight's C.B.
>   For 'drunk and resisting the Guard!'
>   Mad drunk and resisting the Guard –
>   'Strewth, but I socked it them hard!'

'Cells'

When Tom Herodsfoot got drunk he kicked his innocent wife to death; when Tommy Atkins gets drunk he attacks invincible Authority and though he must eventually be defeated, he delights in his moderate success. There is no moral repentence, only the hangover that must be balanced against pleasure obtained:

> I've a head like a concertina: I've a tongue like a button-stick:
> I've a mouth like an old potato, and I'm more than a little
> sick,
> But I've had my fun o' the Corp'ral's Guard . . .

'Cells'

If repentance makes no sense to Tommy Atkins, patriotism is a feeling he well understands. At one and the same time he is both victor and victim:

> Walk wide o' the Widow at Windsor,
> For 'alf o' Creation she owns:

We 'ave bought 'er the same with the sword an' the flame,
An' we've salted it down with our bones.
(Poor beggars! – it's blue with our bones!)

'The Widow at Windsor'

Excitement for Tommy Atkins is usually some form of violence; either in a civilian setting:

For it was: – 'Belts, belts, belts, an' that's one for you!'
An' it was 'Belts, belts, belts, an' that's done for you!'
O buckle an' tongue
Was the song that we sung
From Harrison's down to the Park!

'Belts'

Or a military:

'E rushes at the smoke when we let drive,
An' before we know, 'e's 'ackin' at our 'ead;
'E's all 'ot sand an' ginger when alive,
An' 'e's generally shammin' when 'e's dead.

'Fuzzy-Wuzzy'

What aesthetic sense he possesses is satisfied only by the sharply defined, highly romanticized, exotic scenes he remembers from his service overseas:

Elephints a-pilin' teak
In the sludgy, squdgy creek,
Where the silence 'ung that 'eavy you was 'arf afraid to
speak!
On the road to Mandalay . . .

'Mandalay'

His sense of justice is expedient and poetic:

If the wife should go wrong with a comrade, be loth
To shoot when you catch 'em – you'll swing, on my oath! –
Make 'im take 'er and keep 'er; that's Hell for them both . . .

'The Young British Soldier'

His own particular philosophy of social anarchism is kept in check by upper-class Authority – his most constant enemy – to which he must bow if he is to retain his freedom, even though he can

never properly understand the reason for it. True realization of
the power it has over him comes only at extreme moments:

> 'Is cot was right-'and cot to mine,' said Files-on-Parade.
> 'E's sleepin' out an' far tonight,' the Colour-Sergeant said.
> 'I've drunk 'is beer a score o' times,' said Files-on-Parade.
> 'E's drinkin' bitter beer alone,' the Colour-Sergeant said.

'Danny Deever'

Time and time again Kipling stresses that it is ridiculous to talk
of Tommy Atkins in middle-class terms. Crushed down by incomprehensible social and military forces, both at home and abroad,
he escapes total annihilation by placing his faith in immediate
sensation:

> Ship me somewheres east of Suez, where the best
>   is like the worst,
> Where there aren't no Ten Commandments an' a man
>   can raise a thirst.

'Mandalay'

And continually there is the contrast between life in England and
life abroad. In 'Mandalay' it takes the form of Kipling's own
perennial grouse:

> I am sick 'o wastin' leather on these gritty pavin'-stones,
> An' the blasted Henglish drizzle wakes the fever in my bones.

In 'Tommy' it takes the more significant shape of civilian hypocrisy:

> I went into a theatre as sober as could be,
> They gave a drunk civilian room, but 'adn't none for me;
> They sent me to the gallery or round the music-'alls,
> But when it comes to fightin', Lord! they'll shove me in the
>   stalls!

Here once again it is Kipling himself turning away from the theatre
and towards the music hall; away from the middle and towards
the working class. His association with working-class culture,
coinciding as it did with far-reaching social and political changes,
provided the slum novelists who were to follow with a working-
class archetype which was predominantly 'realistic'. What is most

striking of all about Tommy Atkins is the way he always expresses
himself in simple, commonplace, 'vulgar' metaphors, never bringing into his monologues experiences or sentiments alien to his
way of life. Unlike many of the novelists who came before him,
Kipling did not feel that before a working man could have anything to say he had to be educated – either by self-help or individual
philanthropy. On the contrary, Kipling fully understood the
necessity for the working man to express himself in his own language. In one of his early soldier stories Kipling wrote: 'There is
nobody to speak for Thomas except people who have theories to
work off on him; and nobody understands Thomas except Thomas,
and he does not always know what is the matter with himself.'[55]
The *Barrack Room Ballads* attempted to put this situation right.
The opening dedication acknowledges the debt Kipling felt to
the private soldier:

> I have made for you a song,
> And it may be right or wrong,
> But only you can tell me if it's true;
> I have tried for to explain
> Both your pleasure and your pain,
> And, Thomas, here's my best respects to you!

When expressed in this manner it becomes apparent that there
is more than a little condescension in Kipling's admiration for
Tommy Atkins; an element of *de haut en bas* that it is impossible
to conceal. As we have already seen, this is a common weakness
in working-class fiction, but Kipling's case is significantly different
from that of any earlier writer. He fully recognizes that the
differences between the classes are primarily cultural, and, unlike
Gissing and Besant, refuses to acknowledge that middle-class
culture is inherently superior to working-class culture. Indeed,
there is an important sense in which Kipling believes the opposite
to be true. What he admires in working-class life is its spontaneity
and freedom, qualities which are lacking in his own class. Because
Kipling's work is both intensely personal and sociologically
objective; because he is continually seeking to express his admiration for a way of life that is necessarily foreign to his own inner
experience; the class judgement he reaches comes over to the
reader as a form of cultural envy. This is expressed openly but,
at the same time, is occasionally rendered condescending by the

author's knowledge that he is excluded in every real sense from the way of life he so admires. In the twentieth century this equivocal relationship with the working classes becomes very common and is most strikingly observable in a writer such as George Orwell, but in the nineteenth century it was revolutionary. The *Barrack Room Ballads* explore different facets of Tommy Atkins's personality – his patriotism, sentimentality, ingrained violence, frustrations and social anarchism – with a sympathy that comes from a total understanding of the simple fact that 'single men in barricks don't grow into plaster saints'.[56] Kipling was the first important Victorian writer who was not scared of the working classes.

9 Albert Chevalier singing 'My Old Dutch', *c.* 1895

10 'The Jago', Boundary Street, *c.* 1890

7

Arthur Morrison and the tone of violence

I

In the 1890s Arthur Morrison wrote three books which deal with
working-class life in the East End: *Tales of Mean Streets* (1894),
A Child of the Jago (1896) and *To London Town* (1899). It is in
these novels and short stories that we can most clearly see gathered
together the various literary and social forces which have been
discussed in the preceding chapters. Morrison's work is an amalgam of Besant, who supplies a new image of the East End; Charles
Booth, who clarifies the class structure of that image; and Kipling,
from whom Morrison derives his objective, amoral, literary
method. To these diverse influences he brings considerable
personal experience of working-class life, carefully acquired skill
as a reporter, and a simple but vivid prose style. More than any
other author it is Arthur Morrison who establishes the tone of
slum fiction in the nineties.

Very little of a personal nature is known about his early life,
though it is now possible to construct a sound outline of his
activities in the nineties. His birth certificate shows that he was
born in Poplar, the son of an engine fitter, and from a few obviously
autobiographical remarks in his published writings it seems
reasonable to assume that at least some of his childhood was spent
in the East End, but it is impossible to draw any definite conclusions about this period of his life. Nothing further is known of
him until, at the age of twenty-three, his signature appears on a

M

cash receipt in respect of one month's salary (September 1886) as Clerk to the Beaumont Trustees, the philanthropic foundation that administered the People's Palace. Once again he disappears from the scene until 6 March 1889 when he was appointed sub-editor of the *Palace Journal*, then under the control of Walter Besant, from whom it was later claimed he 'received some hints on the technical ABC of fiction'.[1] As sub-editor of the *Journal* he compiled a weekly column of general information about the Palace and, more interestingly, published three signed descriptive sketches of the East End. After about nine months Morrison relinquished his post as sub-editor and six months later resigned from the Beaumont Trustees.[2] From this time onwards he chiefly earned his living as a free-lance journalist. In October 1891, he published an article in *Macmillan's Magazine* called 'A Street' which, in a revised form, later became the famous introduction to *Tales of Mean Streets*. This article attracted the attention of W. E. Henley who invited Morrison to write a series of working-class stories for *The National Observer*. Apart from the *Mean Street* stories he probably also contributed unsigned articles to the *Observer* and was usually labelled as one of 'Henley's young men' with, among others, Rudyard Kipling, who remained a life-long friend.

The three descriptive sketches published in the *Palace Journal* show Morrison striving, with little success, to develop an individual approach to the difficult problem of writing about the East End. The first of them, 'Whitechapel' (24 April 1889), challenges the 'graphically-written descriptions of Whitechapel, by people who have never seen the place'. Morrison distinguishes between two types of description. The one:

A horrible black labyrinth . . reeking from end to end with the vilest exhalations; its streets, mere kennels of horrent putrefaction; its every wall, its every object, slimy with the indigenous ooze of the place; swarming with human vermin, whose trade is robbery, and whose recreation is murder; the catacombs of London – darker, more tortuous, and more dangerous than those of Rome, and supersaturated with foul life.

This approach, as we have already seen, belongs to the Newgate-novel-Dickens-Kingsley-early-Gissing tradition, and during the late-Victorian period was still commonly used in the working-class romance. The other type of description is that of 'outcast' London:

> Black and nasty still, a wilderness of crazy dens into which pallid wastrels crawl to die; where several families lie in each fetid room, and fathers, mothers, and children watch each other starve; where bony, blear-eyed wretches, with everything beautiful, brave, and worthy crushed out of them, and nothing of the glory and nobleness and jollity of this world within the range of their crippled senses, rasp away their puny lives in the sty of the sweater.

Morrison admits there are places in Whitechapel that fit these descriptions, but because of the size of the district and the variety of life to be found in it, neither can be said to be representative. In order to paint a fair picture of Whitechapel, he argues, one should take into account the ancient industries, colourful street traders, booksellers, and its many literary and historical associations, as well as the suffering poor and the foul slums. This is very similar to the kind of East End image that, under Besant's influence, the *Palace Journal* usually advanced, save at the close of Morrison's sketch a note of despair creeps in. While mocking the 'slummers' Morrison agrees that 'something must be done' about the black spots. But what?

> Children must not be left in these unscoured corners. Their fathers and mothers are hopeless, and must not be allowed to rear a numerous and equally hopeless race. Light the streets better, certainly; but what use in building better houses for these poor creatures to render as foul as those that stand? The inmates may ruin the character of a house, but no house can alter the character of its inmates.

These words, written while Morrison was actually working in 'The Palace of Delight', hardly represent a vote of confidence for Besant's particular brand of optimism, but at this stage of his development Morrison was obviously not sure in his own mind just what attitude he should adopt towards the East End and the working classes. The other two sketches he wrote for the *Palace Journal* show the same uncertainty. 'On Blackwall Pier' (8 May 1889) attempts to describe the strange extremes of life to be found side by side in a working-class setting. The gay coarseness of lovers on a pier is contrasted with the half-drowned body of an attempted suicide that is dragged from the Thames. The third sketch is virtually a plagiarism of Dickens's *A Christmas Carol*, in which tradesmen and shoppers swop jokes amid a plethora of fruit, meat and spirits. In this East End jolly policemen fall over children's slides, gentlemen's hats fly off, bells chime, and the foulness of the slums is made picturesque by a sparkling frost.

By the time Morrison wrote 'A Street' in 1891 he had rid his mind of these conflicting attitudes and had firmly established the compound of realistic observation and quiet despair that he made peculiarly his own:

> There is about one hundred and fifty yards of our street, all
> of the same pattern. It is not a picturesque street; a dingy
> little brick house twenty feet high with three square holes
> to carry the windows and an oblong hole to carry the door is
> not picturesque; and two or three score of them in a row,
> with one front wall in common, represent either side of our
> street and suggests stables.

Morrison has here completely accepted Besant's view that monotony not poverty is the most serious problem of East End life, but he has rejected Besant's cultural antidote. For Morrison monotony is a quality endemic in working-class life; it is not merely a sickness to be cured by building libraries or Palaces of Delight: 'And this is the record of a day in our street, – of any day, – of every day . . . Of every day excepting Sunday . . . This is Sunday in our street, and every Sunday is the same as every other Sunday.'[3]

To the social influence of Besant can be added the literary influence of Kipling, for the tone of *Tales of Mean Streets* owes much to 'Badalia Herodsfoot'. Short, simple, yet rhythmic sentences, tellingly used to create an air of authorial disinterest, is one of the techniques, coming from Kipling, that most distinctly separates the slum novelists of the nineties from their predecessors:

> Nobody laughs in our street, – life is too serious a thing –
> nobody sings. There was a woman who sang once, – a young
> wife from the country. But she bore children, and her voice
> cracked; then her man died, and she sang no more. They

took away her home, and with her children about her skirts
the woman left our street for ever. The other women did not
think much of her. She was 'helpless'.[4]

Morrison himself wrote that he intended 'A Street' to convey 'the
deadly monotony and respectability of the mean streets so characteristic of the East End, for hopeless monotony is more characteristic than absolute degradation such as you find in the Jago'.[5] And
this is the theme of not merely the introduction but the majority
of *Mean Street* tales. This point is of some importance as Morrison's reputation for concentrating upon the violent aspects of slum
life was established even before he wrote *A Child of the Jago*
(1896).

When *Tales of Mean Streets* was first published, critical attention, which was on the whole very favourable, focused so exclusively on 'Lizerunt', the one really violent story in a collection of
fourteen, that Morrison, who was generally shy of publicity, wrote
to one periodical denying that he had 'generalized half London as a
race of Yahoos'.[6] At this time he had already begun to write *To
London Town* which, because of its gentleness of tone, might have
been intended as a rebuke to his critics, but for some unknown
reason he abandoned this work and published instead his study of
East End criminal life *A Child of the Jago*. Once again he found
himself at the centre of a debate on the extent and nature of
violence in working-class life and fiction. Just as he had earlier
pointed out that 'Lizerunt' represented only one part of life in the
East End, now he was forced to explain that *A Child of the Jago*
dealt with a specific East End criminal ghetto, and at no time
had he intended to offer it as representative of working-class life
as a whole.[7] The critics paid little attention to his disavowals, and
the phrase 'Jagodom' (used as a synonym for hooliganism, itself
a word of recent coinage) passed, with 'mean streets', into common
usage. In spite of the fact that the greater part of Morrison's work
was not concerned with the working classes at all, and that most of
his working-class fiction did not deal with violent themes, it was
'Lizerunt' and *A Child of the Jago* that established his literary
reputation in the nineties.

Even today Morrison's critics find it difficult to regard his work
in a rational manner. Julian Franklyn, concentrating entirely on
'Lizerunt', claims that: 'There could be such a monster [as Billy

Chope, the hero] but in *Tales of Mean Streets* one gathers the impression that all Cockneys are like this. To Morrison, poverty and criminality are synonymous.'[8] And Alan Sillitoe, himself an outstanding working-class novelist, ironically in the Morrison tradition, finds that Morrison's characters 'lived in a zoo, and were to be regarded with fear, hostility, and derision'.[9]

Judgements such as these are extremely unfair to Morrison. While it is true that his most successful work is on the violent side of working-class life (in artistic terms *To London Town* is a complete failure), violence is never used for sensational reasons, but is always part of a well-defined total pattern. Furthermore Morrison's novels and stories possess considerable historical importance. When he first decided to write some short stories about the working classes he determined that 'they must be done with austerity and frankness and there must be no sentimentalism, no glossing over'.[10] Almost every working-class novelist before him had vowed the same, but, as we have already seen, in these earlier novels scenes which deal with the more debased or violent aspects of working-class life, such as wife-beating, drunkenness or hooliganism, are so handled as to indicate the author's personal disappropriation of the behaviour described. This may be done in two ways. Either some kind of terrible retribution comes to the debased character, or the way of life of other characters in the novel (either a substitute-working-class or a middle-class hero) provides a constant moral standard against which the debased scenes can be measured. Morrison, following the example of Kipling, rejected these moral middle-men. In his role of 'realist' he demanded absolute freedom to write on whatever subject he wished:

> If the community have left horrible places and horrible lives before [the novelist's] eyes, then the fault is that of the community; and to picture these places and these lives becomes not merely his privilege, but his duty.[11]

As Morrison's reference to the 'duty' of the novelist suggests, he did not believe in the total abnegation of social responsibility, but he interpreted 'responsibility' to mean presenting the simple, objective truth as it appeared to him. He angrily attacked those critics who demanded that in his novels he should always clearly indicate his own moral position:

It is not that these good people wish me to write 'even weeping': for how do they know whether I weep or not? No: their wish is not that I shall weep, but that I shall weep obscenely in the public gaze. In other words that I shall do their weeping for them, as a sort of emotional bedeman.[12]

Morrison owes his historical and literary importance to precisely this – that he refused to be an 'emotional bedeman' for the reading public. Like Kipling, he felt that the only justifiable way of presenting the working classes in fiction was in terms of their own attitudes and values. The East End world that he knew seemed to comprise three main qualities, monotony, respectability and violence. It is the interrelationship of these qualities that Morrison tries to express in his novels and stories.

'Lizerunt' traces the brief life of a factory girl, Elizabeth Hunt, from her courting days, through the early years of marriage and fertile motherhood, to the moment when her brutal husband throws her out of the house to earn money street-walking. Several aspects of his kind of story had already been handled by novelists. The Bank Holiday courtship which is used to contrast the rowdy horse-play of cockney love-making with the brutal violence that takes its place once the marriage ceremony is over, had been used by Gissing in *The Nether World*. And the theme of a feeble, terrorized wife devotedly defending her debased husband had also been superbly handled by Gissing in his portrait of Pennyloaf Candy, by Kipling in 'Badalia Herodsfoot', and by many other writers stretching back to Dickens in *Sketches by Boz*. The tone of 'Lizerunt' owes everything to Kipling. As in 'Badalia Herodsfoot', the action centres upon several violent moments in Lizer's life, each of which is described dispassionately by the author. Moral comment is made obliquely by using incongruous metaphors and images. Thus, Lizer watching two men fighting over her is elated and 'for almost five minutes she was Helen of Troy'.[13] This use of the mock heroic – like pastoral, a technique favoured by many working-class novelists – serves not merely to describe but also to ridicule. The same is true of some of Morrison's observations on working-class behaviour. When Billy Chope meets Lizer in the street he 'caught and twisted her arm, bumping her against the wall':

'Garn', said Lizerunt, greatly pleased: 'Le' go!' For she knew that this was love.[14]

Morrison does not point out (as for instance Gissing does) that rough physical contact is an important part of slum courtship, but allows the incident to speak for itself. The effect, however, is immediately destroyed by the implied sneer in his next sentence.

Yet in spite of these faults 'Lizerunt' is very effective. By concentrating a period of about three years into a series of graphically presented moments, Morrison captures one of the aspects of slum life that had always horrified the working-class novelist – the collapse of a slum girl's feeble prettiness into the shapeless sluttishness of the young slum mother. She is by no means an innocent victim (as are both Badalia Herodsfoot and Pennyloaf Candy), but lives by a moral code little different from that of her husband. Driven solely by mercenary motives, she plays each of her two boy friends off against the other, until the issue is resolved by Billy Chope having Sam Cardew beaten up. For a while she is smitten by something very like conscience, but soon tires of a quiet life and returns to the person responsible for Sam's beating. She is fully aware of what she is doing. The period of enjoyment she can expect from life is short, and to waste time taking oranges to a bandaged, bed-ridden hero, is to make it even shorter. Life with Sam Cardew might have been better than it offers to be with Billy Chope, but in a world where pleasure is immediate and mainly violent, a choice between the two men is, at bottom, meaningless. This, for instance, is one of the courtship scenes:

'Ullo, Lizer! Where *are* y' a-comin' to? If I 'adn't laid 'old 'o ye – !' But here Billy Chope arrived to demand what the 'ell Sam Cardew was doing with his gal. Now Sam was ever readier for a fight than Billy was; but the sum of Billy's half-pints was large: wherefore the fight began. On the skirt of an hilarious ring, Lizerunt, after some small outcry, triumphed aloud. Four days before she had no bloke; and here she stood with two, and those two fighting for her! Here in the public gaze, on the Flats! For almost five minutes she was Helen of Troy.[15]

If a person accepts this as pleasure, and all three participants obviously do, then there can be no complaint when the triumphant girl-friend becomes the victimized wife:

'Two bob? Wot for?' Lizer asked.
''Cos I want it. None o' yer lip.'
'Ain't got it,' said Lizer sulkily.
'That's a bleed'n lie.'
'Lie yerself.'
'I'll break y'in'arves, ye blasted 'eifer!' He ran at her
throat and forced her back over a chair.
'I'll pull yer face auf! If y' don't give me the money,
gawblimey, I'll do for ye!'[16]

For Morrison it is a simple matter of logic that the first of these scenes could quite easily, although not inevitably, lead to the second. The emphasis that earlier writers had placed on the possibilities of escape from the slums disappear in Morrison. Billy Chope is by no means presented as the ordinary working man (Morrison later described him as 'in a minority, a blackguard')[17] but the forces which control his outlook and actions, press down upon, and thus limit, the aspirations of even the most respectable members of the mean streets. When Morrison says, in the introduction, that no one sings in the street and then in the very first story shows Lizer and Billy Chope shouting and dancing with glee at the Whitsun Fair, he is not contradicting himself. He means that no one sings for long as the country girl sang; no one can bridge two separate worlds once they inhabit this street. The country girl sings of a world outside of her present environment; the simple desire she expresses is for gentle happiness, which has no relevance in the East End. Once she suffers some of the everyday tragedies she collapses – she is 'helpless' – she cannot establish a working compromise with her physical surrounding, and anyone who cannot do that must be crushed. It is for this reason that, unlike Besant, Morrison can suffer no aristocrats living in his world, and unlike Gissing, cannot allow his characters to spend their evenings reading Greek tragedy. The slums would not allow such things to happen. If anyone should move in this direction, then, like the country girl, their voices would crack and they would sing no more.

Yet the theme of escape occurs frequently in Morrison's stories – escape from monotony or from violence, from one section of working-class life into another. More than any other author he uses as a framework for his stories the deadening desire for respectability (as passionate as in any middle-class world) that is the only viable means of escape from association with the twin evils of violence and social pity. A majority of the stories in *Tales of Mean Streets* deal with this theme of respectability, and it is indicative of the depth of Morrison's pessimism that all such strivings are shown as pointless or self-defeating.

In 'That Brute Simmons' a farce is enacted in which an intensely house-proud woman believing herself to be a widow marries again. When her first husband reappears and tries to blackmail his successor, the two men vie with each other in trying to run away from this respectable hell. In 'Behind the Shades' a mother and daughter, fallen from a higher social position, starve themselves to death rather than let their neighbours know they can no longer keep up the façade of respectability. 'In Business' and 'All that Messuage' have similar plots. In the former, a family dominated by a respectable mother use a small inheritance to set up a genteel shop in Bromley. In the latter, some hard-saved money is used to buy a house so that a couple can live on the rent. In both cases these plans collapse because of the inability of the working-class aspirants to understand the most elementary commercial principles. 'Squire Napper' is similar but far more successful. A labourer inherits a small sum of money and immediately gives up his work, and while he wonders what to do with his new-found wealth, indulges in the only form of entertainment he knows – drinking. His money slowly disappears and with it the opportunity, of which he is never really aware, to better himself. In one scene, very reminiscent of the Boffin–Wegg relationship in *Our Mutual Friend*, Squire Napper hires a street-corner orator so that he can listen to revolutionary speeches in his own home. In another story 'On the Stairs', a mother, influenced by her neighbours' snobbery, determines to give her dying son a decent funeral. When a sympathetic doctor gives her some money, she saves it rather than spend it on medicine. The son dies and the mother is proud that she can afford the ultimate funereal status symbol – plumes.

These stories with their stale, hackneyed plots, do not live up to the promise offered by the introduction and 'Lizerunt', but they are saved from being excessively sentimental or pathetic by Morrison's terse style and relentless insistence that the slum is an autonomous world which forbids the miraculous character transformation so common in working-class romance. The characters are not fools – in 'The Red Cow Group', for instance, they neatly turn the tables on an anarchist seeking converts – but the environment within which they live has eaten into their souls, so that their social ambitions, humble as they may be, are utterly beyond their capabilities. In one of the best sketches – there is no plot to make it a story – 'To Bow Bridge', the narrator is one of a handful of respectable working-class people taking a bus journey late at night. When the pubs turn out, a crowd of rowdy men and women clamber on to the bus in order to cross to the other side of Bow Bridge where the drinking hours are extended to midnight. Morrison carefully and impartially describes the coarse, drunken, noisy but non-violent behaviour of the crowd until their destination is reached and they get off, leaving the respectable workers to continue their journey. This sketch epitomizes Morrison's attitude in *Tales of Mean Streets*. The journey that all the passengers are making is dull and dreary; for some of them it is only made bearable by hooliganism. The novelist sits by, noting behaviour patterns but passing no comparative judgement. For Morrison the working classes are neither more nor less corrupt than other social groups – at least not in a moral sense. Their behaviour, habits and customs are part of a pattern which possesses its own impetus, scale of values, class system and taboos. Above all else what interested Morrison about working-class life was the way that this predominantly dreary world could suddenly explode into physical violence. In 'To Bow Bridge' he merely stated the problem; in *A Child of the Jago* he tried to explore it fully.

Shortly after the publication of *Tales of Mean Streets* Morrison received a letter of appreciation from the Reverend A. Osborne Jay, vicar of the Holy Trinity, Shoreditch. Jay praised the truthfulness of Morrison's East End portrait and invited the author to visit his parish. At this time Morrison was already planning to write a full-length novel which would explore the effects of heredity and environment on a young boy, but was uncertain where exactly in the East End to set his story. The meeting with Jay helped him to make up his mind, and for a period of eighteen months he frequented Jay's parish, exploring the alleys and courts, sitting with the parishioners in their homes, drinking with them in pubs, and even for a spell letting them teach him how to make matchboxes (at this date still one of the standard occupations for the London destitute).[18] The real name of this tiny area that later came to be called the Jago, was the Old Nichol. It stood on the boundaries of Shoreditch and Bethnal Green, a square block of some half-a-dozen streets containing one of the worst slums in East London.[19] On Charles Booth's maps it is shaded a deep black denoting inhabitants of the 'lowest class of occasional labourers, loafers and semi-criminals', as far removed from the dreary, respectable workers of *Mean Streets* as it was possible to be. Here Billy Chope would have been completely at home. Jay had taken charge of the parish that contained the Old Nichol in 1886 and, realizing the futility of pursuing a purely religious policy in such an area, had gradually improvised an idiosyncratic technique for dealing with his unruly flock. He opened a social club, encouraged boxing matches in which he often took part, painstakingly acquired a working knowledge of criminal language and habits, and wrote three excellent books describing his work: *Life in Darkest London* (1891), *The Social Problem* (1893) and *A Story of Shoreditch* (1896). In the first of these he described a street scene in the Old Nichol:

> Women, sodden with drink, fighting and struggling like wild creatures; men, bruised and battered, with all the marks and none of the pleasures of vice upon them; outcasts, abject and despairing, without food or shelter; the very children, with coarse oaths and obscene jests, watching, like wild beasts, for anything, dishonest or otherwise, which might come their way.[20]

As so much of the criticism later aimed at *A Child of the Jago* questioned the veracity of Morrison's portrait, it is worth mentioning that Jay, although in some ways eccentric, was no sensationalist. He always maintained that the Old Nichol was a special case: that the East End had 'portions which are really delightful',[21] and he later vigorously defended Morrison against his incredulous critics.[22] Neither Jay nor Morrison claimed to be writing about the 'working classes' as a whole. Their subject was Charles Booth's 1.2 per cent of the East End population and unlike many writers before and after they were fully aware that they were dealing with only a minority section of the working classes, albeit a minority that posed a permanent threat to the well-being of its decent neighbours.

Morrison knew that he was compiling a social document in the form of a novel, a work in which problems of character and personality would be subordinated to a sociologically exact, yet at the same time symbolic, image of the Jago. In *A Child of the Jago*, the Jago itself is the true hero. This seems to suggest that Morrison was writing under the direct influence of Zola's dramshop or coal mine, but the novel as it finally appeared is a curious mixture of the English social-moralizing tradition and French naturalistic objectivity. Morrison, for instance, outlining his reasons for writing the novel, sounds just like Mrs Gaskell, Kingsley or Dickens:

> I resolved therefore to write the 'Child of the Jago' which should tell the story of a boy, who, but for his environment, would have become a good citizen; also, the story of the horrible Nichol; and, lastly, I wished to show that Father Jay's method is the only one that is possible in such a district.[23]

And it is interesting to find repeatedly details in Morrison's novel which seem to be unashamedly borrowed from Jay's various slum memoirs.[24] Yet *A Child of the Jago* is not merely a *tendenzroman*. Only at the close of the book is a moral clearly stated. Until that moment Morrison succeeds in absorbing the reader in this strange and violent world, not by pointing a social lesson but by bringing the slum vividly alive.

The long opening description of the Jago shows Morrison rejecting the 'austere' objectivity of *Mean Streets* in favour of the death, disease and hell imagery traditionally found in slum descriptions. But he now has a specific reason for doing this. Unlike Gissing's nether world or Kipling's Gunnison Street, which were representative districts of areas totally rotten, the Jago is a solitary diseased spot which threatens to contaminate the whole of the East End.

> It was past the mid of a summer night in the Old Jago. The narrow street was all the blacker for the lurid sky; for there was a fire in a farther part of Shoreditch, and the welkin was an infernal coppery glare. Below, the hot, heavy air lay, a rank oppression, on the contorted forms of those who made for sleep on the pavement: and in it, and through it all, there

rose from the foul earth and the grimmed walls a close,
mingled stink – the odour of the Jago.[25]

The usual inhabitants of this hell are not the suffering poor but
the very dregs of London: 'What was too vile for Kate Street,
Seven Dials, and Ratcliff Highway in its worst day, what was too
useless, incapable and corrupt – all that teemed in the Old Jago.'
In this world 'cosh carrying was near to being the major industry';
'front doors were used merely as firewood' (which provides as we
later see not merely warmth but easy escape passages from the
police); and 'the elementary Education Act ran in the Jago no
more than any other Act of Parliament'.[26] Law in the Jago is
determined by the feuding gangs of Ranns and Learys who, while
usually content to fight each other, are also capable of joining
forces to face a common enemy; and by Father Sturt (modelled
faithfully on Jay), whose philosophy of good-neighbourliness
interests few of his parishioners. The Perrott family, as new-
comers to the Jago, owe allegiance to neither the gangsters nor
the priest. Josh Perrott, the father, is a tradesman who, having
fallen on evil days, discovers that earning a living Jago-style is
more attractive than plastering. It is his son Dicky who is the 'child'
of the Jago.

In choosing to centre his novel on a slum child Morrison was
following a very conventional line, and it is possible that he
deliberately did this as an implied criticism of the golden-haired
child or the aristocratic changeling of working-class romance. The
novel that set the tone for this romantic mid-Victorian treatment
was *Oliver Twist* which was often seen in the later 'realistic' period
as the father of the slum novel.[27] Certainly there are sufficient
similarities between *Oliver Twist* and *A Child of the Jago* to
suggest that Morrison had the earlier novel in mind. Aaron Weech,
who battens on Dicky Perrott and cunningly trains him as a thief,
recalls Fagin, while Josh Perrott's flight from the police, especially
the moment when he is spotlighted in an upstairs window, is very
reminiscent of Bill Sikes's death scene. Finally, Josh's trial is
virtually a plagiarism of Fagin's. Where the novels differ most is
in their treatment of the slum child. Dicky Perrott could never be
mistaken for a lost aristocrat, nor will he escape by virtue of a
superior education. At times Morrison appears to be mocking
this convention, as when Beveridge offers Dicky some advice:

'Now, Dicky Perrott, you Jago whelp, look at them – look hard. Someday, if you're clever – cleverer than anyone in the Jago now – if you're only scoundrel enough, and brazen enough, and lucky enough – one of a thousand – maybe you'll be like them: bursting with high living, drunk when you like, red and pimply. There it is – that's your aim in life – there's your pattern. Learn to read and write, learn cunning, spare nobody and stop at nothing, and perhaps –' he waved his hand towards the Bag of Nails. 'It's the best the world has for you, for the Jago's got you, and that's the only way out, except the gaol and the gallows.'[28]

The model life being held up for Dicky's approval is that of the High Mobsman: the alternatives, as pointed out by Beveridge, are the gallows and the gaol. Father Sturt's attempt to find Dicky a regular job is frustrated, not simply because Aaron Weech is lurking round the corner, but because the power of the slum is greater than that of the priest. In the Jago crime is attractive, respectability non-existent. There is only the East End Elevation Mission and Pansophical Institute to provide an alternative way of life and this is bitterly satirized by Morrison as a place where 'a number of decently-dressed and mannerly young men passed many evenings . . . in harmless pleasures, and often with an agreeable illusion of intellectual advancement'.[29] The only good it does for the Jago is to provide Dicky with the opportunity to steal a watch. It is his first 'click' and after the sheer joy of this moment he has no chance at all. From now on he accepts as a moral guide the single rule of the Jago – 'Thou shalt not nark' – and he abides by this even when he lies dying, stabbed in a street brawl.

There is much about *A Child of the Jago* that is unsatisfactory. Some of the characters (Pigeony Poll the golden-hearted prostitute, and Aaron Weech the fence, in particular) are conventional and rather wooden figures, while the portrait of Dicky does have, as H. D. Traill pointed out, 'odd touches of old-fashioned melodrama' about it.[30] More seriously, the fatalistic tone is too heavy for the slight structure of the story. Even allowing for the Jago as a special case, the reader feels that the dice are too heavily loaded against the Perrott family, the options open to them unjustifiably narrow and soul-destroying.

What really impresses is Morrison's handling of violence. The gang fights evoke an atmosphere of crude reality that the English working-class novel had never seen before:

> Norah Walsh, vanquished champion, now somewhat recovered, looked from a window, saw her enemy vulnerable, and ran out armed with a bottle. She stopped at the kerb to knock the bottom off the bottle, and then, with an exultant shout, seized Sally Green by the hair and stabbed her about the face with the jagged points. Blinded with blood, Sally released her hold on Mrs. Perrott, and rolled on her back, struggling fiercely; but to no end, for Norah Walsh, kneeling on her breast, stabbed and stabbed again, till pieces of the bottle broke away. Sally's yells and plunges ceased, and a man pulled Norah off. On him she turned, and he was fain to run, while certain Learys found a truck which might carry Sally to the hospital.[31]

It is not so much the actual description that is new as the assumption by the novelist that this kind of behaviour, at least in the Jago, is the norm. So infectious is the battle that everyone is caught up in it:

> As for old Beveridge, the affair so grossly excited him that he neglected business (he cadged and wrote begging screeves) and stayed in the Jago, where he strode wildly about the streets, lank and rusty, stabbing the air with a carving knife, and incoherently defying 'all the lot' to come near him.[32]

Violence of various kinds and degrees dominates the novel. Josh Perrott's boxing match with Billy Leary in Jago Court is a public festival, honoured with the attendance of the High Mobsmen who put up the stake money. Only Mrs Perrott is frightened: for everyone else the fight is a high spot of their week, the moment when Kingship (in a non-criminal sense) is firmly decided. Josh's victory in the fight brings him a larger sum of money than he had ever possessed before, and while he is fêted as a hero, news arrives that his baby has died: 'The rumour went in the Jago that Josh Perrott was in double luck. For here was insurance money without a doubt.'[33] In this world the formula that Gissing felt typified working-class attitudes in *The Nether World* – 'Get by whatever means so long as with impunity' – reigns absolutely. When a later fight breaks out in a pub, the rotten floor gives way

11 'Mean Streets', Tent Street, Bethnal Green, *c.* 1900

12 'Hooligans (A Sketch from Life)', by Jasper Weird, *Pall Mall Magazine*, 1901

and the Jagos and Dove Laners are hurled into the cellar. They immediately forget their feud and plunder the pub. The children born and bred in the Jago naturally follow the example of their parents in forming gangs and settling private quarrels by premeditated violence.

In the Jago there is no tenderness or love – save that professionally administered by Father Sturt – for such emotions would undermine the basic Jago philosophy of social anarchism; they would encourage people to build whereas the only thing the Jagos understand is destruction. Nor, in spite of his careful attempts to recreate the speech of the Jago, does Morrison allow his characters the cockney's traditional fund of wit for fear that this would weaken the horror of his portrait. What he does neatly capture, and make good use of, is the sardonic side of cockney humour, as in the first conversational lines of the book: 'AH–h–h–h,' he said, 'I wish I was dead: an' kep' a cawfy shop;' and in the same character's immediate comment on his friends' refusal to speak to him: 'This is a bleed'n' unsocial sort o' evenin' party, this is.'³⁴ But where Morrison is once again truly successful is in presenting working-class speech at moments of violence:

'Won't sing yer hymn? There ain't much time!
My boy was goin' straight, an' earnin' wages:
someone got 'im chucked. A man 'as time to
think things out, in stir! Sing, ye son of
a cow! Sing! Sing!³⁵

It is one of the main themes of the novel that those who live violently, die violently. Josh Perrott is hanged for a murder of revenge and his son is stabbed in a childish vendetta. These are the victims. But the Ranns and the Learys do not come to grief. When the County Council begins to demolish the Jago, most of the inhabitants move on, seeking a new district as much like the old as possible, for even if they could afford to live in the new flats, they would be unable to change their way of life. Kiddo Cook, now a respectable costermonger and married to Pigeony Poll, does take a council flat. He is the only 'Jago-rat' to escape. It is interesting to compare the end of this novel with that of *The Nether World*. Gissing openly stated that life in the new flats was worse than in the old slums, but this judgement did not fit easily with the working-class life we were shown. It was Gissing talking about himself rather than about his characters. Morrison quite clearly believed that the flats represent a step forward for society, but recognizes that they are not for the Ranns and Learys. This fits in perfectly with the way they have been presented in the novel. The flats would impose restrictions upon them, it would break up the clan basis of their life, it would destroy the only thing they have to enjoy – the vigorous, brutal excitement of slum violence.

In a prefatory note to *To London Town* (1899), Morrison wrote:

> I designed this story, and, indeed, began to write it, between the publication of *Tales of Mean Streets* and that of *A Child of the Jago*, to be read together with those books: not that I pretend to figure in all three – much less in any one of them – a complete picture of life in the eastern parts of London, but because they are complementary, each to the others.

To London Town attempts to strike a balance between the monotony of *Mean Streets* and the criminal violence of *A Child of the Jago*. The opening scenes show the May family living on the borders of Epping Forest which the East End invades in the form of some London visitors getting drunk in a country pub. When the grand father dies the mother and her son Johnny move to the East End where he is apprenticed to an engineering firm, and she remarries. Morrison traces the adventures of Johnny and his mother to the moment when the son falls in love, and the mother's marriage breaks down.

To London Town is perhaps not so dull as this summary makes it sound, but it is certainly less successful than the other two books in the trilogy. Its comparative failure does, however, raise interesting issues regarding the narrow range of working-class experience normally presented in fiction. So long as Morrison is dealing with working-class characters in extreme situations then his fiction comes vividly alive, but the same is not true of his treatment of the more ordinary, less sensational, aspects of working-class life. We have already seen that this is true of most earlier fiction, where street characters, cartoon types, suffering poor, melodramatic villains, or a political mass, act as working-class representatives. The most important contribution made by Kipling and Morrison was to break down the old view that one code of manners could be used to cover the behaviour of different class groups. They showed that drunkenness, swearing, and even violence, could be regarded as genuine forms of expression for people who did not respond to situations in a rational, intellectual or 'educated' way. But this in itself was only a partial solution. If, for instance, a novelist tries to write about working-class life from a point of view other than, on the one hand, violence, and on the other, escape, then what does he place at the core of his novel? What frame of reference can he use to interrelate the various experiences he is describing? This line of thought must be returned to in the next chapter; here we can briefly see how it applies to Morrison, as in *To London Town* he was obviously trying to solve such a problem. Johnny May is the kind of boy Dicky Perrott might have hoped to be had he not been brought up in the Jago. Morrison takes great care when outlining Johnny's development – his apprenticeship, work at night school, membership of a social club and his falling in love – to present him as an 'ordinary' member of the working classes. Johnny's mother is presented in a similar manner. In *Tales of Mean Streets* those working-class women whose highest ambition was to run a small shop had been treated harshly by Morrison. Mrs May, however, has enough business sense to make a success of her shop by providing a much needed service to the working-class community. But when it comes to turning this observed behaviour into material for a novel Morrison's own good sense breaks down. The girl Johnny falls in love with turns out to be, after a series of mysterious disappearances, the daughter of 'Old-Mother-Born-Drunk', the most disreputable character in the neighbourhood; and the man Johnny's mother marries is not merely a drunkard but also a bigamist. The novel is thus a curious mixture of the new realism and the old melodrama.

By the time he came to write this novel Morrison's influence was already at work on other slum novelists of the nineties. In his two early books he had shown that, provided great care was observed, the objective use of violence was a new and fruitful way of presenting the working classes in fiction. He had also shown that working-class characters could be placed at the heart of a novel; that the substitute working-class hero common in earlier fiction was unnecessary so long as the novelist did not entertain ambitious views of presenting a cross-section of society in his work. In this he was following the example of Kipling who had concentrated on the working class as a separate cultural entity by using as his media the short story, sketch and ballad, rather than the full-scale social novel. Morrison had both limited and expanded the scope of working-class fiction, and there were many novelists who were willing to learn from him.

II

Late in life, looking back upon his long career as a novelist, Somerset Maugham wrote of his first novel *Liza of Lambeth* (1897):

> Any merit it may have is due to the luck I had in being, by my work as a medical student, thrown into contact with a side of life that at that time had been little exploited by novelists. Arthur Morrison with his *Tales of Mean Streets* and *A Child of the Jago* had drawn the attention of the public to what were then known as the lower classes and I profited by the interest he had aroused.[36]

Maugham owed a greater debt to Morrison than this would suggest. Apart from the change of setting from East to South London, much of *Liza of Lambeth* suggests Morrison's influence. The three principal qualities that Morrison believed dominated working-class life (monotony, a yearning for respectability and violence) all feature in Maugham's novel. The opening description of Vere Street with its subdued evocation of environmental monotony is typical of the *Mean Streets* approach:

> It has forty houses on one side and forty houses on the other, and these eighty houses are very much more like one another than ever peas are like peas, or young ladies like young ladies. They are newish, three-storied buildings of dingy grey brick with slate roofs, and they are perfectly flat, without a bow-window or even a projecting cornice or window-sill to break the straightness of the line from one end of the street to the other.[37]

The houses themselves are dead, but the street is full of life, with children playing cricket in the road, and women gossiping in doorways. Liza burst upon this scene with great vivacity and humour. She is dressed in the standard coster costume of 'brilliant violet, with great lappets of velvet, and she had on her head an enormous black hat covered with feathers'.[38] Her appearance transforms the mood of the street. She sings Albert Chevalier's latest music-hall song, 'Knocked 'em in the Old Kent Road', jokes with the gossips, flirts with the men, plays cricket with the children, and finally gets the whole street dancing round a barrel-organ. Like Badalia Herodsfoot and Lizerunt, these are Liza's 'days of fatness' and this carefree moment signifies the beginning of her tragic decline.

The most unusual feature of *Liza of Lambeth* is that it deals at some length with a working-class love affair. The Pennyloaf Candy/Bob Hewett and Lizerunt/Billy Chope marriages are not really 'love' matches at all. Gissing and Morrison both merely note what they regarded as rather curious courting habits and then moved the stories on to their violent conclusions. Maugham, however, makes the love affair central to his book, and furthermore treats it seriously and sympathetically. This is all the more unusual because Liza's love for Jim Blakeston is adulterous, and although adultery had long been a stock subject for the novelist, its fictional treatment had been limited to the middle and upper classes. There are two main reasons for this: Gissing's novels can supply one, Kipling's and Morrison's the other. As was pointed out earlier, Gissing usually allowed his working-class heroines to be sexually attractive only in proportion as they possessed upper-class qualities. This was in order that they might be worthy of their substitute working-class lovers. The three genuine working-class girls in his novels are handled in a different manner. Pennyloaf Candy is spineless and totally subservient to Bob Hewett, and is also shown to be physically anaemic. Clem Peckover is extremely sensual but she is more animal than human. Totty Nancarrow in *Thyrza* is much nearer in personality to Liza than Clem Peckover or Pennyloaf Candy, but, for Gissing, her ceaseless chatter and coarse manners made her sexually undesirable. In this respect it is significant that she finally marries Joe Bunce, one of the least important people in the novel. It is impossible to imagine Gissing regarding any of these women as fit subjects for a prolonged, adulterous, love affair. Kipling and Morrison did not share Gissing's snobbery in this respect, but their reason for avoiding the subject of adultery is just as strange. They blindly accepted the belief that working-class sexual amorality was a natural

condition of slum life, and that therefore the term adultery
possessed no meaning. Badalia Herodsfoot is shown to be sexually
attractive, but when her husband leaves her, Kipling goes out of
his way to stress how strange it was that she did not immediately
pair off with someone else: 'With rare fidelity she listened to no
proposals for a second marriage according to the customs of
Gunnison Street, which do not differ from those of the Barra-
long.'[39] Morrison, for all his claims of dealing frankly and fear-
lessly with life in the East End, rarely shows sex to be a part of it,
but that he would have agreed with Kipling on this subject can
be seen from his reference to Dicky Perrott as 'not married, either
in the simple Jago fashion or in church'.[40] In the final instance
Kipling and Morrison are little different from Gissing, for like
him they could not conceive of a working-class couple possessing
the sensitivity or emotional depth which, as participants in an
adulterous love affair, they would require.

Maugham was not so inhibited. All the normal trappings of a
fictional middle- or upper-class love affair are there, simply translated into working-class terms. Liza and Jim meet in the street, on
a Bank Holiday outing, in the gallery of a theatre, and in pubs.
The initial seduction scene is a curious instance of Maugham
interpreting the horse-play of courtship for animal violence:

> He looked at her for a moment, and she, ceasing to thump
> his hand, looked up at him with half-opened mouth.
> Suddenly he shook himself, and closing his fist gave her a
> violent, swinging blow in the stomach.
> 'Come on,' he said.
> And together they slid down into the darkness of the
> passage.[41]

Liza is not presented as a naturally immoral person. She treats
Tom, her faithful working-class suitor, gently; becomes the
outcast object of her neighbours' respectability, and when called a
'prostitute' fights the slanderer. She is also, for the sake of love,
willing to shoulder her guilt, rather than act as, for instance,
Kipling thought natural for one of her class. In this respect Jim
Blakeston is the innocent:

> 'Well, I'll marry yer. Swop me bob, I wants ter badly
> enough.'

'Yer can't; yer married already.'

'Thet don't matter! If I give the missus so much a week aht of my screw, she'll sign a piper ter give up all clime ter me, an' then we can get spliced. One of the men as I works with done thet, an' it was arright.'[42]

Jim's innocence is a form of self-protection. In this world men determine the physical and women the moral code of behaviour. So long as Jim can respond to any situation with an immediate show of strength, he is safe. Liza cannot so easily escape retribution. Because of her adultery she has lost all chance of gaining the much-coveted badge of respectability. For the men she becomes merely an object of their semi-serious bawdry: 'Yer might give us a chanst, Liza; you come aht with me one evenin'. You oughter give us all a turn, jist ter show there's no ill-feelin'.'[43] But for the women Liza is a constant threat to their own marital stability: 'A woman's got no right ter tike someone's 'usbind from 'er. An' if she does she's bloomin' lucky if she gits off with a 'idin' – thet's wot I think.'[44] The public beating that Mrs Blakeston gives Liza is not merely personal revenge; it is a ritualistic cleansing approved by the whole female community of Lambeth. It is only at this moment that Liza, pregnant, physically beaten and rejected by the other women, ever appears to be promiscuous. Moved by Tom's faithfulness, she offers herself to him, but he refuses to understand anything except marriage. At the same time as this conversation is taking place the husbands are reasserting their supremacy. Jim Blakeston knocks his wife senseless, and when a neighbour attempts to get her own husband to intervene, he refuses:

'But 'e's killin' 'er,' repeated Polly, trembling with fright.

'Garn!' rejoined the man; 'she'll git over it; an' p'haps she deserves it, for all you know.'[45]

The relationship between Liza and Jim had been tender and happy, but in this world violence ultimately decides every issue of importance. As a young girl Liza had managed to impose her personality on the neighbourhood, by singing louder, dressing flashier, being cheekier than her friends. The older women can no longer act in this way. They have already faced the brutality and violence that later must also come to Liza, and now they have replaced their early gaiety with a staid, and largely hypocritical, cover of respectability. This is their protection against the physical superiority of the men. So long as Liza strictly acts out the part allotted to her then the older women approve her actions, but once she steps into their domain, they temporarily adopt the masculine form of dealing with trouble and then retreat once again into respectability.

This behaviour pattern is presented directly in Mrs Blakeston's thrashing of Liza, and is also worked out in a more subdued tone through the presentation of Liza's mother. Mrs Kemp has only two aims in life – to be drunk whenever she can, and to be regarded as eminently respectable by her neighbours. She alone of the Lambeth women knows nothing of Liza's affair. When she learns that her daughter has had a miscarriage she can only say, 'Well, you surprise me . . . I didn't known as Liza was thet way. She never told me nothin' abaht it.'[46] She exhibits no emotion on hearing that Liza is dying, but just sits with the nurse discussing the 'respectable' funerals the district has known, and swopping tales about the 'respectability' of their late husbands. Only when Jim Blakeston, huge and bearded, comes to sit by the death bed does Mrs Kemp show any interest: 'Fancy it bein' 'im! . . . Strike me lucky, ain't 'e a sight!'[47]

Maugham's treatment of working-class life is thus very similar to Morrison's. The natural condition of the slums is bleak monotony, and life is only made bearable by adopting rowdiness, violence or respectability as a means of expression. Each of these is self-defeating. They produce a narrow, enclosed, vicious society that will tolerate no deviation from what it regards as normal or everyday. Jim Blakeston's proposed solution of running away to another district is not countenanced by Liza. To do this would be to surrender her individuality. Elsewhere, living with Jim as man and wife she would be obliged to conform to the very hypocrisy she condemns in Lambeth.

If Maugham relies heavily on Morrison for his literary method and philosophy of working-class life, he does instil into *Liza of Lambeth* that genuine sense of working-class humanity so lacking in Morrison's work. Liza's love affair is an obvious example of this, but there is also the greater emphasis that is placed on working-class speech. Maugham captures just as well as Morrison the grim jesting and the free-flowing abuse of the sardonic or the angry cockney, but he also manages to convey raucous humour:

> 'Na, I can't,' she said, trying to disengage herself. 'I've got the dinner ter cook.'
> 'Dinner ter cook?' shouted one small boy. 'Why, they always cook the cats' meat at the shop.'[48]

The humour in *Liza of Lambeth* is the true humour of a realist – it conveys a joke which is funny to the characters rather than to the reader. It also attempts to express briefly but forcefully the truth about their life without passing judgement upon it:

> 'Them's not yer ribs,' shouted a candid friend – 'Them's yer whale-bones yer afraid of breakin'.'
> 'Garn!'
> ''Ave yer got whale-bones?' said Tom, with affected simplicity, putting his arm round her waist to feel.
> 'Na then,' she said, 'Keep off the grass!'
> 'Well, I only wanted ter know if you'd got any.'
> 'Garn; yer don't git round me like thet.'
> He still kept as he was.
> 'Na then,' she repeated, 'tike yer 'and away.
> If yer touch me there you'll 'ave t'er marry me.'[49]

It is by successfully relating moments such as this to the wider framework provided by the monotony-violence-respectability philosophy that Maugham manages to expand, if only slightly, the narrow cultural world of Morrison. One scene in *Liza of Lambeth* shows Maugham falling short of the austere standard set by Morrison in *Jago* and reverting to one of the weaknesses of 'Lizerunt'. The Bank Holiday outing, from which the above extract comes, is at one point sub-titled 'The Idyll of Corydon and Phyllis'. For a few inexplicable pages Liza becomes a 'shepherdess' and Tom her 'swain'. With incongruous irony Corydon and Phyllis are shown swilling beer from a pint pot and when it is finished holding a spitting contest. For all their successful presentation of certain aspects of working-class life, neither Morrison nor Maugham could completely escape the lingering influence of pastoral.

III

The popular success of Kipling's and Morrison's work inspired many writers to try to produce novels and short stories in the same vein, but, apart from Somerset Maugham, they possessed little talent and added nothing new to working-class fiction. Lacking Kipling's profound personal involvement with working-class culture or Morrison's sociological common sense, they were unable to make any worthwhile use of the lessons offered them by 'Badalia Herodsfoot', *Mean Streets* and *A Child of the Jago*. Certain important aspects of these three books – the new system of phonetics to indicate working-class speech, a changing image of the East End, violence as a means of slum expression and the doctrine of authorial objectivity – are widely used by later novelists. But so ignorant do they seem of the real issues involved, so careless are they with the exact social and literary qualifications made by Kipling and Morrison, that instead of further expanding the scope of working-class fiction, they actually pervert their models' original intentions. This process can be understood most clearly by looking at the influence of Morrison on first the working-class romance, and secondly, the later 'realists'.

In the nineties the romance retained its faith in a plot based upon change of identity or individual philanthropy and thus an overall tone of cheerful optimism. It also continued to concentrate on the problems of middle- or upper-class characters acted out against a working-class backcloth, but changed the model for its working-class scenes from the 'Newgate' novel or Dickens to a mixture of Besant and Morrison, with an occasional dash – for the more serious-minded reader – of Mrs Humphry Ward. Some examples of these 'realistic' romances are: Joseph Hocking's *All Men are Liars* (1895) and *The Madness of David Baring* (1900); Harry Lander's *Lucky Bargee* (1898); Richard Whiteing's *No. 5 John Street* (1899); John A. Steuart's *Wine on the Lees* (1899); Robert Blatchford's *Julie* (1900); and Morley Roberts's *Maurice Quain* (1897), which has a special interest in that the middle-class hero living in the slums is almost certainly a portrait of George Gissing. We can see the influence of Morrison by looking at just two of these novels. *Wine on the Lees* tells the story of an aristocratic brewer's conversion to the cause of temperance and in most respects is no different from many such novels written earlier, but there are certain scenes in it that belong only to the nineties. Jenny Goodman, a gentle working-class wife, explains to the woman who once employed her as a maid, why she doesn't want to return to London:

> 'Oh my Lady!' she cried, the tears coming afresh, 'you can never understand what it is to be poor and live in the East End of London. My Lady, you say it is horrible – it's worse, it's worse.'[50]

But she does go back to London and is soon resigned to her fate:

> It no longer paralysed her to come upon groups of muscular sluts whooping and clawing each other's faces, tearing rags from grimy shoulders and dancing jigs on them in the gutter. Marks of death on stairs and pavement ceased to make her sick. Even when in great orgies wives tucked and bled over their fallen men she did not swoon or feel faint.[51]

Here the slum dwellers are no longer the suffering poor, the drearily respectable people of *Mean Streets*, or the ghetto criminals of the Jago – they are the ordinary inhabitants of the East End. Charles Booth's 1.2 per cent has become the whole population, and Morrison's careful attempt to show that slum violence was either a reaction against the bleak monotony of the East End or the normal behaviour of certain kinds of criminal, has been transformed into widespread working-class animalism. Furthermore, in contradiction to the central social philosophy of the realistic romance, there frequently appears a sneering and condescending attitude towards organized philanthropy: 'Missionaries, indeed, there were whose wry, reproachful faces and tactless ways made redemption sour and excited resentment and ridicule.'[52] Here, without any attempt to relate it to a total pattern, is one of the standard ironic devices employed by Kipling and Morrison. Their social criticism is turned into a meaningless platitude.

No. 5 John Street is not so crude a novel as *Wine on the Lees* but it differs in degree rather than kind. An extremely popular novel in its day, it provides a perfect example of the old-fashioned romance that has had elements of the new 'realism' grafted uneasily on to it. Whiteing was an old man when he suddenly attained his first commercial success. Over thirty years earlier he

had written *Mr. Sprouts: His Opinions* (1867), a lively if superficial satire on working-class manners, and in 1888 he had published *The Island*, a satirical examination of English society in the
year of the Jubilee. Whiteing had thus been interested in the
working classes for many years, but there is nothing in *No. 5
John Street* to suggest that his latest novel was a natural product
of artistic development. Like *Wine on the Lees* it has a hackneyed
plot. A wealthy young man determines to find out for himself how
the working classes live. His first thought is to join a settlement in
the East End but 'it proved to be a mere peep-hole into the life I
wanted to see, with the Peeping Tom still a little too much on the
safe side'.[53] As this implies he is obviously on the look-out for
violence and he goes to live in a West End slum, hoping to find the
real workers there. On his first night in the slums he hears a
scream and tries to draw it to the attention of Low Covey, his
working-class friend:

> 'Did you hear that fearful cry?'
> 'Ah!, I 'eerd somethink.'
> 'There's murder going on – a woman, I think.'
> 'Dessay; it's Sat'd'y night.'
> 'I'm going to see.'
> 'S'pose so; you're fresh to the place.'[54]

The meaning of this scene is perfectly clear. The working man
accepts murder as a natural condition of his life, or at least of his
Saturday nights, and the fact that the victim appears to be a
woman does not disturb him in the least. In Kipling, Morrison or
Maugham, there is always a reason specified as to why a working
man might, in a given situation, remain indifferent to a scene of
violence. Whiteing feels there is no need for an explanation of
Low Covey's curious behaviour. In all other respects he is shown
to be gentle and friendly, but by clumsily following what had
come to be a stale literary convention, Whiteing unconsciously
shows Low Covey, in this instance at least, to be morally corrupt.
When the two men do stir themselves they find an 'Amazon'
towering over a sailor who has been knocked to the ground:

> Her gown torn open in the scuffle, exposes the heaving breast.
> Her black hair streams over her shoulders. Her sleeves are
> turned up to the elbows for battle. One stout fist is streaked

with the blood of the man with the knife. The lips are parted with her quick breathing; the flashing eyes outshine the moonlight.[55]

No working-class romance of this time would have been complete without one scene describing a half-naked working-class woman fighting in the streets, and once again this example shows how hollow the convention had become. Clem Peckover, Pennyloaf Candy, Lizerunt, Badalia Herodsfoot, and Liza Kemp, in their different ways, had all been the victims of slum violence. They had suffered and had ultimately been destroyed by either accepting the code of violence or by being unable to avoid it. In *No. 5 John Street* the genuine pathos of these earlier working-class heroines becomes merely a lifeless, romantic posture.

Wine on the Lees and *No. 5 John Street* demonstrate how the working-class romance, in trying to inject itself with new life drawn from Morrison's studies of slum violence, only succeeded in establishing a new set of stale attitudes and conventions. The same is even more true of the writers who produced plagiarisms of *Tales of Mean Streets*. W. J. Dawson's *London Idylls* (1895), Arthur St John Adcock's *East End Idylls* (1897), Edith Ostlere's *From Seven Dials* (1898), J. Dodsworth Brayshaw's *Slum Silhouettes* (1898) and K. Douglas King's *The Child who will Never Grow Old* (1898), attempt to re-create not isolated scenes from Morrison's work but the overall tone of dispassionately described monotony and violence. The stories in these collections exhibit a bizarre mixture of pastoral (strikingly epitomized by the recurrent, ironic use of the word 'Idyll') and objective realism. As with working-class romance the result is a crude perversion of Morrison's original intentions. A closer look at two of these stories will be sufficient to demonstrate this.

Katherine Douglas King's 'Lil: an Idyll of the Borough' tells the story of a slum girl who has the chance to escape from her environment by going to live in 'pagan unconventionality' as the mistress of a wealthy aesthete. Lil's moral dilemma is made acute by the presence of her working-class boy friend, Jim, and her two sisters, Liz, and Louie, a four-year-old cripple. The basic plot is, of course, ages old. Lil's beauty is of 'a restless, passion-swayed, unangelic nature' even though she is only a 'starving seamstress', and her beauty alone gives her the opportunity to escape from slum life. But the trappings of this feeble plot are so brutal, the attitudes that come through to the reader so tasteless, that it could have been written at no earlier period. While trying to decide what to do Lil wonders what her life will be like if she stays in the Borough:

> She knew . . . that a lamp flung by a drunken husband into her face; a kick of his nailed boots on her prostrate body; his fists in her eyes; and a chair-back on her breasts, do not improve a woman's looks, nor compensate for the bearing of many sickly babies.

This will happen to her not because Jim is exceptionally violent but because most of the women in her street have already suffered the same fate. In this story the only kind of response permitted to the working-class characters, in any situation, is violence, if not upon someone else then upon themselves. When Lil's scandalous behaviour is made public, her sister's boy friend takes this opportunity to run away:

> A little quiver passed over Liz's strained stunted features, when Dick's footsteps had died away. Her teeth met on her tongue until her mouth was full of blood . . . When she had washed out her mouth she set about getting tea for Louie.

In the Borough this kind of behaviour represents the norm. In one scene Jim comes to the house to try to discover Lil's new address. At first he attempts to bribe the cripple with sweets and 'custid tarts' but when the four-year-old child bites him in anger, he gives her a 'blow on the ear that half-killed her'. Finally Lil leaves to join her pagan lover and is pursued down the street by Jim swearing he will beat her up while 'his new girl' is waiting for him round the corner.[56]

With stories such as this (and if not always quite so crudely employed, the same elements constantly recur) the portrayal of working-class violence and amorality reaches its lowest point. What makes this story so horrifying is the author's belief that she should not pass any kind of moral or social judgement on the actions of her characters. In Kipling and Morrison objectivity was necessary if they were to show that in certain circumstances slum violence could be exciting for some if not all of the participants.

In 'Lil' the treatment of slum violence is blatantly vicarious. Katherine King's characters behave as they do for no other reason than that they are working class.

In its approach to working-class life Edith Ostlere's 'Any Fla-ars or Po-t Ferns' is just as insensitive as 'Lil' but it shows Morrison's influence working in a slightly different manner. Nell, a local beauty (not idealized like Lil) and flower-seller, is courted by two costers – Bill Gubbins who is ugly but kind hearted, and Jack Standing, who is handsome and rakish. Much to Bill Gubbins's surprise Nell chooses him. The scene then switches to the marriage night:

> A thrill of passion swept over him. His heart felt bursting.
> 'Nell,' he whispered hoarsely, 'there ain't nobody lookin', give us a kiss.'
> 'Lor', Bill, giv' hover, yer fat-'eaded sawney, yer! I ain't a-goin' to do nothink of the sort!'
> All the same she did.

Then one evening he returns from work to find that Nell is missing. She has left a note reading, in part: 'i am goin ome to mother's for a week abart dont kum arter me wen I kum ome Praps i shall ave Sumthink 2 Sho yew.'[57] Neighbouring gossips persuade Bill that his wife has run off with Jack Standing and when ten days later she knocks on the door Jim curses her and drives her away. The next day he meets Jack and the two men fight. Bill is beaten and then learns that Jack has had nothing to do with Nell's disappearance. A year passes while Bill searches for his wife, until one day he sees a street accident involving a woman and a child. They are, of course, his wife and child. Nell dies in agony but not before she has told Bill that she left him to have the baby 'nice an' easy like, an' I'd be no trouble to yer, nor cost yer nothink neither, an' I meant ter bring it back to yer as a s'prise like'. Nell then dies and Bill is left with the baby.[58]

It is impossible to imagine a story like this, completely serious as it is, being written about people of any other class. Unlike the writer of a temperance novel who is able to justify his grotesque treatment of the working classes in moral terms, or the 'Condition-of-England' reformer who can defend his shock tactics on social grounds, Edith Ostlere has no excuse for writing as she does. From Morrison she has learnt the lesson that because of the corrupting effect of the slums upon the working classes they cannot be held responsible for their actions. Therefore, she reasons, one pattern of behaviour is just as plausible as any other. So long as the author does not interfere, the working classes cannot be presented as too degraded or ignorant.

These working-class romances and stories written during the closing years of the nineteenth century are bizarre travesties of Morrison's carefully observed, deeply felt and sociologically qualified work. Although limited, in both artistic and social terms, his novels and short stories were genuinely experimental. More than any other working-class novelist of the late-Victorian period he had broken with past conventions; attacking, though not destroying, the pastoral myth, and claiming the right of the urban working classes to a place in serious fiction. Unfortunately Morrison did not continue to write working-class fiction, and Somerset Maugham, the only important writer of the nineties with a talent similar to Morrison's and a far greater potential as a novelist, also turned to other subjects. With no one to provide a lead, popular novelists seized upon isolated aspects of Morrison's work and by employing them with a crude lack of imagination, crushed all meaning from them. The nineteenth century passed on to the twentieth two distinct images of the working man, both of which were popular corruptions taken from experimental fiction of the nineties. The first, a working man, violent, debased and lacking any decent or humane qualities, came from Morrison; the second, which must be examined in more detail now, came from the Cockney School.

8

The Cockney School

Historians of the English novel often employ the label 'Cockney School' to cover all of those novelists in the nineties who wrote about East End working-class life. Here the term is used more specifically. We have seen that in the early work of Rudyard Kipling two images of the working man emerge. On the one hand there is the violent cockney of 'Badalia Herodsfoot' who looks back to the debased working-class tradition in fiction, and forward to Arthur Morrison; on the other, there is Tommy Atkins who is a composite portrait of the London working classes, a new cockney archetype. He looks back to the age-old tradition of street types, and forward to the small group of writers who, in so far as they wrote about the same subject in a similar manner, can be correctly described as the Cockney School. The writers influenced by 'Badalia Herodsfoot' painted a spiritually cramped, narrow, and one-sided picture of working-class life; the Cockney School, a more optimistic, happy and culturally inclusive portrait.

The first distinctive writer of the Cockney School was Henry Nevinson, who in 1893 was commissioned by J. W. Arrowsmith, the Bristol publishers, to write a series of short stories on working-class life. Although Nevinson's personal experience of the working classes was considerable (he had been an early member of the S.D.F., had helped organize an East End mission, and, on his

o

own initiative, had run English Literature classes in Hackney),
he began immediately to supplement this knowledge by first-hand
research. He attended East London police courts, travelled on
Thames barges, accompanied rent collectors on their rounds, and
even went hop-picking in Kent. By early 1894 he had written
Neighbours of Ours but 'Arrowsmith kept it hanging about for
eleven months before publication (January 1895), thus allowing
Arthur Morrison's *Mean Streets*, treating of similar subjects to
beat us by a week, with the result that mine was praised, and
his was bought'.[1] In so far as these two collections of short stories
attempt to portray East End life objectively and without moral
comment, it is fair to describe them as similar, but in every other
important respect they are completely unlike each other. Morrison's work became sufficiently well known for it to influence the
ways in which many later novelists wrote about the East End.
Nevinson's book received little publicity and while it would
be misleading to regard him as the founder of a 'school' the approach
of *Neighbours of Ours* is distinctive and original; it anticipates
rather than influences several later writers.

All of the stories in *Neighbours of Ours* are narrated by one of
the cockney participants. This method enabled Nevinson to
establish a central working-class viewpoint just as Kipling had
done in *Barrack Room Ballads*. The kind of scene that filled
Gissing with horror, and Morrison with quiet despair, is now
viewed from the inside and a calmer tone prevails, as in this
description of a summer night in one of the poorer parts of the
East End:

> And in some o' them 'ouses I know'd they'd stop talkin' on
> them doorsteps all night sooner nor face the things as they'd
> 'ave to face in their own rooms. And I know'd 'ow, when it
> turned light, the men 'ud mostly go and 'ave a swim in the
> river, and come back to 'ave a bit o' sleep before starting out
> to work; and the women 'ud just fall off asleep where they
> was crowdin' up together if it 'appened to come on cold just
> before the sun risin'.[2]

These people are not objects of social pity, brute animals, cartoon
types, or unemployed layabouts; and, most strikingly, they have not
had all sense of life crushed out of them by a hostile environment.
They are presented to the reader as they might be seen by one

of their slightly more fortunate neighbours. It is not so much the environment that interests the narrator as the working-class response to it, and this he understands and approves.

Nevinson accepts the 'meanness' of the East London streets but never tries to transfer this quality to the inhabitants. Indeed, in *Neighbours of Ours* it is the vigour, variety and colour of working-class life that dictates the tone of a district; that breaks through and imposes itself upon the physical environment. The most significant feature of East End life is shown to be a working-class awareness, everywhere apparent, of belonging to a culturally homogeneous community. This community is divided into a great number of individual yet interdependent units, the most central of which is the family. Beyond the family people are bound together by a common occupation, by friendship, by living in the same street, and ultimately by belonging to the same district and class. Furthermore, individual characters are often seen in relation to an all-consuming interest which may or may not be connected with their work. Parky grows flowers, arranges an elaborate garden display and keeps pigeons; Spotter is an authority on dogs and horses; while Old Timmo is famous for his great knowledge on all matters relating to the river. Through his special interest the individual acquires local distinction and also makes a positive contribution to the wider community; he is the final arbiter of all disputes in his particular field of knowledge and his craftsmanship provides a standard of comparison for the whole neighbourhood:

> And twelve months after, if yer'd passed and saw them scarlet-
> runners twinin' theirselves over sticks, and the jeannies
> 'angin' from the winders, and the balsoms and marigolds,
> with paths and walls o' shell between, and little palin's with
> five-barred gates painted green with white tops, paintin'
> bein' Parky's work, you'd 'ave said it was a respite from the
> cares and troubles of life, same as my mother said as we was
> drivin' through the trees in Pimlico, as bein' out for father's
> Beano.[3]

This does not ring quite true. The description is too slick, the quotation from the narrator's mother too contrived. But it is an attempt to show an aspect of working-class life which reflects a socially contagious form of happiness. This is, of course, only one house in the East End but even so it is difficult to believe that it is in the same city as Morrison's *Mean Streets*. Morrison's belief that the East Ender escaped monotony by either retreating into stultifying respectability or exploding into violence makes little sense when placed in the context of *Neighbours of Ours*. Parky's garden is not even an attempt to escape from monotony. It is an act of joy and is accepted as such by the whole street. For slightly different reasons it is also impossible to imagine Morrison writing the following passage:

> 'What, Jacko! What price a bit of 'oppin'?'
> 'Ger on!' says I, 'd'yer think I'm goin' to demean myself?' that bein' what old Spotter always says when 'e gets an offer of reg'lar work.
> Then Parky comes and takes a 'and in the cricket, bein' a fair wonder afore the wickets, as was made of my coat and weskit with a cap on the top for bails, and by the end o' the game 'e'd fair talked me over, what with 'is 'ittin' the ball so 'ard, and bein' just appointed bin-man by the farmer, and 'avin' to get together pickers for five bins, and askin' all 'is mates together with Mrs. Sullivan and Lina, let alone the coin I might bring 'ome.[4]

This is much more successful. Beginning with the boy's mouthing of old Spotter's perennial joke (which has become a popular catch-phrase in the community) the speech tumbles out, expressing the double excitement of a game of cricket and the thought of going "'oppin", capped with the final sobering thought of the money to be earned. Here once again working-class excitement is expressed in non-violent terms, and as with the case of Parky's garden, going hop-picking is not an escape from monotony. It is made perfectly clear that the boys are happy because a considerable section of their community will be going with them.

This sense of a culturally integrated community life is apparent throughout *Neighbours of Ours*, and can be best illustrated by looking more closely at two of the most successful stories, 'The St. George of Rochester' and 'Sissero's Return'. The first of these deals with an idyllic working-class love affair. Old Timmo, a river captain, meets a woman on the wharf-side who asks him to let her live with him on his barge. She is obviously a 'lady born' and he later learns she is pregnant, but apart from this he knows nothing about her. When the baby is born the three live happily together on board the barge, until one day the baby is accidentally drowned. The woman, nicknamed Erith, then disappears and Old Timmo never sees her again. He tells the story to some friends as he lies dangerously ill.

'The St. George of Rochester' is in some respects similar to Maugham's *Liza of Lambeth*. The love affair between Erith and Timmo is conducted in full public view, but it is not adulterous and it is not stifled by the atmosphere of an enclosed slum. The prominence of the river in East London was an aspect of working-class life curiously neglected by most late-Victorian writers, and with the exception of Nevinson, remained so until the emergence of two slightly later novelists whose work was not limited by the 'discovery' of outcast London, W. W. Jacobs and H. M. Tomlinson. Throughout *Neighbours of Ours* the Thames is regarded as the most important highway in the East End:

> And some 'ow or other the story of us spread all down
> the river, and we sailin' past the other barges, my old mates
> 'ud 'oller out to me, wantin' to know 'ow Grace Darlin' was,
> or what price I'd take for the Piccadilly Belle.

Erith delights in the banter, and soon learns how to deal with it: 'And Erith she only laughed, and told 'em she was quite willin' for 'em to 'ave 'er, only they'd got to catch us fust, and then settle it up with 'er man, meanin' me.'

As in *Liza of Lambeth* the men are cheerfully envious, and it is left to the women to adopt a high moral tone:

> But with their females it wasn't the same thing, acourse not,
> and they soon enough found out as the way to 'urt 'er laid
> through the little lad. So they'd 'oller out, ''Ullo, Timmo!
> and 'ow's that little barstud of yourn gettin' along?' or,
> 'Bought any more second-'and kids up the spank, Timmo?'
> or, 'What price the little backstair Dook?'

But these women will never administer to Erith the kind of public thrashing Liza received. Because she is of a different class she should perhaps fear them all the more, but she is protected by Timmo and by the Thames which continually moves her from one section of the community to another. 'The St. George of Rochester' is not a profound story, but its quiet tone and lack of any kind of didactic or sociological intention, makes it unlike any working-class story that had been written previously. The central theme is romantic but it is handled with a simple realism that allows Erith to become part of the river folk-lore, and Timmo, who is fully aware of the happiness he has experienced, to remain deeply rooted in the East End. Most impressive of all about the portrait of Timmo is the way that Nevinson, unlike Morrison, never sees working-class strength as sooner or later leading to violence. Timmo is both strong and gentle: 'And I couldn't do nothink agen them, barrin' by callin' of 'em undecent names, me never bein' any 'and at breakin' the jaws of females, nor yet carin' to give 'em what for, through fear of me doin' 'em some injury.'[5]

'Sissero's Return' is very different in tone from 'The St. George of Rochester' and shows Nevinson handling the more poverty-stricken and squalid aspects of East End life. It tells the story of Ginger, an ordinary working-class girl save that 'the thing as made 'er famous was she'd married a nigger and couldn't never get over it'. Officially she is known as Mrs Sissero but her neighbours refuse to accept her as a married woman the same as themselves and call her 'Mrs. Kentucky, or Tennesse, or Timbuctoo, or Old Folks at 'Ome, or anythink else 'andy as 'ad connection with the niggers'. There is little plot to the story. Sissero, a sailor, does not return from one of his voyages, and Ginger's neighbours assume that he has run away from his wife – this being what they have expected him to do all the time. Ginger, however, continues to believe in him even though a long time passes and she sinks ever lower into poverty. Then suddenly he returns, satisfactorily explains his absence and is reunited with his wife. Nevinson's main interest is in tracing the effect upon a working-class neighbourhood of a mixed marriage, and this he does with frankness and understanding.

Sissero is popular with the East Enders so long as he is remote, and Ginger is regarded with indifference by the local men, but when they marry the whole district suddenly and inexplicably becomes hostile: 'So all the men was wild, for all they didn't exackly want 'er to theirselves. And all the women was wild, for all they didn't exackly want the nigger neither.' Nevinson is not afraid to point out that Ginger's deep love for Sissero, as well as the men's envy and the women's jealousy of him, is basically sexual. In exploring the responses of various neighbours to the marriage, Nevinson approaches this point from several angles.

Mrs Simon who, 'bein' fond of speakin' serious' usually acts as spokeswoman for the community, puts the case against the marriage: 'Would yer like to see the Tower 'Amlets wake up one mornin' chock full o' little niggers? Cos, if so, yer'e goin' about the right way to do it.' When the marriage is seen to be blissfully happy, the men begin to think that 'it wouldn't 'ave been so bad to 'ave a girl like that, for all 'er red 'air, and thought to theirselves what she wouldn't 'ave done for the likes o' them, considerin' what she did for a nigger.' And finally when it looks as though Sissero has run off, Mrs Britton points the moral: 'Yer can't say I didn't warn yer. It'll be somethink black 'e's after now.'

As a contrast to this sense of community solidarity, Nevinson traces Ginger's descent into poverty. When her savings run out she offers herself, once a week, to the 'Sheeny' rent collector, and when he tires of this method of payment she keeps herself and the children by making flags in order to repay the money earned by her temporary prostitution. Finally Sissero returns home cheerfully telling everyone he had missed his ship in China and ''ad been forced to work on a rose plantation, and 'ad lived all the time with a Chinee girl, till at last he'd managed to slip off in a British Injer ship again'. In a final turn-about of community values the women band together to stop the gossips from telling Sissero about his wife's relationship with the 'Sheeny', justifying their decision on the grounds that Ginger was forced to behave as she did, and anyway, it's not as if Sissero was 'an ordinary man same as other people'.[6]

It would be a mistake to make too much of *Neighbours of Ours*. Some of the stories are sentimental and contrived, while the Cockney dialect, successful in small bursts, is not handled with sufficient imagination to carry the more ambitious spells of narrative. But it does not deserve to be so completely neglected. Like Morrison, Nevinson was determined to present the working classes entirely in terms of their own attitudes and values; but unlike Morrison he found qualities which served not merely as compensation for a predominantly dreary existence, but as positive forces in their own right. Whereas Morrison places stress on monotony, respectability and violence, Nevinson emphasizes variety, respectability and a sense of community. The image of a slum as a trap in which all ambitions, aspirations and desires are crushed and ultimately destroyed is transformed into a self-sufficient, poor, but happy community. What also emerges from *Neighbours of Ours* is a fully rounded portrait of a social type – the cockney.

Like Kipling in *Barrack Room Ballads*, Nevinson's characters are first and foremost cockneys. They are not defined in terms of debased qualities or even of class (although they do, of course, all belong to the same class), and their speech and behaviour patterns are not automatically compared with some absolute standard determined by the author. While making allowance for the natural expression of individuality, Nevinson's characters speak the same dialect, share a similar sense of humour, understand, though not necessarily approve of, their friends' behaviour, and exhibit a common attitude to life in general and English society in particular. The cockney is no longer a stock comic character (as he is in most early- and mid-Victorian fiction) nor a tragic figure (as he is in Gissing and Morrison) but a regional type with personal and group characteristics as pronounced as those of the Scotchman, Irishman or Welshman. It is this belief that most clearly distinguished the writers of the Cockney School from earlier working-class novelists, although similar elements can be found in a novel such as Gissing's *Thyrza* and often in Dickens and Mayhew. They are concerned pre-eminently with the cockneyism of the cockney; with translating the qualities of the private-soldier cockney who is their model into civilian terms.

In 1896 Nevinson published a further collection of short stories called *In the Valley of Tophet* which must be considered a complete failure. The spontaneity of *Neighbours of Ours* could not easily be transferred to working-class life in the Midlands, and the stories in the later collection are slight and sentimental. Although Nevinson was to become famous as a writer, *Neighbours of Ours* remained his only successful work of fiction, and the leadership of the Cockney School was assumed by two slightly later writers Edwin Pugh and William Pett Ridge. Just as Kipling had struggled in India to understand the madness of Private Ortheris, so Pugh and Pett Ridge carefully studied their subject (the cockney) and his natural environment (London) in order to discover the very essence of cockneyism. The frame of mind with which they approached London working-class life was totally unlike Gissing's or Morrison's. Pett Ridge's two volumes of memoirs, *A Story Teller: Forty Years in London* (1923) and *I Like to Remember* (1925), are crammed with details of the cockney's life and leisure. He notes cockney songs, dress, manners, speech and habits, the street games played by children and examples of wit and humour with a skill developed over many years of social observation. His belief that 'the lives of the poor . . . are in the lump brighter and more amusing than those of the well-to-do middle class. Their amusements are enjoyed to the full',[7] expresses a cardinal doctrine of the Cockney School.

Edwin Pugh was an even more conscientious student of cockney life than Pett Ridge. Apart from his many novels he wrote four books devoted almost entirely to the subject, *The City of the World* (1912), *Harry the Cockney* (1913), *The Cockney at Home* (1914) and *Slings and Arrows* (1916), as well as further essays and articles. Like Kipling, Pugh marvelled at the cockney's verbal skill, and saw part of his task as being to capture this in print:

> The average cockney is not articulate. He is often witty; he is sometimes eloquent; he has a notable gift of phrase-making and nicknaming. Every day he is enriching the English tongue with new forms of speech, new clichés, new slang, new catchwords . . . But the spirit, the soul of the Londoner is usually dumb.[8]

Pugh's position was complicated by his own working-class background. It is too often evident that he is repaying a debt of gratitude to the dumb soul of the life from which, ironically, he had escaped. He saw himself very much as the cockney become articulate. We can see that in Pugh's case there is a special reason for his rather self-conscious treatment of the cockney, but the same weakness is also characteristic of the other Cockney novelists. In their constant efforts to define, characterize, typify or place the cockney working man, they frequently sound more like the Kipling of the very early soldier stories, than the Kipling of *Barrack Room Ballads*.

One of the principal reasons for this indecision was their consciousness of a working-class literary tradition. They were writing after Morrison's work had made its impact upon the reading public, and they themselves were impressed and influenced by it in spite of the criticisms they advanced. St John Adcock (the Cockney novelist most influenced by Morrison) while noting that 'Arthur Morrison's grimly realistic stories of London low life have not been surpassed by any living writer', pointed to Pett

Ridge as a writer who presented in his novels a more balanced picture of working-class life;[9] and Pugh felt that Morrison 'was out to shock you all the time, and in every conceivable way'; that his work 'dealt too freely and exclusively with the more bizarre features of mean streets'.[10] The intention of the Cockney novelists was to challenge the popular, violent image of working-class life, not by ignoring the element of truth it contained, but by placing it in perspective, by showing it to be merely a part of a total pattern of cockney culture.

The Cockney novelists' criticism of Morrison's work was given impetus by their avowed admiration for Dickens. Gissing and Morrison both admired Dickens but they consciously struggled against his influence, feeling that his presentation of the working classes was outmoded. As we have seen, in their different ways, *Workers in the Dawn* and *A Child of the Jago* were in part attempts to bring Dickens up to date. The Cockney novelists, however, felt a greater affinity with Dickens than with Gissing and Morrison. The views of Edwin Pugh, as set out in his two interesting studies *Charles Dickens: The Apostle of the People* (1908) and *The Charles Dickens Originals* (1912), can be taken as typical. Gissing had found Dickens's portrayal of the 'virtuous' poor distasteful; Pugh heartily approved it:

> [Dickens] had already learnt the uplifting lesson that the harder one's lot, and the poorer and the more mean and ignorant one's associates, the better and nobler our fellow creatures will prove themselves to be. For wherever there is great suffering there is always great love also . . .[11]

Equally significant is Pugh's attitude towards Sam Weller:

> Though you search London you shall not find a Cockney who is half such a Cockney as Sam Weller . . . who never existed, but who yet remains and will forever remain the typical Cockney.[12]

Gissing had criticized Sam Weller for being 'unreal', an idealized portrait of the London working man. Pugh regarded him as a genuine type who had long since disappeared from the streets of London, but whose spirit was still to be found in the late-Victorian cockney. Believing this, it was natural that Pugh should criticize Cruikshank's and Phiz's illustrations of Dickens on the grounds that they were largely responsible for his reputation as a caricaturist and praise the more straightforward work of Fred Barnard, Marcus Stone and Luke Fildes.[13]

Dickens's influence on the Cockney novelists can be seen not only in this resurgence of interest in a more cheerful image of the cockney, but also in descriptive passages:

> Some delay occurred before Alfred found himself able to leave the room, because one of the workman's wives, having announced her willingness to sing, and being thereupon begged to go onto the platform, refused flatly to do this, declaring that she had never been one of your saucy minxes (which was, indeed, not a title that one could have applied to her appropriately), and being still urged to comply with the usual procedure, suddenly changed her mind and decided not to sing at all, but to sulk instead.[14]

The style of this seems old-fashioned when set beside the terse prose of Kipling and Morrison. It is an attempt to apply techniques learnt from Dickens (especially the indirect speech and parenthetical asides to the reader) but lacks entirely Dickens's imaginative genius. At times the influence is even more blatant, as in this plagiarism of *Bleak House*:

> The sun blazed down from a sky of burnished steel. There was not so much as a huffle of wind to temper the steady glare. Dust upon the paving stones, dust upon the roads, dust in the air, dust everywhere. Men of dust in a city of dust, breathing dust under clouds of dust. From dust they were; to dust should they return. Eyes and throats and ears all full of it. A faded odour of dust to offend the nostrils. A faded hue of dust to colour the outlook. A very plague of dust.[15]

But dependence on Dickens to the extent shown in this passage is unusual: *Mean Streets* still remained the model for slum descriptions:

> It was such a street as you might find in a dozen or more districts of London; grimy, dreary, gloomy. The houses were four-storeyed and without architectural ornament of any kind. Doors and windows were each a rigid oblong divided into four smaller oblongs of panel and pane. A few of the windows

vaunted pots of flowers and muslin curtains tied with ribbon, but most were naked and blank save for a drooping, discoloured blind, perhaps.[16]

Where the Cockney novelists really differ from Morrison is in their treatment of the inhabitants of these mean streets. Jane Findlater, the most perceptive late-Victorian critic of working-class fiction, greeted their books with fervour. Instancing Pett Ridge and Clarence Rook, she claimed that they were more successful than Gissing, Kipling, Morrison or Maugham in presenting 'nearly the ultimate truth about slum dwellers'. She continues: 'There comes the truth; every slum-dweller is not entirely depraved, or desperately miserable – and Mr. Pett Ridge, by boldly breaking away from the tragic convention of the slums, has come into a new kingdom.'[17]

Jane Findlater is being a little too enthusiastic here, but in stressing the Cockney novelists' rejection of the 'tragic convention of the slums' she does indicate the most distinctive feature of their work. Together with Henry Nevinson's *Neighbours of Ours*, the following books can be classified as products of the Cockney School: Edwin Pugh's *A Street in Suburbia* (1895), *The Man of Straw* (1896), *Tony Drum: A Cockney Boy* (1898) and *Mother-Sister* (1900); William Pett Ridge's *Mord Em'ly* (1898), *Outside the Radius* (1899), *A Son of the State* (1900) and *A Breaker of Laws* (1900). It has already been mentioned that Arthur St John Adcock's *East End Idylls* (1897) was inspired by Morrison's *Mean Streets*, but his first full-length working-class novel, *In the Image of God* (1898), shows him trying to present an inclusive picture of working-class life more in the manner of Pugh and Pett Ridge than Morrison. Clarence Rook's *The Hooligan Nights* (1899) can also be classified with the Cockney School. Although Rook claimed, in an introduction to *The Hooligan Nights*, that his book was not a work of fiction but a collection of factual reports and interviews, his method is dramatic, and the considerable skill he exhibits in telling the story of Alf the burglar owes more to the techniques of fiction than sociology. One further writer whose early work in some respects belongs to the Cockney School is W. W. Jacobs.[18] From these books (no one of which would stand up to extensive critical study) we can take two aspects which are of particular interest. First, the attempt to convey what Jane

Findlater called: 'The wild joys and excitements of slum-life';[19] and secondly, the image of the cockney that is advanced.

In contradiction to Morrison, the Cockney novelists found that contentment and happiness were qualities more natural to the slums than violence. Usually this conviction is expressed indirectly, but it sometimes appears as an open challenging statement:

> Pandora Buildings, despite its bare passages and blank
> asphalted yards and drafty balconies, all suggesting that it
> was a place where people were sent for some infraction of the
> law, was, nevertheless, for its inhabitants sufficiently cheerful,
> and there were very few of them who were not happy.[20]

Like Nevinson, it is stressed repeatedly that working-class happiness is dependent upon a central community, to which people can belong and in which they can participate. When Private Ortheris says: 'I'm sick for London again; sick for the sounds of 'er, and the sights of 'er, an' the stinks of 'er', he is expressing a basic yearning that the Cockney novelists understood, approved and at times seemed to envy. Ortheris is not homesick for any particular street, house or person, but for an indefinable atmosphere, a way of life that has a soul and personality of its own; that can command the loyalty and affection of those who are born and bred in it. As with the novels of the Morrison School (though for totally different reasons), the theme of the exceptional working man trying to escape from slum life virtually disappears from the novels of the Cockney School.

In *Mord Em'ly* slum life is presented as exciting and happy, and the various attempts by individuals and institutions to help the heroine 'better' herself are frustrated by her continual longing for home. The novel opens with a description of a fight between two gangs of young girls, which, although in deadly earnest, lacks the brutal violence found in Morrison. For the girls, belonging to a gang is a badge of distinction, a means of expressing themselves within a wider community, a way of announcing their hostility to any form of authority that is not of their own choosing. When Mord Em'ly is found a job as a maidservant in a respectable middle-class house in Peckham, she is haunted by memories of the Walworth streets, music halls and her friends. She eventually runs away 'deftly unpinning her fringe as she went, and combing it over her forehead',[21] thus replacing the symbol of middle-class respectability by a working-class symbol of freedom. Later in the novel she is sent to a reform home after carrying out a 'dare' to steal some cakes, and once again she runs away, drawn back to the streets of Walworth.

Mord Em'ly is by no means a criminal type, nor is she the innocent victim of brutal parents. When her mother is drunk she praises the Conservatives and the Queen, and outlines maudlin plans for the improvement of her daughter. Mord Em'ly listens, jokes and goes her own way. She desires nothing that she cannot find in South London.

As a contrast to Mord Em'ly's uninhibited love of freedom, Pett Ridge contrasts the staid, dreary, middle-class world of Peckham. The women who employ Mord Em'ly as a housemaid are crudely satirized:

> 'Are you a hard worker, my girl?'
> 'Fairish, miss. I ain't afraid of it anyway.'
> 'I think we shall decide to call you Laura if you stop with us.'
> 'Whaffor?' demanded Mord Em'ly.
> 'We always call our maids Laura,' explained the eldest of the ladies complacently. 'It's a tradition in the family. And my youngest sister there, Miss Letitia, will look after you for the most part. My other sisters are engaged in -er- literature; I myself, if I may say so without too much confidence, am responsible for' – here the eldest sister looked in a self-deprecatory manner at the toe of her slippers – 'art.'[22]

This scene is not simply a device to emphasize Mord Em'ly's vivaciousness; it represents a basic attitude of the Cockney novelists who take the element of cultural envy in Kipling's work a step further and frequently imply that working-class life is morally superior to that of the middle classes. The most stinging insult Mord Em'ly can hurl at anyone is 'city clerk'. This is very similar to Orwell's repeated use of the adjective 'little' to signify someone who has surrendered his working-class heritage and replaced it by a façade of respectability.[23] In *Outside the Radius*, a collection of short stories satirizing middle-class philistinism, Pett Ridge makes this same point even more directly when he mentions the slum area of a fashionable suburb:

It supplies all the police news to the local Mercury, engages
the attention of missions; and the general feeling of our
suburb is that the place contains nothing but misery, the fact
being that the Old Town folk have an uncommonly good time
of it, and get more enjoyment out of their lives than does the
average sympathiser.[24]

The idea, here implied by Pett Ridge, that at least part of the
excitement of working-class life comes from a cheerful acceptance of
petty criminality, is also taken up by Clarence Rook:

Poetic justice demands that young Alf should be very
unhappy; as a matter of fact, he is nothing of the sort. And
when you come to think of it he has had a livelier time than the
average clerk on a limited number of shillings a week.[25]

He has 'a livelier time' because he never knows what it is to be
bored; every day has its special interest and possibility of the
unexpected. It is for this reason that Alf, like Mord Em'ly, values
above all else his freedom. As paternalistic representatives of the
middle-class way of life, the missionaries also come in for criticism
from the cockney novelists:

'Concernin' wot the lawst speaker said,' he began. 'Ez fur ez
I could mike art 'e wuz on'y atryin' it on. Nar, I arst yer,
mates all, is that fair pl'y? We come 'ere ter be elevated, an'
a bloke gits up an' talks a lot o' boomin' rot.'[26]

Morrison had satirized the slum missions because they were
irrelevant to the true social problem of the working classes.
Edwin Pugh satirizes them because they are an intrusion on
working-class life, and shows this by allowing one of the working
men in the audience to complain ironically that he is not being
'elevated'.

In the later nineties working-class novelists who did not really
belong to the Cockney School often picked up this more attractive
working-class image and inserted it into their predominantly
Morrison-influenced work. G. T. Kimmins's only novel *Polly
of Parker's Rents* (1899), is a sentimental, melodramatic picture of
slum life. Like Mord Em'ly, Polly works as a servant, but is
obliged to run away when it is believed she has been involved in a
burglary. She goes back to the slums, and while she is making up

her mind whether to call on her old friends, she helps a blind man cross the road:

> He thanked her in the old rough way, but striking his foot against the kerb, swore at her in the familiar language of Parker's Rents; then, with marvellous instinct made off in the direction of that quarter. Polly watched him with a hungry look in her eyes, and with difficulty refrained from making herself known to him. That she had come back to her own people she knew but too well; the invisible cords of her childhood were drawing her into the old ways; she had been living a kind of ticket-of-leave existence these last few years, and now she was back once more in the prison world of the slums.[27]

The final phrase fits uneasily on to the rest of the passage. There is no reason why the author should suddenly introduce the image of the slum as a prison. By doing so she is refusing to face the social truth she has already expressed.

Edwin Pugh's *Mother-Sister* can be regarded as the most typical product of the Cockney School. The basic plot is extremely simple. Dan Mamory in the mistaken belief that his wife has run off with a friend beats him up and is sent to prison. The novel then traces the attempt by Dan's fifteen-year-old daughter Maddie (the mother-sister of the title) to look after the family. The setting of the novel is entirely working class, with Sam Belvidere, a flashy, vulgar bookmaker, and Mr Blackaby, a builder, representing the highest social types in the book. Both of these men are shown to be completely at home with working-class people, and both, in their different ways, hold positions of responsibility in the district. The various children in Maddie's family symbolize different aspects of working-class life. Maddie herself stands for solid, ultra-respectable home values. Dood, the younger brother, becomes a street-corner layabout; and Bridget, the elder sister, is used to show the temptations that can befall a pretty girl in the slums. Around the family there radiates a gallery of rather strange working-class types, and beyond them there is a strong consciousness – especially in moments of distress – of a wider community that shares, and tries to alleviate, the suffering of individual members.

In discussing *To London Town*, it was noted that Morrison had been unable to construct a satisfactory working-class novel once he had rejected the themes of violence and escape. The same is true of *Mother-Sister*, and indeed of all the cockney novels. Although Pugh succeeds in building up a recognizably real working-class atmosphere in the early sections of the novel, he found it necessary to move the plot on to an attempted seduction of Bridget which recalls the worst excesses of working-class romance. What impresses about *Mother-Sister* is the ring of sociological truth possessed by occasional scenes, as when Dood returns home from a Bank Holiday outing, having been rooked:

'O, Dood!'
'Don't mag,' said he. 'Gimme some supper and lemme go to bed. I bin in the pie shop today and got sold.'
Maddie fell silent. Presently, Dood went wearily to bed.[28]

The way that Dood and his sister, in moral terms completely unlike each other, still share a basic understanding about what is and what is not possible in their way of life, comes through very clearly. Or again, when Dood comes into some money, he takes a friend into a shop where they buy all sorts of useless knick-knacks:

'What's that there bead thing for?'
'That's a lamp mat.'
'All right ain't it Billy! How much?'
'Tenpence-ha'penny.'
'Yuss, I'll have that. Billy, ain't you going to buy nothing to cheer yourself up with?'[29]

The essential emptiness of Dood's way of life is well shown here. He is not a violent thug or a frustrated intellectual, but a person with, on the one hand, no education, and on the other, no settled home life from which he is able to derive a sound set of values. If he has money he might as well buy a lamp mat as anything else.

But however successful individual scenes are, the book itself is a failure. The attempts by novelists in the nineties to rid the working-class novel of substitute heroes, to make working-class characters, who express themselves in terms of their own attitudes and values, the centre of attraction, fail because in the final instance these characters are invariably seen as types first and human beings second. The writers of the Cockney School deliberately set out to humanize the cockney by studying his psychological make-up. They succeeded in creating a further stereotype of the working man.

From Egan, through Dickens to Milliken and Kipling, the first characteristic of the cockney is his skilful use of words. The Cockney novelists follow this tradition but try to break away from the idiolects used by Sam Weller and 'Arry, and to re-create instead the everyday language of the streets. Mord Em'ly, for instance, when in a sullen mood, takes the opportunity to strike at authority by interpreting every word literally:

> 'How old might you be?'
> 'I *might* be a 'undred and forty nine', said Mord Em'ly looking at herself anxiously in a square of unframed looking-glass on the wall. 'I *am* jest close upon thirteen.'[30]

Sometimes Pett Ridge shows her using this particular habit to extend a conversation, rather than cut it short, as when she finds her gang leader with a young man:

> 'Where did ye find it?' asked Mord Em'ly of Miss Gilliken, with a satirical accent.
> 'Who are you calling "it"?' demanded Mr. Barden aggressively. 'P'r'aps you'll kindly call me 'im and not "it"?'
> 'P'r'aps I shall do jest as I like,' replied Mord Em'ly. She turned to Miss Gilliken. 'Did you win it in a raffle?'
> 'I'll tell you presently,' said Miss Gilliken.
> 'Sometimes they give 'em away,' said Mord Em'ly thoughtfully, 'with a packet of sweets. I 'ave seen 'em offered instead of a coker-nut or a cigar at one of these Aunt Sally –'
> 'Look 'ere!' interrupted Mr. Barden crossly. 'You think you're jolly clever, no doubt.'
> 'Think?' repeated Mord Em'ly. 'Don't I know it.'[31]

As a piece of 'realism' this is very successful. The sullen jealousy of a thirteen-year-old cockney girl, awkwardly trying to get at the person she thinks has supplanted her, is exactly conveyed. There is no attempt to make the reader laugh, as there is in the following more laboured piece of cockney understatement:

'Was she a woman with -er- inebriate tendencies?'
'Pardon, sir.'
'I say, was she a woman who had a weakness for alcohol?'
The sergeant interpreted. Did she booze?
'She liked her glass now and again, sir,' said Mrs. Rastin
carefully.
'That is rather vague,' remarked the coroner. 'What does
"now and again" mean?'
'Well, sir,' said Mrs. Rastin, tying the ribbons of her
rusty bonnet into a desperate knot. 'What I mean is, whenever
she had the chance.'[32]

This represents a typical device of the Cockney novelist – showing
the cockney inhibited by officialdom. Clarence Rook was more
interested in the cockney taking complete control of a situation, as
in this scene when Alf tries to pass some 'snide' in a shop:

'Arf-a-dozen eggs, missus, an' new laid,' I says. 'We always
keep 'em fresh,' says the ole woman. 'Well, I want 'em for
someone that's snuffin' it,' I told 'er. 'Wort you mean?' she
chipped in not 'ankin.' 'Well, peggin' out,' I eggsplained. So
she says, 'Dyin', I s'pose you mean 'an' 'andin' me the
wobblers. Down I planks a two-hog piece, an' she picked it
up an' fair screamed. 'That's bad,' she calls out. 'I've 'ad one
like it afore to-day,' she says – the old geezer. 'Bad, missus!'
I says. 'I'd like to 'ave a cartload of 'em.'[33]

Apart from the unfortunate phonetic spelling of 'explained', this
is superb. The cockney's ability to tell a story is exploited to the
full, and the sharpness of his wits is shown in the last sentence.
Before he runs away he must make a play on the woman's words.
It is this constant concern with words that most distinguishes the
cockney's humour, often turned against himself:

'Sit down Maddie,' said Holy Jo, handing her a chair. 'Ben,
be one of us. Make yourself at home.'
'Always am at home when I'm out,' said Ben.[34]

Finally, a further example of the cockney in court, only this time,
not cowed:

'Were you a witness of this assault?'
'Yes, your worship, I was.'

'What happened?'
'Dan just mopped the road with him, your honour.'
'You mean he knocked him down?'
'Knocked him down ain't the word for it.'
'What is the word for it?'
'Lumme! how should I know if you don't.'[35]

These examples of cockney humour indicate many of the qualities that impressed the Cockney novelists. Quick-witted, scornful of authority and jealous of his liberty, he is, like Tommy Atkins, apolitical, simply because being naturally cynical he cannot believe that any social change could be for his benefit. On the rare occasion when the subject of politics is mentioned the cockney appears enthusiastically uninterested:

'The Kinservatives 'ave won, mother,' said Mord Em'ly as she unlaced her boots.
'Ooray!' said Mord Em'ly's mother sleepily. 'Sooner they got in than them blessed old Tories.'[36]

The dominant image is of a 'rough diamond'. The violent nature which had so fascinated Morrison is now tempered by some gentleness, considerable good-neighbourliness, and a great deal of sentimentality on the part of the novelist. Clarence Rook decided that Alf's girl friend was 'loyal, strong, and courageous, possessing all the virtues but virtue. Rough and coarse, if you please, and foul of tongue when the fit seizes her; but we may call the roughness honesty, and the foulness slang, without being far wrong.'[37]

This quotation is particularly interesting because in it can be found the basic ingredients for one of the most popular images of the cockney that the nineteenth century (after, as we have seen, considerable preoccupation with the subject) passed on to the twentieth. In one sense it is the same old portrait of the rough but honest working man which can be found in all literature at all times, but there are important variations to be noted, for this cockney is peculiar to an age of democracy. Besant's undemanding class mass is now being broken down into individual units. It is accepted that the cockney should be allowed to follow any code of behaviour which seems reasonable to him, short of actually breaking the law. The fact that Alf's girl friend is promiscuous, foul-mouthed and vulgar matters little, because the sociologically

aware observer can quite easily give these qualities other, less
emotive, labels; while, at the same time, the fictional framework
ensures that class control is effectively maintained. In spite of this
sympathy, admiration, and even envy of working-class life, the
Cockney novelists, like the great majority of their predecessors,
finally advance an image of the working man as someone who is
socially harmless if handled in the right manner. This comes
through in two distinct ways.

First there is the part now played by the State in governing
working-class life. Pett Ridge's *A Son of the State* has virtually the
same story as *Mord Em'ly*. Like her, Bobbie Lancaster is a social
anarchist and his love of the London streets eventually places him
in a reform home. But unlike Mord Em'ly (who, slightly improved
by her stay in the home, marries a boxer and emigrates), Bobbie
fully responds to the school discipline which is a mixture of
persuasion and indoctrination: 'Thus it was that when appeals
to a boy's sense of honour or his sense of decorum failed, an appeal
to his appetite proved effective.'[38] The cockney's inclination to
enjoy his amusements to the full (a quality which Pett Ridge
claimed to admire greatly) is gradually squashed out of Bobbie
until he has been turned into a socially acceptable person:

'I think I shall be all right, sir. I've improved wonderfully
in the years I've been here.'
'Made a man of you, have we?'
'You have that, sir,' said Bobbie.[39]

Bobbie joins the navy and in an unbelievably 'stiff upper lip' scene
saves his admiral's life in a native skirmish.

The second way that the Cockney novelists render socially
harmless the subject they profess to admire in his natural state,
can be seen in a short story by Edwin Pugh, 'Bettles: A Cockney
Ishmael!'[40] One day the narrator goes into a riverside pub where
he sees a loud-mouthed and vulgar cockney called Bettles thrown
out for fighting. Two years later the same narrator is sitting in his
club talking about 'cockney pluck' and he cites his riverside pub
experience as an unpleasant example of the cockney. He is then
told that Bettles had recently been killed while fighting the natives
in the Sudan, and that he died setting an example of courage to his
fellow soldiers.

Finally, a slightly different example can be taken from Annie

Wakeman's *The Autobiography of a Charwoman* (1900). In this book, which might be considered a satire on naturalism were it not perfectly serious, an upper-class woman invites her charwoman to tell her life story. While the charwoman cheerfully talks, the author sits by, taking notes and carefully refraining from any kind of intrusion. The whole of the story is written in cockney phonetics and the adventures are described solely in terms of working-class attitudes and values. Because there is no standard of comparison offered in the book itself the author required a preface to make her own position clear.

> Do not expect the daughter of a dissipated mother and a cruel father to picture a life as beautiful as, with all its advantages, yours has doubtless been; nor hope that this patient struggler of the mews can fashion her words into a style as glittering as yours would surely be; nor anticipate that sordid actions can be decked in a sheen of romance that shall captivate the drawing room or charm a maiden's heart.

Save for the slightly ironic tone which warns the reader that he is shortly to be brought face to face with *real* life, this is not unlike the attitude expressed by the authors of temperance-reform pamphlets or mid-Victorian working-class romance. In this case, however, it is necessary to show that the charwoman is both hard and gentle. To do this Annie Wakeman once again uses the preface:

> She was a sunny optimist and her brave courage never flagged. She delighted in music, and sometimes stole into Covent Garden gallery, away from care and hunger. She loved flowers, and they bloomed in her window often when the larder was empty. She was persistently industrious, a natural cook, a born nurse. Her voice was as soft as the cooing of a dove, and her touch as soothing as a gentle anodyne. And finally, there was great personal dignity in this Gentlewoman of the Slums.

We are then told how this 'Gentlewoman of the Slums' was seduced as a housemaid, later had several illegitimate children by different men, and nearly starved in an East End workhouse. When she does finally achieve her long frustrated amibition to marry, it is to a brutal drunkard. It was pointed out earlier that this kind of violence in the working-class novel, made vicarious by the studied objectivity of the author, became common in the later nineties through the misapplied influence of Arthur Morrison. But novels such as *The Autobiography of a Charwoman* differ from those of the Morrison School in that they attempt to show not merely the violence but the moral courage of the cockney. Annie Wakeman's charwoman possesses 'great personal dignity' simply because she has suffered such terrible experiences. This is no social-conscience novel: at no time does the author suggest that society might be held responsible for such a way of life. On the contrary, it is impossible to avoid the conclusion that the charwoman is being held up to the reader as a superior moral being, for suffering has turned her into a philosopher: 'Life is mostly darns and patches, till we've wore out our needles and our 'earts in the doin'.'[41] It was exactly this quality that the Cockney novelists so admired in the working man. Because of his determination to remain free he has developed the ability to take whatever life has to offer without complaint; take it wittily, cheerfully or philosophically. Such a man is of inestimable use to a democratic society. So long as his wit, drunkenness, violence, sentimentality and love of freedom are expressed in individual terms, he is socially harmless; so long as these qualities are viewed from a distance he is even attractive and picturesque. Because he now possesses the vote he is expected to accept the existing social structure, just as the upper classes accept him, and the working man who claims the right to challenge the political *status quo* is necessarily a fool or a crook.[42] These particular people can be easily outwitted, they are no threat to society. Much more dangerous are those working men whose social anarchism (in itself usually an object of admiration) gets out of hand. Ultimately these too are rendered harmless by the new beneficent state machinery, controlled by the upper classes. No longer is the street ragamuffin allowed the fictional option of either fairy-godparents or the gallows, but instead is given a second chance to hold his place in society. The reform home and the army now serve to mould the cockney into a socially acceptable person, not by attempting to eliminate his cockneyism (the working man who ends up as a banker or collector of rare books has now completely disappeared), but by playing on and manipulating his individuality. The loud-mouthed, violent working man who causes brawls in riverside pubs is disgusting in his natural environment but splendid on the field of battle. The nerve and wit of a street raga-muffin trying to pick up a living are obviously just the qualities required by a person who, after the reform home has worked its magic, is to save his officer's life in a native skirmish. And the broken-down and rather stupid charwoman can be easily advanced as a perfect example of human courage in adversity. That almost all working-class novels are basically works of class propaganda is as true of late- as of early-Victorian fiction. The changes that have taken place are less significant than they at first appear to be. For although it is now fully agreed by novelists that the working classes should be presented in the novel in terms of their own attitudes and values, an extreme self-consciousness about class distinctions is still everywhere apparent.

> Good evenin'm. It's a treat to be arsked out to 'ave a cup
> o'tea, and me and the maid 'as enjoyed it proper. I never was
> a gad-a-bout, and wot with work and one thing and the other
> I don't git much time fur visitin'. Thanks'm, I *will* sit down,
> and wile I'm a-talkin', if you don't mind, I'll jest mend young
> Dick's stockin's.[43]

No longer does the novelist believe he has the right, by virtue of his superior social position, to lecture the working man on manners or behaviour, no longer does he teach, guide or berate him. Instead, from his still superior position, the novelist accepts that all men are equal and merely records details of working-class speech and behaviour, with the result that one form of condes-cension makes way for another, less direct, more subtle and equally divisive. The old stereotypes and conventions are replaced by new stereotypes and conventions. Whereas the one typified an oligarch-ical society so the other reflects a dangerously new democracy. At the close of the nineteenth century, as at the beginning, the most important single fact about the fictional working man is his class.

9

Industrialism, urbanism and class conflict

'I tell you what,' said Mick, with a knowing look, and in a lowered tone, 'The only thing, my hearties, that can save this here nation, is – a —— good strike.'[1]

The fear that many working men might share Dandy Mick's relish for violent class conflict as a solution to their problems is never completely absent from Victorian working-class fiction, but it was only at those moments when novelists were naggingly aware of the workers as a mass force that the subject of class conflict was brought into the open and acknowledged as a matter of central importance. It is most apparent in the industrial novel where this kind of awareness is everywhere present. As was pointed out in Ch. 1, the industrial novelists were exploring a received mass image of the working classes which made it impossible for them to regard the industrial worker as other than a class representative. He could be placed topographically in his northern cities, which seemed to have no other reason for existing than their industries; ideologically, with Chartism; and occupationally, because everyone worked at, or was associated with, similar jobs. The fact that these jobs were instinctively linked in the public mind with symbols of power and strength – the furnace, engine and factory – added a further frightening element to his mass identity. It was his suffering to which novelists drew attention, but his potential power that was their true concern. The possibility that the workers might have ideas of their own about the uses to which this power could be put was discountenanced by the novelists. On this subject they had made up their minds long before they began their journeys north or put pen to paper. First and foremost they were determined to prove misguided anyone who thought like Dandy Mick.

For reasons already examined in the preceding chapters, none of this is applicable to the novel of urban working-class life written before 1880, though here, as in earlier discussions, it will be seen that *Alton Locke* has much in common with industrial fiction. The clearest example of the contrasting attitudes towards urban and industrial workers in the mid-Victorian novel is provided by Dickens. In *Hard Times* the workers are automatically given a mass identity. The description of Coketown as a place of uniform monotony and meanness, Slackbridge addressing large union meetings, the effective isolation of Stephen, and Dickens's concern with the ideology of industrialism, are all elements in the novel which serve to emphasize the solidarity of the industrial working class. There is nothing similar in Dickens's London novels where even the mob is ignored as a contemporary phenomenon and reserved for treatment in his two historical works, *Barnaby Rudge* and *A Tale of Two Cities*.

Dickens does frequently point out that slum conditions in London might breed violence, but such warnings are too localized, too rooted in the fate of a sympathetically presented working-class individual or group, for the reader to feel that class conflict is a real possibility. A good example is the moment in *Bleak House* when Jo and a drover's dog are shown together listening to some street musicians. Dickens estimates that the dog's aesthetic sense is at least as great as Jo's, and comments: 'Turn that dog's descendants wild, like Jo, and in a very few years they will so degenerate that they will lose even their bark – but not their bite.'[2] The implication is clear but within the novel as a whole it can be regarded as little more than a rhetorical flourish. Jo himself is a danger to no one (save symbolically as a carrier of disease) and there is no sense of a *class* of urban working men speaking or acting on his behalf. It is, however, particularly significant that the one person in *Bleak House* acutely conscious of the workers as a mass force is Sir Leicester Deadlock, for whom the mere thought of Mr Rouncewell, the ironmaster, awakens images of Wat Tyler and 'a body of some odd thousand conspirators, swarthy and grim, who were in the habit of turning out by torchlight two or three nights in the week for unlawful purposes'.[3] These fears are evoked by 'smoke and a tall chimney' not by a tumble-down slum and destitute crossing-sweeper; by industrial not urban life. Much later in the novel when George Rouncewell journeys from Chesney Wold to his brother's iron foundry, 'fresh green woods' are left behind and 'coal pits and ashes, high chimneys and red bricks, blighted verdure, scorching fires, and a heavy never-lightening cloud of smoke become the features of the scenery.'[4] This is similar to the description of Margaret Hale's return journey to Milton in *North and South*, and like Mrs Gaskell, Dickens is examining contrasting attitudes towards the new and old worlds and acknowledging, if not fully approving, the ultimate victory of the new. The industrial workers themselves hardly appear in *Bleak House* but the atmosphere of industrialism is vividly realized. Set against the strength, power and potential of this world, the inhabitants of the London slums are seen to be of no account whatsoever, as either a political or a class force.

In *Bleak House* we are made aware of the political passivity of the urban working classes only by implication in *Little Dorrit* our attention is deliberately drawn to it. This is the only one of Dickens's novels in which London is regarded, in part at least, as an industrial city. Characteristically the factory in Bleeding Heart Yard is presented not as a thriving symbol of progress but as an incongruous relic of the past: 'Two or three mighty stacks of chimneys, and a few large dark rooms which had escaped being walled and subdivided out of the recognition of their old proportions';[5] and the factory workers are shadowy figures, described only once, as they are seen by Arthur Clennam: 'patient figures at work . . . swarthy with the filings of iron and steel that danced on every bench and bubbled up through every chink in the planking.'[6] What is curious about this aspect of the novel is that having taken the unusual step of introducing a London factory, and having placed it so carefully, Dickens then dissociates the inhabitants of Bleeding Heart Yard from it. We are doubtless meant to understand that many of them work in the factory, but the only man presented in any detail is Mr Plornish, a plasterer who works outside the Yard: and, using an image common in the literature of urban exploration, Dickens describes the inhabitants collectively as: 'Poor people who set up their rest among [the Yard's] faded glories, as Arabs of the desert pitch their tents among the fallen stones of the Pyramids.'[7] Allowing that Daniel Doyce's firm is not a very prosperous concern, this hardly describes the kind of workmen he would have needed to employ. Their down-trodden social state also firmly fixes them as urban rather than industrial workers. Dickens's discussion of the 'political position of the Bleeding Hearts' contains one of his most bitter and explicit assaults on the ruling classes. In spite of their apparent incompetence and stupidity, the Barnacles and Stilt-stalkings retain absolute power in the country because they have 'carefully trained' the working classes in a set of beliefs which serve to keep them politically impotent: 'They believed that foreigners had no independent spirit, as never being escorted to the poll in droves by Lord Decimus Tite Barnacle, with colours flying and the tune of Rule Britannia playing.'[8] Flattered, trained and duped, the Bleeding Hearts accept poverty as the price to be paid for the glorious privilege of being English. Their political passivity is rendered grotesquely pathetic by the qualities of friendliness and human sympathy which they are shown to possess in such abundance. Dickens presses the point home by following his political analysis with one of Mrs Plornish's hilarious attempts to communicate with her Italian lodger.

This view of the urban working classes as lacking the kind of mass identity possessed by their industrial counterparts is common throughout Victorian fiction. Nor does the situation change significantly after 1880. The discovery of the East End gave the urban workers a mass identity, but an identity compounded of suffering and passivity rather than suffering and power; they were still regarded as too completely down-trodden to evoke much sense of class fear. There were, however, a few late-Victorian novelists who took an entirely different view. For them the East End stirring into life represented a new, eagerly anticipated stage in class relationships: it seemed that at long last the Bleeding Hearts were about to rebel against the Barnacles and Stiltstalkings. Before considering the work of these novelists, we must look at some of the ways the subject of class conflict is handled in industrial fiction.

II

Scenes of physical violence between employers and employees abound in the industrial novel. In *Mary Barton* Mr Carson's son is murdered by a Chartist; in *North and South* John Thornton is baited by a mob of strikers possessed with 'the demoniac desire of some terrible wild beast'; in *Sybil* one of the Wodgate employers beats his employees with anything that comes to hand, splitting open their heads and faces, and in a scene which anticipates Zola's *Germinal*, the Wodgate tommy shop is destroyed by a mob, the owner dying in the fire. In *Michael Armstrong* Sir Matthew Dowling systematically tortures the young factory boy he brings to live in his house, though Sir Matthew's behaviour is good-hearted compared to the treatment Michael is later to receive at the 'prison Prenticehouse' in Deep Valley; and in *Helen Fleetwood* a young girl is crippled by a brutal overseer. The direct portrayal of violence plays no central part in Harriet Martineau's *A Manchester Strike*, but a revealing scene during the strike shows the workers' children playing their favourite game of cotton-spinners with 'a big boy frowning and strutting and personating the master, another with a switch in his hand being the overlooker'.[9] *Alton Locke* and *Felix Holt* as 'Condition of the People' novels both give prominent places to riots. *Hard Times* is an exception to this general pattern though Stephen Blackpool's death, largely brought about by Bounderby's indifference and union hostility, serves a similar function. In the urban tradition where there is observable no clearly defined employer–employee relationship such scenes do not occur; instead, urban working-class violence is almost always rooted in personal or domestic relationships.

What is particularly noticeable about violence in industrial fiction is the amount of blame allotted to the employers. This is not because the novelists are adopting a working-class viewpoint; on the contrary, these are very much novels about the condition of England as seen from above. The reason lies rather in the limited social philosophies of the novelists. Changes are desired but not changes of too radical a nature. They are demanding a revolution in class relationships without any alteration in the balance of power. By personalizing class conflict and placing blame on the human failings of individual employers and employees, sympathy is aroused for the workers' appalling conditions without this being taken to imply that there is anything fundamentally wrong with the social structure as a whole. Mrs Gaskell, for instance, shows her principal employers, Mr Carson and John Thornton, gradually growing to understand that the labour troubles they have experienced were in no small degree the result of their own ignorance of working-class life. A change of heart, we are led to believe, will transform the relationship between Capital and Labour. In *Mary Barton* this is merely a hint for the future: in *North and South* we watch the incredible transformation take place. Dickens similarly shows Bounderby and Gradgrind as men with much to say about industrial life from very little knowledge of it; while Disraeli, Mrs Trollope and Mrs Tonna all make it clear that their vicious employers and overseers are sadists and either roundly condemn them or allow them to meet suitably gruesome ends. With such men out of the way there is hope that things will improve: a point they all reinforce by carefully introducing scenes which describe model factories run by model employers.

The workers of course are not left blameless. They too must offer up scapegoats or bow in repentance if the necessary class balance is to be achieved. Mrs Gaskell was particularly conscious of this. In answer to the criticism that *Mary Barton* was biased in favour of the workers, she replied: 'No one can feel more deeply than I how *wicked* it is to do anything to excite class against class; and it has been most unconscious if I have done so . . . no praise could compensate me for the self-reproach I shall feel if I have written unjustly.'[10] It is impossible to doubt Mrs Gaskell's sincerity of purpose in either this statement or her two industrial novels; but it is precisely this refusal to face the class implications of the situation she is analysing that ultimately weakens the power of *Mary Barton*. She relies, in common with the other industrial novelists, on personalized relationships to make her point, and it is in the contrived nature of these relationships – in the unbelievable class balance they are meant to symbolize – that the bias is to be found. John Barton dies clasped in Mr Carson's arms; and Higgins, in *North and South*, is so convinced by John Thornton's change of heart that hearing his master heave a 'suppressed sigh' over some shoddy workmanship, he returns to the factory at night to do some unpaid overtime. Disraeli, as Louis Cazamian has pointed out, was more ruthless than Mrs Gaskell in allotting a share of the blame to individual members of the working classes.[11] After drawing an unusually accurate portrait of an intelligent, articulate, working-class radical in Stephen Morley, Disraeli gratuitously sacrificed him to the ideals of Young England, while Dandy Mick he treated with heavy irony. Throughout the novel Mick has consistently expressed a primitive form of Marxist delight in worsening social conditions, but when the eagerly anticipated riot takes place he remains loyal to Sybil, is rewarded by Lord Marney, and becomes a 'capitalist'. Mrs Trollope and Mrs Tonna simply followed the conventions of working-class romance. Having handed their factories over to respectable reformers they allow their central working-class characters to escape from industrial life: Michael Armstrong inherits a fortune and Helen Fleetwood dies.

By placing blame for class conflict on the character weaknesses of individual employers and employees, and by supporting the reform of factory conditions, the industrial novelists were able to present any attempts by the workers to act or speak for themselves as totally unnecessary. Strikes, mass demonstrations or any expression of working-class solidarity, however understandable the motivating grievances are shown to be, are naturally condemned. Condemnation may be made directly, though more subtle techniques are also employed. The most common is to ensure that any mass demonstration gets out of hand and leads to arbitrary violence or looting so that the initial sympathy is replaced by horror. In *North and South* and *Mary Barton* this effect is achieved when the strikers viciously attack non-union workers: in *Hard Times* union solidarity helps bring about Stephen's death: and in *Sybil*, *Alton Locke* and *Felix Holt*, mass demonstrations disintegrate into bloody riots. In these three novels especially it is important that the working-class hero or heroine survives finally as someone still capable of arousing the reader's sympathy, and the riot is therefore used to allow him to dissociate himself from the mass. Alton Locke and Felix Holt both receive prison sentences for the parts they have played in riots, and are sufficiently chastened to accept a view of society which denies the possibility of the workers acting as a class or expressing a mass viewpoint. Alton Locke accepts Lady Ellerton's interpretation of the situation:

Not from without, from Charters and Republics, but from within, from the Spirit working in each; not by wrath and haste, but by patience made perfect through suffering, canst thou proclaim their good news to the groaning masses, and deliver them, as thy Master did before thee, by the cross, and not the sword.[12]

Felix Holt is similarly shown adopting a view of the working classes which places full emphasis on the need for individuals to reform themselves, thus denying the power possessed by the workers as a whole. Even before the riot he believes the majority of workers to be morally corrupt, but does none the less conceive of them in mass terms: 'I want to be a demagogue of a new sort; an honest one, if possible, who will tell the people they are blind and foolish, and neither flatter them nor fatten on them.'[13] After the riot his tone is entirely changed: 'I don't mean to be illustrious, you know, and make a new era . . If there's anything our people want convincing of, it is, that there's some dignity and happiness for a man other than changing his station. That's one of the beliefs I choose to consecrate my life to.'[14] The demagogue has become a local, small-time teacher, and *the* people have become *our* people. George Eliot thought Felix Holt's recantation of his part in the 1832 election riot so important that thirty-six years later she brought him from retirement to address the newly enfranchised working men of England. His address is a perfect example of praising the individual at the expense of the mass:

We could groan and hiss before we had the franchise: if we had groaned and hissed in the right place, if we had discerned better between good and evil, if the multitude of us artisans, and factory hands, and miners, and labourers of all sorts, had been skilful, faithful, well-judging, industrious, sober – and I don't see how there can be wisdom and virtue anywhere without those qualities – we should have made an audience that would have shamed the other classes out of their share in the national vices.[15]

If this means anything it is that for George Eliot, as well as for Felix Holt, the majority of workers are unskilful, faithless, injudicious, lazy and drunken: a view which confirms her statement in another essay: 'That delicious effervescence of the mind which we call fun, has no equivalent for the northern peasant, except tipsy revelry; the only realm of fancy and imagination for the English clown exists at the bottom of the third quart pot.'[16] In this essay – the purpose of which was to deplore the idyllic presentation of the lower classes in art – George Eliot chooses Scott and Kingsley as exceptions among English novelists because through their fiction they were capable of 'linking the higher classes with the lower' and 'obliterating the vulgarity of exclusiveness'. This well describes the social purpose of *Felix Holt*, though it places George Eliot as a successor to Kingsley rather than Scott, in that the classes are brought together only by denying the workers any cultural viewpoint of their own, and making their representative exceptional.

Sybil's conversion is similar to those of Felix Holt and Alton Locke, though made less dramatic by Disraeli's refusal ever to associate her in any credible way with the working classes. Disillusionment comes with her understanding that 'the world was a more complicated system than she had preconceived. There was not that strong and rude simplicity in its organization which she had supposed.'[17] The workers' delegates she discovers constitute 'a plebeian senate of wild ambitions and sinister and selfish ends, while the decrepid authority that she had been taught existed only by the sufferance of the millions was compact and organized, with every element of physical power at its command, and supported by the interests, the sympathies, the honest convictions, and the strong prejudices of classes influential not merely from their wealth but even by their numbers.'[18] She is now ready to agree with Egremont that the aristocracy are the true leaders of the People: the ensuing riot merely confirms her in this belief.

The kind of treachery discovered by Sybil in the People's delegates is echoed in other industrial novels. It serves as a further means by which the mass of workers can be separated from their leaders and broken down into individual, and thus harmless, units. Disraeli's treatment of Stephen Morley has already been mentioned: the union leaders in *Hard Times* and *A Manchester Strike* are discredited in a similar manner. The names they are given, Slackbridge and Clack, are alone sufficient to indicate their untrustworthy natures. Beyond this they are openly described as morally and physically inferior to the workers they claim to

Q

represent, dangerous demagogues interested only in self-glorifi-
cation and trouble-making. Even Mrs Gaskell sneers when she
introduces a trade union leader:

> Then the 'gentleman from London' (who had been
> previously informed of the masters' decision) entered. You
> would have been puzzled to define his exact position, or what
> was the state of his mind as regarded education. He looked so
> self-conscious, so far from earnest, among the group of eager,
> fierce, absorbed men, among whom he now stood. He might
> have been a disgraced medical student of the Bob Sawyer
> class, or an unsuccessful actor, or a flashy shopman. The
> impression he would have given you would have been
> unfavourable, and yet there was much about him that could
> only be characterised as doubtful.

This 'gentleman from London' smirks at the men, wins them over
by supplying tobacco and beer, further treats them to 'a burst of
eloquence, in which he blended the deeds of the elder and younger
Brutus, and magnified the resistless might of the "millions of
Manchester"', and then the true purpose of his visit is revealed –
he pays out money to help cover the delegates' expenses. Mrs
Gaskell does not attempt to conceal her astonishment at such
honest behaviour from such a vulgar man.[19]

The saddest working-class leader in all of the industrial novels
is Allen in *A Manchester Strike*. Unlike Clack, who when there is
no more money to be squeezed from the impoverished strikers can
move on to cause trouble elsewhere, Allen is shown to be genuinely
devoted to his family and the improvement of his fellow workers'
conditions; an intelligent and skilled workman. His sole fault is
that he has tried to challenge the inviolable laws of Political
Economy and for this Harriet Martineau gradually strips him of all
self-respect. The novel ends with him sweeping the gutter as his
only means of earning a living.

In consistently playing down the mass power of the workers and
discrediting their leaders, the industrial novelists were not simply
responding from fear of physical violence: they had an ideological
point to make as well. The real danger lay in the possibility of the
workers consolidating their position by mass adherence to any
social philosophy which tended to accentuate class differences.
To the novelists there was little difference in effect between

Chartism, Socialism, Communism or Trade Unionism: all of them weakened the social viewpoint they themselves wished to advance – conciliation between the classes on terms put forward by exemplary employers. Any working man who persisted in believing otherwise was transformed into a Stephen Morley, Clack or Slackbridge. Mrs Tonna, as usual, can be relied on to state bluntly a fear that the more skilful of the industrial novelists only allowed to emerge indirectly:

> Lately a new and an almost unutterable curse has been added to those already felt in the mills. A man of whom it is hard to think otherwise than as of Satan, had been among them personally, and had circulated by his delegates a vast deal of his infernal doctrine in that and other manufacturing districts. It will suffice to say that some half dozen of the young men in that mill had become Socialists. Beyond this it was impossible to go – Socialism is the *ne plus ultra* of six thousand years' laborious experience on the part of the great enemy of man – it is the moral Gorgon upon which whomsoever can be compelled to look must wither away: it is the doubly-denounced woe upon the inhabitants of the earth – the last effort of Satanic venom wrought to the madness of rage by the consciousness of his shortened time.[20]

Mrs Gaskell brought to her study of John Barton's moral collapse a degree of sympathetic understanding that no other industrial novelist was capable of attaining, but even so there are moments when she refuses to face the inevitable consequences of her own analysis and begins to sound like a subdued Mrs Tonna. In this scene John Barton, recently laid off work, walks the streets looking for employment while his son lies dying at home. In a state of near starvation he watches his ex-employer's wife buying mounds of food for a party. Mrs Gaskell comments:

> You can fancy, now, the hoards of vengeance in his heart against the employers. For there are never wanting those who, either in speech or in print, find it their interest to cherish such feelings in the working classes; who know how and when to rouse the dangerous power at their command; and who use their knowledge with unrelenting purpose to either party.[21]

The second sentence in this passage follows on from the first as though forming a logical connection, but really the introduction of working-class agitators ready to take advantage of John Barton's grief is irrelevant to the situation as it has been presented to us. Mrs Gaskell is anticipating the moment when John Barton takes the final deadly step:

> John Barton became a Chartist, a Communist, all that is commonly called wild and visionary. Ay! but being visionary is something. It shows a soul, a being not altogether sensual; a creature who looks forward for others, if not for himself.[22]

The half-hearted qualification here does little to alleviate Mrs Gaskell's fear, for the 'others' in this particular visionary's scheme of things are the working classes, and, as we have seen, any movement towards solidarity on the part of the workers is destructive of Mrs Gaskell's own social philosophy. For her the division of society into classes of men hostile to each other has got nothing to do with the pressures of industrialism or the struggle for power in a rapidly changing society, but rather results from the indifference and ignorance of employers. Had they treated the workmen as 'brethren and friends' and explained that 'it was the wise policy of the time' for sacrifices to be made on both sides,[23] then the misunderstanding that is the root cause of class conflict would have been removed, and all Chartists and Communists shown up as the cranks they are. In one way or another this view of society was shared by the other industrial novelists. It was far more 'wild and visionary' than anything conceived of by John Barton.

There were a few novelists of the 1840s and 50s who tried to reverse the tendencies discussed here and speak for the working classes as a whole, and specifically for the cause of Chartism. In dedicating his novel *Sunshine and Shadow* (1849) to Fergus O'Connor, Thomas Martin Wheeler pointed out the power of fiction to convey a class or ideological viewpoint: 'The fiction department of literature has hitherto been neglected by the scribes of our body, and the opponents of our principles have been allowed to wield the power of imagination over the youth of our party.'[24] But Chartist fiction is too blatantly propagandist, and artistically too close to working-class romance, for its interest to be other than historic. It does not even justify its claim to provide a unique inside view of working-class life: in the words of Thomas Frost it 'conducts us in turn to the comfortless dwelling of the working-man, the elegant drawing-room of the profit-monger, and the luxurious saloons of the aristocrat'.[25] In both tone and quality it recalls the work of G. M. W. Reynolds, the dominant literary influence on Chartist fiction. For our purposes here interest lies in the particular nature of its class bias. The workers fall into two main groups – the intelligent artisans who are Chartists, and the debased poor. Members of the upper classes are presented as bloated, debauched capitalists battening on the poor and actively working to undermine Chartism. The crudeness of their portraiture recalls Shaw's gibe at Dickens's treatment of trade unionism in *Hard Times*: 'All this is pure middle-class ignorance. It is much as if a tramp were to write a description of millionaires smoking large cigars in church, with their wives in low-necked dresses and diamonds.'[26] The upper-class characters in Chartist fiction, one feels, are quite capable of behaving like this. In complete contrast to the industrial novelists, total emphasis is placed on the rightness of class conflict as a means of solving working-class problems. In this the Chartist novelists interestingly anticipate several later writers.

III

W. E. Tirebuck's *Miss Grace of All Souls* (1895) was the most important industrial novel to be published in England since *Hard Times* almost exactly forty years earlier, and the most successful portrayal of industrial working-class life since *Mary Barton*. In addition it is the only worthwhile English novel about coal-miners written in the nineteenth century. While it would be a mistake to make extravagant critical claims for *Miss Grace*, the industrial tradition in Victorian fiction is too thin for it to remain completely neglected.

Like many other genuinely working-class writers of this period, little is known of Tirebuck's life, though two memoirs written by friends shortly after his death do provide some basic information.[27] He was born in Liverpool of 'humble parents' in 1854, left school at the age of twelve to work as an office boy, and later worked in an iron foundry and telegram office before becoming a journalist and professional novelist. In the eighties and nineties he wrote a large number of novels and short stories, mainly on regional themes, and late in his life, according to Hall Caine, was ambitious to become 'the novelist of Wales'. This ambition was never realized and now sounds foolish when baldly stated, but his fiction, hastily written as much of it appears to be, does show a keen appreciation of regional ways of life which might well have matured had he not been forced by circumstances to be so prolific. Two of his novels still retain considerable power. *Dorrie* (1891), the story of a Liverpool girl's descent into prostitution, is in the tradition of working-class romance but distinguished by occasional scenes of grim, even grotesque, realism; and *Miss Grace of All Souls*.

Miss Grace traces the history of a northern mining village during the lock-out of 1893 when an attempt to reduce wages by 10 per cent was opposed by the newly formed Miners' Federation. Apart from being set in the north of England the locality of Tirebuck's village is left deliberately vague. Beckerton-beyond-Brow epitomizes all of the Beckertons throughout the country 'that were in the same struggle that labour was making to speak and make itself heard, to act and make itself felt'.[28] The Ockleshaw family, on which the novel centres, is also intended to represent the working classes as a whole, and divisions within the family indicate the changes which have taken place during the nineteenth century. Dan Ockleshaw, the grandfather, brings to this new kind of class confrontation a lifetime's experience of defeat and compromise, accepting the masters as naturally superior to the men. His son Ned dismisses such thoughts as relics of the past: 'No, fayther, it's no use; your owd way of lookin' at things has gone out by the back-door. Pity it couldn' be kicked owt by the front!'[29]

Where Tirebuck differs most strikingly from earlier industrial novelists is in his determination to show the rightness of the workers' case. As in Chartist fiction, upper-class society (consisting here of the owners and the local vicar) is regarded as corrupt and irresponsible. Mr Brookster, the coal owner, deliberately manipulates the strike so as to force up coal prices, and the vicar, turning his back on the workers in order to retain Brookster's patronage, is concerned solely with the value of his coal shares:

Far away he saw, as he paused on the hilly side of the park to look down the busy, smoky, and still beautiful little valley, the smoke of Rasselton Mill curling up like, to him, the financial incense of $7\frac{1}{2}$ per cent.[30]

The belief that the workers exist solely for the benefit of the owners and that the church connives at this state of affairs by preaching a gospel which keeps the workers poor and docile, is held not merely by the radical young miners, but by Tirebuck himself. It lies at the heart of the novel and renders it, in spirit if not always in form, totally unlike the work of Mrs Gaskell or Disraeli. When the Ockleshaw family join together to sing 'Rock of Ages Cleft for Me' Ned points out that the title should be changed to 'Rock o' Ages, cleff for mesters', because 'that's what *aw* seem to hide in it for!'[31] Old Dan and the women may still look to 'the quality' for charitable help but the younger workers have long since lost all faith in the owners: 'They'd wear us to the bone on'y for our bit o' brain that's beginnin' to put us right.'[32]

Full blame for the lock-out is placed on the owners. Long before breaking point is reached, Mr Brookster has begun systematically to aggravate the workers, bullying the married rather than the single men, constantly moving the piece-workers from seam to seam, and setting men to work on hard coal after telling them it was soft. When eventually the owners meet to formulate a policy for a 25 per cent reduction in wages (a 15 per cent increase on historical accuracy which indicates clearly enough Tirebuck's position), the men are already aware that conflict is unavoidable. The employers 'met much as European monarchs sometimes meet, with the smile of peace masking the grin of war',[33] and the workers also recognize the need for solidarity to ensure that the Capital–Labour conflict is transformed from a local to a national, even international, struggle. For inspiration they look to the Federation which links the pits of Lancashire, Yorkshire, County Durham and Wales; and beyond England to the moral and financial support that streams in from foreign labour organizations. The *class* nature of this conflict is never in doubt: unlike earlier industrial fiction there is no attempt to obliterate central issues by focusing attention on the personal problems of individual characters.

The greater part of *Miss Grace* traces, at times movingly and in great detail, the progress of the lock-out from the first early enthusiasm for the Federation to the moment when the poverty-stricken miners accept a compromise and return to work at the old rates of pay. Ned is killed by soldiers called in to keep order, and the vicar dies murmuring words of repentance for his neglect of the workers. The novel ends with the marriage of Ned's son, Sam, and the vicar's daughter, Grace. To conclude *Miss Grace* in this manner (with the death of one upper- and one working-class father, followed by the marriage of their children), makes it sound as though this novel is firmly in the tradition of 'Condition of the People' fiction, but this is not so. Certainly the ending is clumsy and the excessive idealization of Miss Grace a major flaw, but in spite of this Tirebuck retains a consistent point of view. The marriage of Grace and Sam does not have the same kind of symbolic purpose that, say, John Barton dying in Mr Carson's arms, Sybil's marriage to Egremont, or Higgins's unpaid overtime for John Thornton, are meant to have. Nobody can believe in these relationships as solving any but the most artificial forms of class conflict, whereas Sam's marriage to Grace makes perfectly good sense. It is symbolic in that it signifies Grace's failure to unite the two nations, and thus her realization that divided allegiance being impossible she must change sides. To the marriage she brings a superior education and sufficient knowledge of working-class life gained during the lock-out, to inspire Sam to better things for both himself and his class: 'If he were only a success – something *worth* having – on the board of the Federation – on the County Council . . . ah, if he were a Labour Candidate – *a Labour M.P.* – a worker, a doer, a practical reformer of the cruder members of his own kind.'[34]

In showing Grace Waide as willing, even eager, to surrender her own class background and commit herself fully to the working-class cause, and most strikingly, in allowing her to achieve these ends, Tirebuck was reacting against the attempts by earlier novelists to play down the existence of the workers as a separate power group. *Miss Grace* is as much a work of class propaganda as *A Manchester Strike* or *Sybil*, but it is propaganda in favour of the employees as against the employers. Tirebuck has no interest in uniting the two nations. He proclaims the rightness of the workers' cause, their ability to manage affairs for themselves, and the probability that they will eventually take power into their own hands. In this he differs not simply from Mrs Gaskell,

Dickens and Disraeli, but from Kipling, Morrison and the Cockney novelists as well. *Miss Grace*, of course, stands almost alone as a late-Victorian representative of the industrial tradition, and this apart, it is too slender a work to bear the various generalizations I have made. But Tirebuck was not the only late-Victorian novelist writing fiction within this particular ideological framework. He has several counterparts in the urban tradition.

IV

In Ch. 4 and earlier in the present chapter, it was pointed out that despite the potentially explosive state of class relationships in London during the eighties, the attention of novelists centred almost exclusively on the 'outcast' aspects of working-class life. While the creation of a Palace of Delight and the exploration of mean streets encouraged many writers to turn to working-class fiction, events such as the Trafalgar Square riots and the strikes by match girls and dockers were relatively ignored. The reason for this bias lies partly in the power and attractiveness of the mean streets image, partly in the personal outlook of the most important urban novelists of the eighties and early nineties, and partly in the slow development of an image of the urban workers as a distinct power group. That side of London working-class life described in utopian retrospect by William Morris in *News from Nowhere* does, however, appear in a few late-Victorian novels. Although their intrinsic merit is slight, they retain some interest for the modern reader because, in certain important respects, they anticipate the class viewpoint of Robert Tressell and other twentieth-century working-class writers. The work of just two novelists, Constance Howell and Margaret Harkness, can be taken as representative. In ideological terms it stands completely apart from the mainstream of late-Victorian urban working-class fiction.

Both Gissing and Besant were strongly conscious of the underlying strain of class hostility in working-class life, but Besant's particular social philosophy was dominated by the belief that the working classes were incapable of governing themselves, and Gissing came to the same conclusion albeit from a different line of reasoning. If we exclude a few idealistic scenes in *Workers in the Dawn*, it is fair to say that Gissing and Besant always treat the working-class political aspirant with disdain. A similar attitude is to be found in working-class romance. The upper-class Socialist and the crazy, usually foreign, anarchist, are common figures in late-Victorian fiction, but the working man who claims a passionate interest in politics inevitably turns out to be either a fool, or more often, a crook. This much the urban and industrial traditions share in common. The case of Rudyard Kipling and his followers in both the Morrison and Cockney Schools, is entirely different. Although Tommy Atkins is a composite portrait, politics play no part in his make-up. To show a positive interest in politics would be to suppose a person capable of conceiving and planning for a future society. But the various aspects of Tommy Atkins's personality (his violence, sentimentality and patriotism) are all given their particular tone by his spontaneous reaction to events. The happiness he experiences always comes from the satisfaction of an immediate need. He has, and can have, no sense of constitutional refinement: he is a social, but not a political, anarchist.

Constance Howell and Margaret Harkness (who wrote under the pseudonym of John Law) saw and tried to describe other aspects of London working-class life. Like Tirebuck, and the Chartist novelists before him, they were committed to a working-class point of view. Faced with a question such as that posed by Engels – 'Every year England is brought nearer face to face with the question: either the country must go to pieces, or capitalist production must. Which is it to be?' – they would both have answered unhesitatingly, capitalist production.[35] The special tone of their novels is one of joyful realization that the traditional image of the London working classes as lethargic and politically passive is in the process of being destroyed by a new mood of active, mass militancy: the change of attitude noted by Engels in 1889:

Hitherto the East End was bogged down in passive poverty. Lack of resistance on the part of those broken by starvation, of those who had given up all hope was its salient feature. Anyone who got into it was physically and morally lost. Then last year came the successful strike of the match girls. And now this gigantic strike of the lowest of the outcasts, the dock labourers . . . For lack of organisation and because of the passive vegetative existence of the real workers in the East End, the gutter proletariat has had the main say there so far. It has behaved like *and has been considered* the typical

representative of the million of starving East Enders. That
will now cease . . . In brief it is an event . . . a new section
enters the movement, a new corps of workers . . . Hurrah![36]

Constance Howell's *A More Excellent Way* (1888) is the most
interesting of several novels written at this time which explore the
conversion of a member of the upper classes to Socialism.[37]
Whereas Grace Waide's conversion had been instinctive, the result
of personal involvement in the suffering caused by a lock-out,
Otho Hathaway's conversion is intellectual. Brought up as a
free-thinker, his first real contact with the workers comes as he
watches a 'mob' returning from a Trafalgar Square meeting. As
the mob disappears he begins to wonder where the individual
members of it have gone, and his thoughts lead him to the library
where he reads Marx, Engels and Kropotkin, and from there to
membership of the National Socialist Federation. His upper-class
friends regard Hathaway's connection with Socialism as degrading
and gradually break with him, but not before he has tried to
persuade them that it is they rather than the workers who constitute the 'dangerous' class because of their blindness to the fact
that: 'Collective Socialism is the next development in the evolution
of society; necessarily so, because of what has gone before. It
may be resisted, but it cannot be prevented.'[38] This much his
friends can accept as eccentricity. They come to regard Hathaway
as a traitor to his class only after he hails as martyrs some Nihilists
who have tried to assassinate the Czar, and boasts that the English
police and soldiers are secretly on the side of the workers.

Hathaway's relationship with his new working-class friends is
reminiscent less of Marx and Engels than of Ruskin, Arnold
Toynbee or William Morris; its dominant characteristic being
one of class repentance, of abasement before those who have been
wronged for so long:

> It is I, and such as I . . . who oppress you. We shirk the
> productive labour of the world and leave it all to you. You
> have been taught to consider yourselves dependent upon us;
> it is untrue; it is you who support us, and we are your
> pensioners.[39]

The novel ends with Hathaway accepting ostracism by the upper
classes, and making preparations to devote his life and money to

the propagation of Socialism. He is convinced that the revolution will come before the end of the century:

> It is not praise and thanks we Socialists must look for . . . but rather misapprehension and blame. If I were giving the workers my life in another way. If I were fighting by their side, shedding my blood, under the red flag, that would be a glorious death to die! And yet this must be better, because it is more useful. The time has not yet come to give my life for the people. I will give my life to the people.[40]

Here is the more excellent way of the novel's title.

This new faith in the urban workers as an incipient revolutionary force is also apparent in the novels of Margaret Harkness who, unlike Constance Howell, deals directly with working-class life. She herself is an even more shadowy figure than Morrison or Tirebuck, though there is no reason to believe that her own background was working class. Virtually the only biographical information known about her is that she played an important if mysterious part in helping to resolve the 1889 dock strike. Today she is remembered if at all as the recipient of Engel's famous letter explaining why he considered Balzac a greater realist than Zola.[41] As John Law, she wrote three novels which are relevant here: *A City Girl* (1887) which prompted Engels's letter, *Out of Work* (1888) and *In Darkest London* (1890). These novels are a curious hotch-potch of literary influences and revolutionary ideas. In them can be found Dickensian types and speech patterns side by side with occasional scenes which anticipate the more realistic studies of Kipling and Morrison; a fascination with social movements in the East End (*In Darkest London* is probably the most sustained attempt by a late-Victorian novelist to write a novel centred upon the Salvation Army); elements of working-class romance; and an obvious familiarity with Zola as well as Marx and Engels. The one constant they possess is Margaret Harkness's enthusiasm at the awakening class consciousness of the East End workers.

One of her characters expresses what were undoubtedly her own feelings:

> The West End is bad, or mad, not to see that if things go on like this we must have a revolution. One fine day the people

about here will grow desperate; and they will walk westwards,
cutting throats and hurling brickbats, until they are shot
down by the military. I know perfectly well that my ideas
would be called exaggerated if I put them into print – people
prefer to read the pretty stories about the East End made up
by Walter Besant.[42]

Besant was also the object of her criticism in the following description of the Queen opening the People's Palace:

No one would speak about the hisses which the denizens of
the slums had mingled with faint applause as her Majesty
neared her destination; no one would hint that the crowd
about the Palace of Delight had had a sullen, ugly look which
may a year or so hence prove dangerous.[43]

In these novels the ordinary working man, not merely the exceptional artisan, fully understands what is at stake: he knows who
his enemies are, and that time is on his side. Most unusual of all
is his appreciation of the degrading role he is at present obliged
to play in the social structure:

''ave you 'eard what we unemployed's got to do Jubilee
day?' continued the same young man, turning to the others.
'What then?'
'We've got to walk two and two down Cheapside afore the
Queen; we've got to do penance in white sheets and candles;
so I've read in the newspapers.'
Then the men began to sing: –
'Starving on the Queen's Highway'[44]

This sounds remarkably like *The Ragged Trousered Philanthropists*,
and indeed Margaret Harkness advances exactly the same political
argument as Tressell – that the condition of the workers is as bad
as it can be; no longer can they trust any of the existing political
parties to speak for them; they must therefore openly proclaim
themselves Socialists and fight for the revolution that is, in any
case, inevitable:

Competition has had its day; it *must* give place to co-operation,
because co-operation is the next step in the evolution of
society; it has a scientific basis. Individualists may try to stop
it, but it cannot be stopped. The organisation of labour and

the brotherhood of men are scientific truths which *must* be demonstrated. Join them in the struggle. Be Socialists.[45]

The debased scenes in her novels (as brutally direct as anything in Gissing or Kipling) should be considered in relation to her political beliefs:

> An old woman came to us last night and asked if we would take her to the doctor. Her little grandchild led her in. Her husband had knocked her eye out. She is stone blind now; for he knocked out her right eye when she was fifty, and last night he knocked her left eye out of its socket. I know six women close by this house whose husbands have knocked their eyes out.[46]

People such as these are debased not simply because they conform to a pattern of behaviour created by a hostile environment: they are victims of a capitalistic system which is slowly but surely crumbling. Their viciousness is a sign that they can sink no lower, that at last the revolution is on its way. The terrible picture of the East End in Margaret Harkness's novels is therefore, in a very special sense, optimistic.

It follows naturally from this that Margaret Harkness found much to admire in working-class life, and she does make a serious attempt to show the light side as well as the dark. Her ideological conviction prevents her from observing much variety or colour, but occasionally she exhibits sound common-sense, as when she writes: 'It is commonly supposed that men of his class feel a sort of general spooniness, mixed with a good deal of animalism, for their sweethearts.' She mocks this idea, later to be so important to Kipling and Morrison, that working-class sexual behaviour is essentially different to that of other classes.[47] And in *A City Girl* which examines a slum girl's devotion to her illegitimate baby, she bitterly denounces the conventional attitude (expressed by herself elsewhere) that East End mothers do not experience the normal feelings of love for their children.[48] Most interestingly, in *Out of Work* she describes a Sunday afternoon in Victoria Park, noting exactly the same details that a year later were to surprise Charles Booth. Margaret Harkness naturally gives pride of place to the political orators and the sharp repartee that takes place between them and their audience, but she does not fail to mention the smartly dressed courting couples, the music and laughter. These aspects of East End life together with the revolutionary aspirations of at least some of the workers are positive qualities of a very different kind to those found in Morrison's work, and link her, in part, with the Cockney School.

But ultimately interest in Margaret Harkness is ideological. The tradition to which her work belongs is a very minor one in the nineteenth century, though it gathers force and becomes more prominent later. Together with the Chartist novelists, W. E. Tirebuck and Constance Howell, she attempted to reverse the class bias of industrial fiction and correct the blindness of late-Victorian novelists to the urban workers' revolutionary potential. In neither was she successful. Like many minor novelists the value of her work lies in the illumination it casts on the mainstream of English fiction.

10

The phonetic representation of Cockney

I

Of all the difficulties facing the slum novelists of the nineties in their attempt to draw a true picture of the working man, none caused them more concern than how to reproduce on the printed page the curious verbal sounds they heard in the streets. To make their characters appear to speak Standard English would have been an affront to the doctrine of realism, while the working-class speech used by earlier novelists seemed to have little in common with that which they themselves observed.

There were three main problems. First, could Cockney be regarded as a genuine dialect or was it merely corrupt Standard English? Secondly, should swear words ('the common flowers of rhetoric in that world', as Gissing called them)[1] be openly presented in fiction, and if so, how? And thirdly, how could phonetics be used so that the general reader would both catch the exact sound of a voice and understand what was being said?

Irish, Scotch, Welsh and regional dialects had long been accepted in the English novel, and the use of phonetics to differentiate these dialects from Standard English, especially with regard to the speech of lower-class characters, had been successfully employed by many writers, most notably Scott, Mrs Gaskell, George Eliot and Hardy. Indeed, as the century progressed, novelists became increasingly interested in exploring the manners, customs and speech of specific areas of the country with which they were closely acquainted. Lucien Leclaire, in an exhaustive study of the subject, has estimated that while the period 1800–30 produced no English regional novel to rival Sir Walter Scott's and John Galt's tales of life in Scotland, or Maria Edgeworth's of life in Ireland, by 1870 the regional novel was well established in England as a distinctive genre.[2]

If we take Pierce Egan's *Life in London* as the archetype of the London novel, then we can see that the cockney had been accepted in fiction as a regional type (in so far as he is shown to live in a specific area and speak a distinctive dialect) for as long as other regional types.[3] The difference lies in the inferior social status automatically allotted to him. In a novel by Scott, Mrs Gaskell or George Eliot, a regional dialect symbolizes a whole way of life, and may be spoken by all classes of a given society, save usually the very highest.[4] It serves as a cultural link between the various social groups. In *Life in London* all of the characters use slang (one of the principal aims of the book was to show how 'flash' had permeated all ranks of society) but only the speech of the lower classes (the costermongers and the 'Cadgers' whom Tom and Jerry visit in the 'back slums') is represented by phoneticized Cockney. The reason for using Cockney is thus completely unlike the reason for using other regional dialects. It divides rather than unites the classes; it serves to heighten social divisions rather than lessen them; it indicates a type of speech common in a specific area, but shows a lack of 'culture' on the part of the speaker. In Victorian fiction, until about 1890, Cockney is employed either to show that a person is lower class or vulgar, or it is used humorously to emphasize that someone possesses the special status of a 'character'. The slum novelists rebelled against this narrow usage. They were not directly involved in the historical debate on questions such as when exactly cockneys stopped transposing v and w, and whether or not Cockney was a genuine dialect.[5] These were tasks for philologists; but the slum novelists' firm determination to trust their own ears rather than literary conventions, has given a considerable historic importance to much of their work. Their contribution to English literature, in this respect at least, is that they provided a new system for the transliteration of London working-class speech which is used to this day.

They accepted as a social fact that Cockney was spoken only by the London working and lower-middle classes, but recognized

R

that it possessed the same cultural value as a regional dialect. It was a form of speech with its own inflections, grammar, slang and idiosyncrasies; a means of communication which was the product of an urban way of life and which, while different from Standard English, was not necessarily inferior to it in range, colour and expressive power.

If Cockney, the language of the slums, was to be openly presented as a class dialect, the problem of obscenity loomed large. In 1889 Charles Booth had observed that the street language of the East End was 'stuffed with oaths, used as mere adjectives', but had quoted no actual examples.[6] The slum novelists were aware of the same peculiarity but were not satisfied with simply ignoring it. As usual it is necessary to distinguish between attitudes of the eighties and nineties. Gissing frequently referred to 'that vituperative vernacular of the nether world, which has never yet been exhibited by typography and presumably never will',[7] but it is safe to assume that he would not have used swear words extensively even if public opinion had allowed it. As we have seen, he was not personally attracted to working-class life and drew sharp distinctions between the intellectual-respectable working man who would never have 'stuffed' his conversation with oaths and his debased neighbour who certainly would have done. In such a case Gissing relies on indirect speech, as in the following example: 'His forte was the use of language so peculiarly violent that even in Shooter's Gardens it gained him a proud reputation. On the slightest excuse he would threaten to brain one of his children, to disembowel another, to gouge out the eyes of the third.'[8] Like Gissing, Besant placed an exaggerated stress on the value of Standard English pronunciation, and always skirted the problem of swear words. His own attitude can be clearly seen in the type of comparison he draws: 'As for their conversation, it grows continually viler, until Zola himself would be ashamed to reproduce the talk of these young people.'[9]

It was as well for Gissing and Besant that they were not committed to fight this particular battle in the name of realism, for public opinion, with the Vizately trials fresh in mind, would have been extremely hostile. The authors of the *Bitter Cry* fully realized what was at stake: 'We have been compelled to tone down everything, and wholly to omit what most needs to be known, or the ears and eyes of our readers would have been insufferably outraged.'[10] To overstep the undetermined line would be to forfeit public sympathy; while to understate the case might well destroy the power of the argument. It is worthwhile comparing the *Bitter Cry* statement with one made by George Sims six years later:

> There are many of us who have seen with our own eyes, and heard with our own ears, things so revolting that we can only hint at them in vague and hesitating language. Were I, even now that public attention has been thoroughly aroused to a greater danger, to go into the details of ordinary life in a London slum, the story would be one which no journal enjoying a general circulation could possibly print.[11]

Sims obviously felt that some change in public attitudes had taken place but as yet not to such a degree that he would be able to speak the simple truth. The hysterical and rhetorical tone that has been noted as characteristic of both fiction and sociological writing of the eighties, often acted as a substitute for the straightforward presentation of facts. The one was 'literary' and thus acceptable; the other was 'realistic' and thus indecent.

The slum novelists never really solved this problem, nor indeed is there anything like agreement on it even today. They did, however, reject rhetoric as an alternative. Even their apologies are more gentle and less condemning than those of Gissing and Besant. Edwin Pugh remarked that 'untranslatable language was sometimes used'. Somerset Maugham made the same point, breaking with his usually strict code of objectivity, to do so: "That is not precisely what she said, but it is impossible always to give the exact unexpurgated words of Liza and other personages of the story; the reader is therefore entreated with his thoughts to piece out the necessary imperfections of the dialogue.' Rudyard Kipling believed that Tommy Atkins 'really ought to be supplied with a new Adjective to help him to express his opinions' and elsewhere shows Mulvaney 'cursing his allies with Irish fluency and barrack-room point'.[12] These quotations stand in marked contrast to those of Besant and Gissing. None of the slum novelists is adopting an attitude of censure. They are rather pointing out to the reader that a compromise has been struck so that the eyes and ears of the public are not desecrated, and the authors' realism is not entirely sacrificed.

If the slum novelists could not bring about a revolution, they did introduce franker language than had appeared previously in the Victorian novel. Arthur Morrison peppers his stories with 'bleed'n', frequently uses the nouns 'bleeder' and 'cow' and has one of his characters call his wife an "eifer'. Both Kipling and Nevinson use 'bastard' as a term of abuse, and Pugh uses 'bitch'. Some writers, such as Pett Ridge, chose a traditionally weak way out: 'It's a (several adjectives) lie'; while Kipling, in 'Badalia Herodsfoot' employed dashes, sometimes with good effect, to indicate the coarsest language: 'The curick won't care a ——— for me.'[13]

The dread of totally compromising the authenticity of street language led, on the one hand, to a rejection of the theatrical oaths common in the 'Newgate' novel, and on the other, to a distrust of euphemism. The more domesticated oaths were used, though, with economy and care. But if the slum novelists were frustrated in their desire to present unexpurgated street language, they felt that it was possible to overcome this limitation by a judicious use of genuine slang,[14] together with a form of phonetic representation which attempted to convey to the reader the very sound of a working-class voice. It is this important aspect of their work which must now be looked at.

II

In the main the speech of the poor and working-class characters in Dickens's novels is represented by Standard English with occasional pronunciation differences noted. The number of variants employed differs greatly from character to character, but fundamentally the Plornishes speak this kind of pidgin Standard English, as do Betty Higden, Gaffer Hexam, Bill Sikes, Nancy, Boffin, Silas Wegg and Polly Toodles. Their speech is differentiated from that of other characters by occasional cockney or rustic (often interchangeable) variations, the most common being the v/w transposition; certain conventional lower-class mispronunciations (e.g. 'fur', for; 'arterwards', afterwards); grammatical confusion, especially in verb tenses (e.g. 'know'd', knew; 'says', said); and a few colloquial expressions such as 'this here'. Lower-class criminals use 'flash' or 'cant' and melodramatic oaths, and Dickens sometimes employs a form of phonetic spelling to mock aristocratic accents.[15] The use of these variants is rarely consistent. A lower-class character may at one moment be allowed to pronounce the most elaborate sentence immaculately, and then a few pages later have every other word of his speech phoneticized. With the exception of Jo – who is a special case – only the Wellers and Sairey Gamp are shown as speaking at least a consistent form of lower-class London speech. But this distinction is clearly not based on a class differentiation: they are portrayed as 'characters' and thus, while their speech is clearly recognizable as Cockney, they speak idiolects rather than dialect.

With Mrs Gamp, Dickens superbly catches the rhythms of Cockney:

> 'Mrs. Harris often and often says to me, "Sairey Gamp,"
> she says, "you raly do amaze me!" "Mrs Harris," I says to
> her, "why so? Give it a name, I beg." "Telling the truth
> then, ma'am," says Mrs. Harris, "and shaming him as shall
> be nameless betwixt you and me, never did I think till I
> know'd you, as any woman could sick nurse, and monthly
> likeways, on the little that you takes to drink." "Mrs.
> Harris," I says to her, "none on us knows what we can do
> till we tries." [16]

The only examples here of phonetic spelling are 'raly', 'none on (of) us', and 'Sairey'. In conveying the sound of Mrs Gamp's voice Dickens relies almost completely on her use of grammar, syntax and muddled verb tenses. She retains all her aspirates and manages all vowels and diphthongs in spite of the complexity of her sentences.

The most distinctive note in Sairey Gamp's speech is the idiosyncratic pronunciation of certain groups of words. Sibilants are often replaced by 'g', and soft final syllables are hardened. So she believes that it is only 'natur' that we have 'creeturs' who are 'bragian'. She closes the 'shetters' after looking out at the 'para-pidge' and talks about 'Rooshans' and 'Prooshans'. She describes her job as that of a 'nuss' and would think an 'individge' 'imperent' who called her 'orkard'. She eats 'cowcumbers', places her bottle on a 'mankelshelf' and later watches a ship set sail for 'Ankworks'. Ernest Weekley, after comparing Mrs Gamp's pronunciation and sentence construction with that of Lady Wentworth, reached the conclusion that: 'Mrs. Gamp, who must have learnt to talk in the generation which preceded the publication of Walker's *Dictionary*, spoke English very much after the fashion of a lady of quality of 1700–1750.'[17]

The Wellers share many of the same characteristics. They would describe Mrs Gamp as a 'ooman' and Mr Pickwick as a 'gen'lm'n' because he had undergone a thorough 'eddication'. Other similar words they use are 'wentur' (venture), 'manafacter' (manufacture), 'sassages' (sausages), 'Merriker' (America) and 'fort'ns' (fortunes). But with the Wellers Dickens does approximate much more closely to a form of phonetic representation, although this quotation is exceptional:

> The family name depends wery much upon you, Samivel, and I hope you'll do wots right by it. Upon all little pints o' breedin' I know I may trust you as vell as if it was my own self. So I've only this here one little bit of adwice to give you. If ever you gets to up'ards o'fifty, and feels disposed to go a-marryin' anybody – no matter who – jist you shut yourself up in your own room, if you've got one, and pison yourself off-hand. Hangin's wulgar, so don't you have nothin' to say to that. Pison yourself, Samivel, my boy, pison yourself, and you'll be glad on it arterwards.[18]

The most important characteristic here is the transposition of v/w; but also very noticeable is Dickens's use of 'i' in place of diphthongs and other vowels (pints, pison, jist); he also observes the glottal stop on middle and final consonants. Like Mrs Gamp, Tony Weller pronounces 'of' as 'on', and uses phrases such as 'this here' to advance his narrative. His speech, as a whole, flows less easily than Mrs Gamp's partly because Dickens is less concerned with cockney syntax, and partly because of the inconsistent use of liaison and elision (aspirates are all maintained), the glottal stop and the transposition of diphthongs. It should also be stressed that variants noted in this passage are not necessarily employed in other dialogue.

The presentation of Jo is especially interesting because of the class role he plays in *Bleak House*. He pronounces many individual words in a manner similar to Mrs Gamp and Sam Weller (wunst, horsepittle, thankee, Inkwich, dustn't, berryin'), and his speech as a whole is extremely simple, even for long stretches monosyllabic, with the repetition of 'wos', 'wot', and 'ses' giving it a rather hard tone. Even here, however, Dickens makes no attempt to employ phonetics consistently, but relies on the idiosyncratic spelling of particular words: 'I don't know how to do nothink, and I can't get nothink to do. I'm wery poor and ill, and I thought I'd come back here when there warn't nobody about, and lay down and hide somewheres as I knows on till arter dark, and then go and beg a trifle of Mr. Snagsby.'[19] It would be impossible for someone reading this aloud to convey the sound of Jo's voice as being lower-class cockney simply by pronouncing the words as spelt by Dickens. He would need to bring to his reading knowledge of how Cockney is spoken outside *Bleak House*, and adjust Dickens's spelling accordingly. Jo is given a special speech pattern not because he is a lower-class Londoner, but because the role he plays in the novel – especially his outcast social position and pathetic death – demands it. When he returns to Tom-All-Alone's and is discovered there by Allan Woodcourt and the brickmaker's wife, the woman speaks Standard English throughout, and Jo alone speaks his curiously stilted, probably eighteenth-century, Cockney.

Dickens, then, employs Cockney as a class dialect, but uses phonetics extensively only in very special circumstances. He never uses Cockney to indicate working-class vulgarity, nor does he mock cockneys for being uneducated. When there are jokes against the Wellers' pronunciation the laughter is genial:

'What's your name, sir?' enquired the judge.
'Sam Weller, my Lord,' replied that gentleman.
'Do you spell it with a "V" or a "W"? enquired the judge.
'That depends upon the taste and fancy of the speller, my Lord,' replied Sam, 'I never had occasion to spell it more than once or twice in my life, but I spells it with a "V".'
Here a voice in the gallery exclaimed aloud, 'Quite right too, Samivel; quite right, – Put it down a we, my Lord, put it down a we.'[20]

The tone of this is in marked contrast to Thackeray's treatment of the cockney Charles Yellowplush in *The Yellowplush Papers* (1837), who can serve as a useful link between the archetype Sam Weller and the archetype 'Arry.[21]

The phonetic spellings used by Thackeray fall into three main groups. First, the extremely large number of words which acquire aspirates (e.g. hera, hobvious, hofficer, hangel, hacting, hogre). Secondly, idiosyncratic pronunciations (e.g. orfin, poppylation, laffin, disrepettable, suckumstance, melumcolly). And thirdly, alternative spellings which make no difference to the Standard English pronunciation (e.g. sellybrated, bloo, kix, trix, vertyou, vail, seen). The second of these groups is the same type of usage common in Dickens, but the addition of the aspirate and the alternative spellings, when used to an exaggerated degree, represent something quite different, leading as they do to a humour based on feelings of class or educational superiority.[22] When, for instance, Thackeray has a character say 'I bloo the bellus of the horgin', then he is making no attempt to present the actual sound of an actual voice, but is adopting a special form of phonetics for the purpose of class caricature. Likewise when Charles Yellowplush says, 'Let us draw a vail over the seen', or speaks of his 'sellybrated' employers, then here there is an attempt at phonetic representation only in order to indicate the speaker's inferior social status. While both Dickens and Thackeray use Cockney as a class dialect, in the one it leads to the creation of predominantly eccentric characters, in the other to mockery of lower-class vulgarity.

We can thus see that, with the regard to the use of Cockney, there are two main lines of tradition in Victorian fiction. One leads from Pierce Egan, attains its finest expression in Dickens, and is continued in the sociological work of Henry Mayhew, and the now unread novels by writers such as Augustus Mayhew and James Greenwood. Henry Mayhew's *London Labour and the London Poor* is especially interesting because of the vast knowledge of working-class London that the author possessed; but in spite of his instinctive grasp of working-class slang, idiom and speech patterns, he rarely attempts any extended phonetic representation, remaining content with variant spellings of occasional words in a manner similar to Dickens.

The other line of tradition descends from Surtees[23] to Thackeray, via *Punch*, and attains its clearest expression in Milliken's 'Arry cartoons. The stress in this tradition is on 'lower' rather than 'working-class' speech; it is vulgarity that is under attack and this often results from too much rather than too little money. The representation of 'Arry's speech contains little that is new, save that the v/w transposition is less frequent than in former models. Its place is taken by an equally exaggerated use and misuse of aspirates, together with the customary alternative spellings. The tendency we noted in Thackeray to use the cockney accent as a joke for a predominantly middle-class audience is taken a step further with 'Arry's self-appointed role as critic of society, art, politics or any major issue of the day:

> That's wot I call life; true feelosophy, plain
> > common-sense, and no paint;
> But Muggs our top card at the crib – you know
> > Muggs – who's a bit of a saint,
> Swears Society's got a bad fit on, a sort of low
> > Music-Hall fever.
> If *he* ain't a 'umbug at heart, may yours truly be
> > blowed tight for hever.[24]

As was pointed out earlier, the first 'Arry cartoon appeared in 1877 and he immediately challenged Sam Weller as the most popular cockney archetype. When the slum novelists rebelled against the phonetic systems used by earlier writers, it was 'Arry more than any other figure they had in mind, but they were also dissatisfied with the other cockney models discussed here. The slum novelists of the nineties broke almost entirely with the past. They experimented with a form of phonetic spelling which could be justifiably employed in a realistic narrative, and the method they developed is still followed today. They brought about an important technical change in fiction but they themselves were not the formulators of the manifesto. During the eighties two men, seemingly independent of each other, challenged the traditional phonetic representation of Cockney. The first was a theoretician, Andrew Tuer; the second, a practitioner, Rudyard Kipling.

III

In 1900 George Bernard Shaw added a note to *Captain Brassbound's Conversion* to explain his phonetic treatment of Drinkwater's Cockney dialect. He acknowledged the important role Andrew Tuer had played in the formation of the new ideas:

> When I came to London in 1876, the Sam Weller dialect had passed away so completely that I should have given it up as a literary fiction if I had not discovered it surviving in a

Middlesex village and heard of it from an Essex one. Some time in the eighties the late Andrew Tuer called attention in the Pall Mall Gazette to several peculiarities of modern Cockney, and to the obsolescence of the Dickens dialect that was still being copied from book to book by authors who never dreamt of using their ears, much less of training them to listen.

He goes on to note some contemporary practitioners:

> Then came Mr. Anstey's cockney dialogues in Punch, a great advance, and Mr. Chevalier's coster songs and patter. The Tomkins' verses contributed by Mr. Barry Pain to the London Daily Chronicle also did something to bring the literary convention for Cockney English up to date.[25]

Shaw's recognition of Albert Chevalier's part in the changing image of the cockney is perfectly just, but Anstey and Pain are less important figures, their phonetic systems being a mixture of old and new. What is most surprising about Shaw's list is the total omission of the working-class novelists, for at this late date he could also have named Kipling, Morrison, Maugham, Pett Ridge and many others, all of whom were experimenting with the phonetic representation of Cockney long before Shaw made such personal capital out of it. Furthermore the role played by Andrew Tuer was far more significant than Shaw gives him credit for.

The importance of Tuer is twofold. First, he pointed out that the standard representation of Cockney had become a static convention, with writers copying past literary models rather than noting the peculiarities of speech for themselves. Secondly, he wrote two small books, *The Kawkneigh Awlminek* (1883) and *Thenks awf'lly* (1890), in which he sketched out a completely phonetic rendition of Cockney as he himself heard it spoken in London. To these two books should be added a third, *Old London Street Cries* (1885), which contains several observations, incidental to the main purpose of the book, but important to a discussion of Tuer's ideas.

As we have seen the two main features of mid-Victorian Cockney were the transposition of v/w and the addition of an aspirate to words beginning with a vowel. Tuer not only pointed out that the former usage was obsolete but claimed that 'in regard to the use of the letter V for W, "Bevare of the viddy, Samivel my boy, bevare of the viddy," Mr. Weller was exceptional in his pronunciation'.[26] On the second characteristic Tuer was equally dogmatic: 'The popular idea as to the average Cockney indiscriminately scattering his "Hs" is a delusion . . . he settles the problem by ignoring them.'[27] Having dispensed with these traditional features Tuer places full emphasis on the sounds of distorted vowels and diphthongs. The result was that for the first time Cockney was given a life of its own, being used for neither purely comic effect, nor as a mark of vulgarity:

> Now; dawgs is aout er mah lahn. It wuz fer a-priggin' uv a
> ly-deez wrop thet I got aout uv a owpin kerridge frem
> be'ahnd w'en I thought she wasn't a-lookin', bet she wuz
> a'settin' on a bit uv it, en felt the teg. She looked raound en'
> shaouted, en' a blowke oo wuz a-passin' 'eld me till a
> pleeceman tuk me awf.[28]

Understandably Tuer felt the need to print a Standard English word-for-word translation together with the phonetic version, but even without this we can immediately notice certain differences from the earlier examples. There is no bizarre pronunciation of just one type of word; there are none of the visual changes so common in Thackeray, and only in two cases does the phonetic rendition change one word into another with a completely different meaning, 'Now' (No) and 'bet' (but), neither of which could lead to a misunderstanding. The v/w transposition and the use of aspirates before words which do not usually employ them, go entirely. What is most striking about Tuer's Cockney is the way that he uses vowels and diphthongs together with the glottal stop to produce the curiously fast-flowing yet uneven rush of the cockney voice. William Matthews has estimated that Tuer introduced five new sounds into cockney phonetics:

Long a pronounced long i:
   myke, engyged, relytions, eyen't, acquynetince.
Long i pronounced ah or oi:
   tahm, quaht, nahn, mah, bah; or noight, loike, moine, foine, toime.

Long o pronounced ow :
   owm (home), Jowve, now (no), sowp, down't, bouth, stoun.
Ow pronounced ah or aow :
   flahs (flowers), paounds, naow, abaout, craown.
Short u pronounced like short e :
   entil, ether, kentry, seppers, inselt, etc. [29]

With much close searching it would doubtless be possible to find isolated examples of many of Tuer's 'new' sounds in the work of earlier writers. Joseph Saxe, in a comparative study of some cockney verses in mid-Victorian *Punch* and Bernard Shaw's plays, reached the conclusion that Shaw's innovations were not so striking as is often supposed. [30] Even allowing for the fact that Saxe completely ignored Tuer, such a study misses the main point; for what is really new is the consistency of Tuer's phonetic representation; the way that Cockney is placed on a par with regional dialects. It is the total pattern rather than the individual parts that is important.

That Tuer took his pronunciations from first-hand experience can be seen in *Old London Street Cries*, where he occasionally breaks from the traditional method of transcribing street cries into Standard English or into a totally different sentence, and uses his own system of phonetics. For instance, J. T. Smith, in *The Cries of London* (1839), pointed out that the cry 'Holloway Cheese Cakes' was pronounced 'All my teeth ache'. Quoting this, Tuer remarks: 'The philologist will find the pronunciation of the peripatetic Cockney vendor of useful and amusing trifles . . . worthy of careful study.' His own phonetic rendition of certain street cries shows the same kind of difference between himself and Smith as is to be found, for instance, between Thackeray and Morrison. 'A Handy Shoe Horn for a Penny' pronounced 'En endy shoo-awn frer penny'. Or one could instance Tuer's treatment of the new 'Under Street Cries': 'Ferrinden Street, Oldersgit Street, Mawgit Street, Bishergit, Ol'git, Mark Line, Monneym'nt, Kennun Street, Menshun 'Ouse.' [31]

The full significance of Tuer's work is to be found in the way these phonetic spellings can be used to represent a total dialect – the eccentricities which turned a class of people into a composite caricature are removed and a way of life is expressed in the speech. Of course Tuer's own books must be seen primarily as phonetic exercises. The working-class novelists realized that fiction written in such a style would be comprehensible only to a trained phonetician. Furthermore, Tuer was eager to point out that he was offering no universal cure for a moribund convention. He hoped to encourage others to listen for themselves, to note variations and to describe truthfully what they heard.

In 1892 Milliken collected together many of the ''Arry' ballads which had been so popular for the previous fifteen years and published them as a book. In the introduction he entered into a defence of his own phonetic representation. Although Tuer is not mentioned by name, it is perfectly clear to whom Milliken is referring:

> As regards 'Arry's diction, his pronunciation, his
> orthography, it is hardly needful, perhaps, to observe, that no
> attempt has been made to be accurately phonetic. No possible
> combination of letters will really render 'Arry's
> pronunciation of such words as 'lady', 'game', 'Charlie',
> 'daisy', 'down', or 'trousers'. To besprinkle these pages with
> such orthographical combinations as 'lidy', 'goime', 'Choarlee',
> 'doisy', 'daoun', or 'trersers', would (in my opinion) make
> them a perplexing, eye-wearying phonetic puzzle, without
> attaining absolute orthoepical accuracy. It would, of course,
> be quite possible to approximate more closely to 'Arry's
> pronunciation, but only, I think, at the cost of making my
> verses hideous to look at and hard to read. Rightly or
> wrongly, I have deliberately abstained from the attempt.[32]

Within the context of *Punch* one can sympathize with Milliken's defence, but the novelists of the nineties were concerned with taking the cockney out of the artificial environment in which 'Arry had been enthroned, or rather to keep 'Arry but reject 'Arryism. On one point Milliken was clearly right. The new phonetic system could not be used as Tuer had written it. Milliken however implies that so long as some modified form must be used, then his is as good as any other, and this the slum novelists would have completely denied. No one was to claim that he had achieved an exact medium, but the best of the slum novelists could at least say that their modifications were based upon personal research and an intimate knowledge of the way of life they were describing.

IV

There is no external evidence to show that Kipling had read Tuer's writings and the internal evidence suggests that he had almost certainly not done so. It seems reasonable to assume that Kipling developed a personal system of phonetics from his study of the private soldier, slum dweller and music-hall coster. In his early soldier stories the Cockney dialect is a mixture of old and new:

> 'E's gone an' 'ired six men to carry 'im, an' I 'ad to 'elp 'im into 'is nupshal couch, 'cause 'e wouldn't 'ear reason. 'E's gone off in 'is shirt an' trousies, swearin' tremenjus – gone down the road in the palanquin, wavin' 'is legs out o' windy.'[33]

In this passage all aspirates and many final consonants are dropped. The aim is to capture the rapid but jerky speech of the cockney (produced by the omitted aspirates and glottal stop) and Kipling achieves this successfully. But unlike Tuer, he does not phoneticize vowel sounds (gone, off); he uses one alternative spelling which is little different from its Standard English pronunciation (nupshal), and there are three idiosyncratic pronunciations (trousies, tremenjus, windy), all of which are common in earlier literature. We can compare with this Ortheris's speech in a later story:

> 'Jock's no more than a 'ayrick in trousies. 'E be'aves *like* one; an' 'e can't *'it* one at a 'undred; 'e was born *on* one, an' s'welp me 'e'll die *under* one for not bein' able to say wot 'e wants in a Christian lingo'.[34]

'Trousies', the least bizarre of the three idiosyncratic pronunciations noted above, remains, but there are no alternative spellings and the italicized words and elision (s'welp me) serve to move the speech along quickly and realistically. The phonetic spelling of 'what' ('wot') is justifiable in the transliteration of Cockney, for although the aspirate is not sounded in Standard English it does serve to soften the vowel whereas the cockney ignores the aspirate, thus hardening the vowel. With Badalia Herodsfoot's speech Kipling attains his greatest success:

The men they'll shif' for themselves. That's why Nick
Lapworth sez to you that 'e wants to be confirmed an' all
that. 'E won't never lead no new life, nor 'is wife won't get
no good out o' all the money you gives 'im. No more you can't
pauperise them as 'asn't things to begin with. They're
bloomin' well pauped.[35]

There is much greater stress here on grammatical structure than
in the earlier examples. Badalia uses two double negatives in the
same sentence, inverts the following sentence, and finally makes
up an adjective from a verb which she uses correctly. This
grammatical confusion neatly captures the slum girl's attempt to
explain what for her are complex ideas.

From these examples we can notice several important points
about Kipling's use of Cockney. First, it is not treated as corrupt
Standard English, but as a dialect in its own right. In the soldier
stories, Ortheris's dialect is placed on a par with those of the
Irishman and the Yorkshireman. Secondly, it is not phoneticized
in order to make the reader laugh. In spite of the differences in
tone, the writers in both the Dickens and the Thackeray traditions
did use Cockney for this purpose. Thirdly, the transliteration is
consistent throughout. And fourthly, by concentrating on a consistent use of only one or two important cockney characteristics and
largely eschewing the transliteration of diphthongs and vowel
sounds, Kipling succeeded both in capturing the sound of a
cockney voice and in making it comprehensible to the general
reader.

Benefiting from the general discussion of Cockney dialect
initiated by Tuer and from the practical example offered by
Kipling, the working-class novelists of the nineties all employed,
in varying degrees, the new forms of phonetic representation. We
can most clearly see how they differ from the past by comparing
them with novelists of the eighties. George Sims uses phonetics
extensively but with the kind of inconsistency that disappears in
Tuer and Kipling:

'What bizerness 'as he to summings me,' she says, pointing
to the officer, 'just cus my boy ain't bin fur a week? He's
'arsh and harbitury, that's what he is. 'Arsh and harbitury.'[36]

Harsh and arbitrary are just the words to describe Sims's phonetics.

The speech does not flow, the alternative spellings do not contribute to the rhythm of the sentences, and the use and misuse of aspirates is nonsensical. Most important of all there is a self-consciousness about the use of phonetics that is noticeable in most pre-1890 novelists except Dickens. Margaret Harkness, for instance, employs one of her characters to convey to the reader how difficult it is to capture the sound of Cockney:

> 'So I made some balls of frozen snow, and licked the skins round 'em. I sold 'em for injins, and got my night's lodging.'
> 'What's injins?' asked Jos.
> 'Inions, of course.'
> 'Onions!'
> 'Well, call 'em what you like. I'm not particler.'[37]

Gissing provides a more interesting example. In his early work he often uses phonetics:

> 'I know it's 'ard on yer,' pursued honest Ned, 'to stop horff yer little 'musements like, but you see Mike don't like to 'ev his rooms sp'iled. An' then he thinks as 'ow you ain't quite goin' on as you should, wastin' yer time, an' sich like.'[38]

In some respects this is very similar to the kind of phonetics used in the nineties. Gissing notes the unusual pronunciation of vowels and diphthongs, adds one aspirate quite successfully, but inexplicably leaves the aspirates on 'he' and 'his'. What is most surprising about Gissing's use of phonetics is its extreme inconsistency. Elsewhere in the same book working-class speech patterns are mainly Dickensian:

> 'Oh, quite sure, sir. Yer know the parish doctor ain't over pertikler in comin' just when he's wanted. But he won't be long now. Maybe you'd take a drop yerself, sir? No! Well, it don't suit everybody's stomach, certainly. So 'ere's yer very good 'ealth, sir, an' the 'ealth of the poor gentleman too.'[39]

Gissing usually follows the example of earlier working-class novelists in allotting phoneticized speech to characters according to the role they play in the novel rather than the environment they live in. But even in this he is inconsistent. Clem Peckover, one of the most debased characters in *The Nether World*, is often allowed to speak in Standard English save for an occasional alternative spelling.[40] Her speech is differentiated from that of the more respectable working-class characters by its faulty grammar. As we have seen, Gissing stopped writing working-class fiction in 1889, but during the nineties he did occasionally contribute short stories about working-class life to periodicals. One of these shows that he had completely adopted the new phonetic representation:

'I always said you was good-looking Lou, but to see you now fair tikes my breath away, s'elp me gawd! What 'a' you been doin' with yourself all this time? . . .

'There ain't no use in making a bother. I cawn't help lookin' at yer, Lou. You're that 'endsome, I wouldn't 'a' believed it.'[41]

Although much of this is still in Standard English, the changes made by Gissing are significant. Vowels and diphthongs are phoneticized, aspirates dropped, and the sentences flow much more easily than in his earlier work. An even more striking convert to the new system was Richard Whiteing, whose writing life spanned a longer period than any other of the slum novelists:

'And afore I could say Jack Robinson the old party with the hook nose and the eyeglass puts her harm in mine, and in this here stoopid fashion we galliwanted downstairs.'[42]

This was written in 1867. Just over thirty years later Whiteing was transcribing working-class speech in the following manner:

'Other sahd o' the sea. Reg'lar bunch of 'em. 'Arf as big agin as this 'ere country; and this a pretty big un, I kin tell yer, if yer try to walk through.'[43]

In addition to this simplified system Whiteing frequently alters vowels and diphthongs in much the same way as Tuer (e.g. cawnah (corner), awf (off), affawd (afford), cawfee (coffee), mike (make) and many others. At this late date, 1899, the system of phonetics used by Whiteing had been universally accepted. Just as he had earlier followed the literary convention established by Dickens, now he followed that established by Kipling and Morrison.

Morrison especially had built up the simple system made popular by Kipling, mingling phonetics with slang and swear words:

'That's all right, ol' cock,' roared Bill Napper, reaching toward the guv'nor. 'You come an' 'ave a tiddley. I'm a bleed'n millionaire meself now, but I ain't proud. What, you won't?' – for the guv'nor, unenthusiastic, remained at the door – 'You're a sulky old bleeder. These 'ere friends o' mine are 'avin' 'arf a day auf at my expense: unnerstand? My expense. I'm a-payin' for their time, if you dock 'em; an' I can give *you* a bob, me fine feller, if you're 'ard up. See?'[44]

There is a naturalness to this unlike any other example quoted so far. Morrison catches exactly the uneven flow of speech produced by liaison, elision and the glottal stop: 'These 'ere friends o' mine are 'avin' 'arf a day auf at my expense.' There are no idiosyncratic pronunciations, no alternative spellings, and the tone is not funny or melodramatic; neither like Sam Weller nor Bill Sikes. Furthermore, because there is no standard of class comparison in the story, all characters speak like Bill Napper. They speak dialect not idiolects.

Somerset Maugham follows a similar system, except that he places greater stress on long vowel sounds which tends to pitch conversation into a higher key, slows it down slightly, and makes it more suitable to convey ordinary, everyday dialogue:

'I never seen anything so good, I can tell yer. You tike my tip, and git Tom ter tike yer.'
'I don't want ter go; an' if I did I'd py for myself an' go alone.'
'Cheese it! That ain't 'alf so good. Me an' 'Arry, we set together, 'im with 'is arm round my wiste and me 'oldin' 'is 'and. It was jam, I can tell yer!'
'Well, I don't want anyone sprawlin' me abaht; thet ain't my mark!'[45]

This characteristic was also widely used by novelists of the Cockney School, but Clarence Rook, explaining hooligan life, uses harsher phonetics, a technique which is especially effective when Alf makes a point of social criticism: 'Fort they was goin' to see 'orrors . . . an' they didn't see nuffink. I know that sort. Come down jest as if they was goin' to look at a lot o' wild beasties.'[46]

Neighbours of Ours is written entirely in phoneticized Cockney which obliged Nevinson often to convey working-class speech indirectly through his narrator. At times this is done with considerable skill, as in this passage where Ginger draws begrudging praise from her usually hostile friends because of her obvious love for her absent Negro husband:

> And I've 'eard the women say as she was gettin' almost as decent-lookin' as any of 'em. And as for the men, there was plenty willin' to take 'er now, babies and all, through 'avin' a kind of an interest in the way she'd been goin' on. And one on 'em 'avin' lost 'is wife some weeks earlier, makes bold to go up to 'er and offer to take 'er on till Sissero came 'ome, and then give her up again; or to keep 'er for good and all, if 'e didn't never come 'ome. But she just laughed, and told 'im it wasn't 'ardly worth while makin' no change for the little bit of 'er waitin' time as was left, but thankin' 'im for 'is kindness, as she was willin' to be grateful for.[47]

Nevinson's use of phonetics is very similar to Kipling's; almost total stress being placed upon dropped aspirates and final consonants, together with the establishment of an individual, though not idiosyncratic, use of syntax. Where Nevinson really succeeds is in employing the cockney dialect to bring out, in passing, certain values and attitudes accepted as normal within this working-class community, which would appear bizarre if presented in Standard English spelling and grammar.

Alone among the working-class novelists of the nineties, Edwin Pugh uses extremely simple phonetics with a great deal of slang, both rhyming and ordinary:

> 'I ain't bin getting on,' replied Harvey. 'I bin copping out on about the thickest streak o' drive-me-mad as ever I know. Talk about Barney's bull! He never was so busted up as I bin. No tommy. No lotion. No kip. No posh. No nothing. Not even the option. Look at last Monday week. No, I can't tell you about it. It's enough to make an honest pad turn snider, so it is. This is about the roughest bit o' luck I struck. And I reckon it's come for keeps I'm saying "Fainitz" soon.'[48]

But this is not the speech of all working-class characters:

'In the ordinary way,' said Holy Joe, 'he'll come up afore
the beak to-morrow morning and be remanded for a day or
two, p'r'aps a week, p'r'aps a fortnight. I dunno. Then he'll
come up again, and p'r'aps be remanded again. Then
he'll come up once more and they'll either give him the drag
or a sixer – '
'Easy on wi' the slang,' said Maddie. 'Talk English.'
'Three months or six months, I mean, o' course.'[49]

By the middle years of the nineties the new phonetic system had
been fully accepted by all novelists. Just as the working-class
romance had taken over from Morrison a violent image of the
cockney, and from the Cockney School a more cheerful image of
the cockney, and in both cases had made spurious the genuine
originals, so the writers of romance now seized upon the new
system of phonetics and rendered that bizarre also:

'She's er lidy; see 'er white vile.'
''Ow's that fer hair?'
'See yer bloomin' gloves 'arf wye up 'er harm?'[50]

The terrible confusion here comes from the author understanding
neither the new system nor his subject. In the following example
it comes from an attempted amalgamation between the old and
the new:

'Mister Bloomfiel? Lor' lummy! there ain't no misters 'ere.
We're all dooks an' markisses. "Mister" in a tup'ny doss-
'ouse! Bloomfiel' – never yeard the nime. Wot sorter covey?
Tall an' thin, yer say? Wot, wiv long white 'ands, an' black
'air – Yus! Why that's Satan, Why didn't yer say so at
fust?'[51]

In trying to develop a system of phonetics which would exactly
capture the sounds of London working-class voices, the slum
novelists were affirming a shared belief that the Cockney dialect
was an integral part of a total cultural pattern. It has already been
sufficiently stressed that in English fiction before 1880 the urban
working man is usually presented, in one way or another, as an
exceptional member of his social group, and this prejudice is
reflected in the kind of speech pattern allotted to him. If he is
superior, in education or intellect, to the majority of his class, he

speaks Standard English; if he is very poor or debased, his speech is made correspondingly ugly by crude phonetics; if he is exceptional by virtue of personal eccentricity, then he is given an idiolect. The same is not true of the industrial worker whose speech is presented as a genuine dialect rather than as corrupt Standard English. After 1880 the urban novelists become concerned more with the ordinary than the exceptional working man. Their attack on the pastoral nature of earlier working-class fiction encouraged the belief that Cockney should take its place in fiction as a distinct, instantly recognizable dialect, but in spite of their considerable success Cockney continued to differ from other dialects in that its use depended, almost exclusively, on the class of the speaker. As Edwin Pugh pointed out, the cockney himself was fully aware of this discrimination against him:

> For centuries the witlings have been telling him that his accent is 'vile', and he believes that it is vile. Certainly it would never occur to him to be proud of his accent as an East Anglian or a Man of Kent, a Cornishman or a Cumbrian is proud of his burr . . . The Cockney alone blushes for the twang that brands him as a citizen of the greatest city of the world.[52]

The establishment of a consistent phonetic system to represent the cockney's speech thus bred new problems, for in giving a character this particular dialect it meant that he was automatically classified as working class rather than as a Londoner. This particular problem did not greatly worry the late-Victorian novelists who were mainly concerned with gaining a place for the working man in serious fiction, and employed phonetics enthusiastically because it helped them to achieve this end. Edwin Pugh, however, did realize that by continually drawing attention to Cockney as a *class* accent, novelists appeared to be opposing rather than supporting the fact that 'the Cockney accent is not a whit more inaccurate than the University accent; and that the East End speaks with the same disregard of the mother-tongue as the West End'. As Pugh goes on to argue, the only way to correct this imbalance would be for phonetics to be used to represent upper- and middle- as well as working-class speech,[53] a solution which would produce philological exercises incomprehensible to the general reader. Pugh's warning can now be seen as perfectly sound, for with the general acceptance in twentieth-century England of the Standard English accent as representing the normal mode of speech, and with the rapid decline of regional dialects,[54] Cockney has become (in literature, drama, cinema and television) the customary accent for any character who is required to play a part combining lack of formal education and a sharp, natural wit. A regional dialect could serve the second purpose but not the first. The phonetic system used in the twentieth century is that established by the late-Victorian working-class novelists. Just as Morrison's attempt to treat seriously in fiction the true nature of slum violence led directly to a new debased image of the working man; just as the Cockney School's attempt to describe the non-violent 'wild joys and excitements' of working-class life led to a new cockney stereotype; so their common determination to raise the status of Cockney to that of other regional dialects rebounded upon them, and became irrevocably established as the language of the uneducated.

Notes

1 The two traditions, 1820–80

1 'Charles Dickens', *Inside the Whale* (1940), 11–12.
2 Not all of the industrial novels are actually set in Manchester: *Sybil* is set in the Midlands, and Dickens's Coketown is deliberately generalized. But Manchester features in the novels by Harriet Martineau and Mrs Gaskell, it is eulogized in *Coningsby*, and Mrs Trollope made it the first stop on her fact-finding tour of the north. Whether specifically named or not, it is the image of Manchester more than any other city that dominates the industrial novel. For the symbolic importance of Manchester during the early-Victorian period, see Asa Briggs's *Victorian Cities* (1963), Ch. 3.
3 Apart from several historical romances the principal Chartist novels are: Thomas Martin Wheeler, *Sunshine and Shadow: A Tale of the Nineteenth Century*, serialized in the *Northern Star*, 1849–50: Thomas Frost, *The Secret*, serialized in the *National Instructor*, 1850: and Ernest Jones, 'The Working-Man's Wife', *Woman's Wrongs* (1855). A late-Victorian novel which possesses many of the same characteristics as Chartist fiction is H. J. Bramsbury's *A Working Class Tragedy*, serialized in *Justice* from June 1888 to April 1889.
4 'Proletarian Literature', *Some Versions of Pastoral* (1935), 3.
5 Letter dated April 1888. George J. Becker (ed.), *Documents of Modern Literary Realism* (Princeton, 1963), 484.
6 *Some Versions of Pastoral*, 6.
7 Hall Caine, 'Memoir of W. E. Tirebuck', preface to Tirebuck's posthumous novel *'Twixt God and Mammon* (1903).
8 The most notable exception to this generalization is Disraeli's portrayal of 'The Temple of the Muses' in *Sybil*, Bk. III, Ch. X. In *Hard Times* Sleary's circus is employed deliberately to heighten the monotonous life of the Coketown workers.

9 See Charles W. Camp, *The Artisan in Elizabethan Literature* (New York, 1924), and F. W. Chandler, *The Literature of Roguery* (2 vols., 1907).

10 Boswell, *Life of Johnson*, ed. G. Birkbeck Hill, 1934, vol. IV, 201.

11 Asa Briggs, 'The Language of "Class" in Early Nineteenth Century England', *Essays in Labour History*, ed. Asa Briggs and John Saville (1960), 41.

12 *The Novel and Society* (1966), 41.

13 Briggs, 'The Language of "Class" . . . ', 43. See also Raymond Williams, *Culture and Society* (1958), Introduction.

14 Briggs, *Victorian Cities*, 57; G. D. H. Cole and Raymond Postgate, *The Common People 1746–1946* (University Paperbacks, 1964), Ch. XXXVII.

15 *The Newgate Novel 1830–47* (Detroit, 1963), 33.

16 *The Life of Charles Dickens* (1893), Bk. VI, Ch. 2.

17 Gissing, *Charles Dickens* (1898), 90; *Workers in the Dawn* (3 vols., 1880), I, 247.

18 Introduction to his edition of *Life in London* (1869). All page references are to this edition.

19 *Life in London*, 46.

20 *Ibid.*, 45.

21 *Ibid.*, 47.

22 *Ibid.*, 259.

23 *Ibid.*, 320.

24 *Sartor Resartus*, Bk. I, Ch. 3.

25 *The Spectator*, 26 December 1836.

26 *The Immortal Dickens* (1925), 20.

27 *Charles Dickens*, 40.

28 *David Copperfield*, Ch. XXXIX.

29 *Alton Locke*, Ch. VIII.

30 *Bleak House*, Ch. XI.

31 *Our Mutual Friend*, Ch. XVI. The phrase refers specifically to Betty Higden.

32 *David Copperfield*, Ch. XL.

33 *Fiction for the Working Man 1830–1850* (1963), 1.

34 *Ibid.*, 18.

35 *The Uses of Literacy* (1957), 20.

36 *The Nether World* (3 vols., 1889), I, 166.

37 Augustus Mayhew, *Paved With Gold* (1858), Ch. 2.

38 *Charles Dickens*, 15.

2 New lines and continuing traditions

1 *Life and Labour of the People*, Vol. 1, East London (1889), 157.

2 *Helen Fleetwood* (1841), Ch. IV.

3 *Sybil*, Bk. II, Ch. X; and Disraeli's 'Advertisement' to the first edition.

4 *Mary Barton*, Ch. III.

5 *Coningsby*, Bk. III, Ch. 1; *Sybil*, Bk. II, Ch. VIII; *Hard Times*, Bk. I, Ch. XI. For an interesting analysis of this kind of imagery, see Jean-Paul Hulin, 'Exotisme et Littérature Sociale au Début de L'Ère Victorienne', *Etudes Anglaises* XVI (1963).

6 *Hard Times*, Bk. II, Ch. VI.

7 *Sybil*, Bk. III, Ch. VI.

8 *North and South*, Ch. XLIV.

9 *Meliora* IV (1862), 298–9.

10 Preface to *London Labour and the London Poor* (1861).

11 'Urban Sociology in Great Britain: A Trend Report', *Current Sociology* IV (1955), Part 2, 8.

12 George Godwin, *London Shadows: A Glance at the 'Homes' of the Thousands* (1854), 1.

13 Hector Gavin, *Sanitary Ramblings* (1848), 3.

14 Charles Manby Smith, *Curiosities of London Life* (1853), preface.

15 Godwin, *London Shadows*, 1.

16 Godwin, *Town Swamps and Social Bridges* (1859), 1.

17 See Ch. 4 (III).

18 *Illustrations of Political Economy* (9 vols., 1832–4), preface.

19 Mrs Ranyard, *The Missing Link: Or Bible-Women in the Homes of the London Poor* (1859), 1–2. See also: Catherine Marsh, *English Hearts and English Hands* (1858); Mrs J. B. Wightman, *Haste to the Rescue* (1862); and Mrs Bayly, *Ragged Homes and How to Mend Them* (1859).

20 *Told with a Purpose* (1880), 55.

21 *Step by Step* (1882), 27.

22 *On the Doorsteps* (1880), preface.

23 *The New Antigone* (3 vols., 1887), III, 11–12.

24 *Ibid.*, 176–7.

25 Anarchy or anarchism is treated most centrally in the following romantic and futuristic novels: William Le Quex, *Strange Tales of a Nihilist* (1892); E. Douglas Fawcett, *Hartmann the Anarchist* (1893); Charles Gleig, *When All Men Starve* (1898); H. Barton Baker, *Robert Miner: Anarchist* (1902). The subject is treated with a little more seriousness in Joseph Hocking's *The Madness of David Baring* (1900), which is virtually a compendium of late-Victorian social issues.

26 David Christie Murray, *A Life's Atonement* (3 vols., 1880), I, 248–9.

27 *Ibid.*, III, 56.

28 Murray's most interesting book is *The Making of a Novelist* (1894), which contains details of his early contacts with working-class life, including a period as a private soldier in the Irish Guards. One passage about his portrayal of Bolter's Rents is relevant here: 'I thought the picture rather like at the time, within limits; but I never had the heart – or the stomach – to be a realist. Feebly as I dared to paint it, I had to reform it in fancy before the book was finished' (p. 90).

29 *The Notebooks of Henry James*, ed. F. O. Matthiessen and Kenneth B. Murdock (New York, 1961), 68.

30 *The Princess Casamassima* ('The Chiltern Library': John Lehmann, 1950), preface. All page references are to this edition of the novel.
31 *Henry James: The Middle Years 1884–1894* (1963), 116.
32 *Ibid.*, 107: *Notebooks*, 69.
33 Preface to *The Princess Casamassima*.
34 *Dickens and his Readers* (Princeton, 1955), 210.
35 *The Princess Casamassima*, 70.
36 *Ibid.*, 107.
37 *Ibid.*, 172.
38 *Ibid.*, 283.
39 *Ibid.*, 379.
40 *Ibid.*, 410.
41 *Ibid.*, 313.
42 *Politics and the Novel* ('New Left Books', 1961), 145.
43 *Henry James: The Middle Years*, 116.
44 *The Princess Casamassima*, 233.
45 *Ibid.*, 231.
46 *Henry James: The Middle Years*, 126.
47 *The Princess Casamassima*, 60–1.
48 *Ibid.*, 62.

3 *George Gissing*

1 Algernon and Ellen Gissing (ed.), *Letters of George Gissing to Members of his Family* (1927), 184.
2 *Ibid.*, 73.
3 *Ibid.*, 83.
4 *Ibid.*, 128–9.
5 *Ibid.*, 228.
6 *Ibid.*, 81.
7 *Ibid.*, 124.
8 *Ibid.*, 179.
9 *Ibid.*, 182.
10 *Ibid.*, 199.
11 *Ibid.*, 169.
12 *George Gissing* (1912), 61.
13 *Ibid.*, 46.
14 *Workers in the Dawn*, I, 1–9 *passim*.
15 *The Unclassed* (Ernest Benn Ltd., 1930), 95. All page references are to this edition.
16 *Thyrza* (Smith, Elder & Co., 1907), 37. All page references are to this edition.
17 *Ibid.*, 112.
18 *Ibid.*, 53.
19 *Ibid.*, 25.
20 Morley Roberts, *The Private Life of Henry Maitland* (The Richards Press, 1958), 239.
21 *Workers in the Dawn*, I, 141.

22   *Family Letters*, 79.
23   *Ibid.*, 53.
24   *Workers in the Dawn*, III, 170.
25   *Ibid.*, 371.
26   *Ibid.*, 190.
27   *Ibid.*, I, 108.
28   *Ibid.*, III, 370.
29   *Ibid.*, I, 149.
30   *Thyrza*, 14.
31   *The Unclassed*, 112.
32   *Ibid.*, 157.
33   *Ibid.*, 201.
34   *Thyrza*, 190.
35   *Ibid.*, 67–8.
36   *Family Letters*, 172.
37   *Demos* (Wayfarer's Library edition, n.d.), 30. All page references
are to this edition.
38   *Ibid.*
39   *Ibid.*, 38.
40   *Ibid.*, 39.
41   *Ibid.*
42   *Ibid.*, 44.
43   Jacob Korg, *George Gissing* (1965), 41.
44   *Ibid.* and *Workers in the Dawn*, III, 371.
45   *Family Letters*, 79.
46   *Charles Dickens*, 75.
47   *The Immortal Dickens* (1925), 209.
48   *Ibid.*, 241.
49   *Ibid.*, 50.
50   *Charles Dickens*, 88–9.
51   *Ibid.*, 91.
52   *Ibid.*, 206.
53   *Ibid.*, 64.
54   *Workers in the Dawn*, I, 103.
55   *Ibid.*, II, 292.
56   *Ibid.*, 304.
57   *The Unclassed*, 65.
58   *Demos*, 95.
59   *Ibid.*, 31.
60   *Ibid.*, 353.
61   *Thyrza*, 54.
62   *Ibid.*, 25.
63   *Ibid.*, 71.
64   *Ibid.*, 97.
65   *Ibid.*, 113.
66   *Ibid.*, 193.
67   *The Nether World*, I, 144.
68   *Ibid.*, 125.

69 *Ibid.*, 57-8.
70 *Ibid.*, 25.
71 *Ibid.*, II, 25.
72 *Ibid.*, I, 178.
73 *Ibid.*, II, 109.
74 *Ibid.*, I, 153-4.
75 *Ibid.*, 229.
76 *Ibid.*, 248.
77 *Ibid.*, II, 211-12.
78 *Ibid.*, 235.
79 *Ibid.*, III, 106.
80 *Ibid.*, I, 174-5.
81 *Ibid.*, 267.
82 *Ibid.*, 256.
83 *Ibid.*, 274.
84 *Ibid.*, 275.
85 *Ibid.*, 18.
86 *Ibid.*
87 Korg, *George Gissing*, 74-5.
88 *The Nether World*, III, 31.
89 *Ibid.*, I, 273.
90 *Ibid.*, II, 64.
91 *Ibid.*, III, 187.
92 *Ibid.*, 221.
93 *Ibid.*, 199.
94 *Ibid.*, 58.
95 *George Gissing: Grave Comedian* (Cambridge, Mass., 1954), 118.
96 *The Nether World*, III, 309-10.
97 The short stories on working-class life which Gissing published in the nineties are: 'Letty Coe', written in 1884 but first published in *Temple Bar* XCII (August 1891), repr. *Stories and Sketches* (1938); 'Lou and Liz', *The English Illustrated Magazine* X (August 1893), repr. *A Victim of Circumstances* (1927); 'Fleet-footed Hester', *Illustrated London News* CII (Xmas 1893), repr. *A Victim of Circumstances*; and 'The Day of Silence', *The National Review* XXII (December 1893), repr. *Human Odds and Ends* (1915). He had published one similar story much earlier: 'Phoebe', *Temple Bar* LXX (March 1884), repr. *Stories and Sketches*.
98 *Family Letters*, 169.
99 *Born in Exile* (1891), Part III, Ch. V.

4 *Walter Besant and the 'discovery' of the East End*

1 *Autobiography* (1902), 244.
2 *Ibid.*, 247-8.
3 *Ibid.*, 248-9.
4 *All Sorts and Conditions of Men* (Chatto & Windus, 1898) 330. All page references are to this edition.

5   *Ibid.*, preface.
6   *Autobiography*, 246.
7   *Ibid.*, 247.
8   *Children of Gibeon* (Chatto & Windus, 1887), 100. All page references are to this edition.
9   *Ibid.*, 279–80.
10 *All Sorts and Conditions of Men*, 200.
11 *Children of Gibeon*, 45.
12 *All Sorts and Conditions of Men*, 130.
13 *Children of Gibeon*, 187.
14 *Some Versions of Pastoral*, 11.
15 *Charles Dickens*, 10.
16 *Changes and Chances* (1923), 78.
17 *Victorian Cities*, 325.
18 See Besant, *East London* (1901), 127; Booth, *In Darkest England* (1890), 11; J. A. R. Pimlott, *Toynbee Hall* (1935), 6; Barry, *The New Antigone* (1887), III, 14; and Sims, *How the Poor Live and Horrible London* (1889), 114. For an interesting analysis of this kind of imagery see Eric Domville, 'Gloomy City or the Deeps of Hell', *East London Papers* VIII (December 1965), No. 2.
19 *As We Are and As We May Be* (1903), 248.
20 *My Apprenticeship* (1926), 154.
21 *All Sorts and Conditions of Men*, 18.
22 See Fred W. Boege, 'Sir Walter Besant: Novelist', Part 1, *Nineteenth-Century Fiction* X (March 1956), 266–9. Also the obituary of Sir Edmund Hay Currie, *East End News*, 13 May 1916. Many of Currie's friends took the opportunity afforded by his death to point out that he had played a more influential role than Besant in the founding of the People's Palace.
23 Besant, *As We Are and As We May Be*, 247.
24 Sir Baldwyn Leighton (ed.), *Letters and other Writings of Edward Denison* (1872), 8, 46, 29.
25 *Tales of Mean Streets* (1894), 7.
26 *The Parson in Socialism* (Leeds, 1910), 173.
27 Henrietta Barnett, *Canon Barnett* (2 vols., 1918), I, 68.
28 *The Poor in Great Cities* (1896), viii. Two years earlier than this George Bernard Shaw, returning from a visit to Italy, noted with characteristic cynical perception the secular nature of this religious revival: 'Religion was alive again, coming back upon men, even upon clergymen, with such power that not the Church of England itself could keep it out' (Preface to *Plays Pleasant* (1898)).
29 Frederick How, *Bishop Walsham How* (1899), 129.
30 See Stephen Mayor, *The Churches and the Labour Movement* (1967), 53–8.
31 Leonard Huxley, *Life and Letters of Thomas Henry Huxley* (2 vols., 1900), I, 16.
32 *Fors Clavigera*, *The Works of John Ruskin*, ed. E. T. Cook and Alexander Wedderburn (39 vols., 1907), XXVII, 15.

33 *Canon Barnett*, I, 152–5.
34 *Changes and Chances*, 79–80.
35 *My Life* (1928), 130.
36 *Canon Barnett*, I, 302.
37 Barnett, quoted Pimlott, 142.
38 *Canon Barnett*, II, 14.
39 A. F. Young and E. T. Ashton, *British Social Work in the Nineteenth Century* (1956), 233.
40 *Toynbee Hall*, 95.
41 *As We Are and As We May Be*, 51.
42 *Palace Journal* III, 16 January 1889, 850.
43 Quoted K. S. Inglis, *Churches and the Working Classes in Victorian England* (1963), 176.
44 *Ibid.*, 187.
45 *A Story Teller : Forty Years in London* (1923), 234.
46 Quoted Robin Odell, *Jack the Ripper in Fact and Fiction* (1965), 51.
47 Tom Cullen, *Autumn of Terror* (Fontana Books, 1966), 243.
48 Cole and Postgate, *The Common People*, 428.
49 *East London*, 6. The second volume of *Life and Labour*, which examined East End poverty in relation to that of London as a whole, appeared in 1891.
50 *Ibid.*, 591–2.
51 *Ibid.*, 32–62 *passim*.
52 *Life and Labour*, II, 25.
53 *East London*, 66.
54 Booth's criticism of the People's Palace was especially prophetic: 'Here then is a huge growth in the short time since the institute was opened. It must be said that there is about both method employed and results obtained a sort of inflation, unsound and dangerous. Hitherto success has justified the measures taken, but nevertheless a slower growth for such an institution is much to be preferred, and it has even yet to be proved whether the People's Palace is to be regarded as an example or as a warning' (*East London*, 119).
55 *Ibid.*, 160.
56 *Ibid.*, 113.
57 *Ibid.*, 146–9.
58 *Life and Labour*, II, 18–39 *passim*.
59 Sherwell argued that poverty of the kind found in certain areas of central London was potentially more subversive than that in the East End: 'There the colour of life, if deadly dull, is more even; it knows nothing of those violent extremes of luxury and want which fix irrevocably and hopelessly before the worker's eyes the gulf which divides the classes. Here are gifts and treasures innumerable – art, knowledge, beauty, wealth – but they are not for the poor' (*Life in West London*, 7).
60 *The Poor in Great Cities*, 2.

61   *Autobiography of a Fast Man* (1863), 86.
62   'One of the most popular pastimes of the long-ago sixties was
going the rounds of the dens of infamy in the East End' (*London in
the Sixties*, by 'One of the Old Brigade' [Captain Donald Shaw]
(1908), 91). Shaw gives an interesting upper-class view of the
changing pattern of London's night life: 'So extensive indeed has been
the transformation, that, if any night-bird of those naughty days were
suddenly exhumed, and let loose in Soho, he would assuredly wander
into a church in his search of a popular resort, and having come to
scoff, might remain to pray, and so unwittingly fall into the
goody-goody ways that make up our present monotonous existence'
(*ibid.*, 1). Besant makes the same point in *All Sorts and Conditions of
Men*. When Angela Messenger tells Lord Jocelyn that she lives in
Whitechapel, he murmurs 'Do you belong to that remarkable part of
London?' Remarkable because he associates it in his mind with his
'Corinthian days' when he had often 'repaired to Seven Dials to see
noble sportsmen *chez* Ben Caunt, and rat-killing and cock-fighting,
and many other beautiful forms of sport' (p. 170). The violence of
working-class life in the mid-Victorian East End is captured superbly
by Arthur Morrison in *The Hole in the Wall* (1902).
63   *My Apprenticeship* (1926), 298.
64   E. Beresford Chancellor, *The London of Charles Dickens* (1924),
foreword.
65   *Oliver Twist*, Ch. XIII.
66   *Sketches by Boz*, Ch. XXII.
67   *In Strange Company* (1873), 180-1.
68   *Robert Elsmere*, Ch. XXXII.

5   *French naturalism and English working-class fiction*

1   'The Limits of Realism in Fiction', *Questions at Issue* (1893),
152-3.
2   'Zola: The Man and His Work', *The Savoy* I (January 1896), 74.
3   'Reticence in Literature', *The Yellow Book* II (July 1894), 262.
4   W. C. Frierson, 'The English Controversy over Realism in
Fiction 1885-1895', *PMLA* XLIII (June 1928), 548. See also W. C.
Frierson, *The English Novel in Transition 1885-1940* (New York,
1965); Clarence R. Decker, 'Zola's Literary Reputation in England',
PMLA XLIX (December 1934); *The Victorian Conscience* (New
York, 1952).
5   'Zola's Literary Reputation in England', 1149.
6   Quoted F. W. J. Hemmings, *Émile Zola* (2nd ed. rev., Oxford,
1966), 112, n. 1.
7   'Germinie Lacerteux', *Mes Haines* (Paris, 1866), 81. Zola later
made the same point more explicitly: 'In *Germinie Lacerteux* they
were the first to study the common people of Paris, depicting the
suburbs and the desolate landscape of the outlying areas, daring to
say everything in a refined language which gave true life to people and

things' ('Naturalism in the Theatre' (1880), Becker (ed.), *Documents of Modern Literary Realism*, 206). The key qualifying phrase is 'in a refined language'. It was this more than anything else that Zola was to challenge in *L'Assommoir*.

8   Quoted Hemmings, 110.
9   Preface to *L'Assommoir*.
10 Quoted Hemmings, 85.
11 *L'Assommoir*, preface.
12 Quoted Hemmings, 121.
13 See George H. Ford, *Dickens and His Readers*, 35–43; K. J. Fielding, *Charles Dickens* (2nd ed. rev., 1965), 32–46.
14 *L'Assommoir*, preface.
15 'The Experimental Novel', Becker (ed.), *Documents of Modern Literary Realism*, 165–81 *passim*.
16 Hemmings, 151–2.
17 'The Limits of Realism in Fiction', *Questions at Issue*, 144; see also Robert Gorham Davis, 'The Sense of the Real in English Fiction', *Comparative Literature* III (Summer 1951), 200–17.
18 'Our adversaries alone play us this villainous trick of only speaking of our "Germinie Lacerteux" and our "Assommoirs", keeping silent about our other works. We must protest, we must show the general whole of our efforts.' Zola goes on to point out that he has 'undertaken to show in a series of novels the picture of a whole epoch'; and assures his readers that *L'Assommoir* 'will remain a single note in the midst of twenty other volumes' ('Les Frères Zemganno', *The Experimental Novel and Other Essays*, trans. Belle M. Sherman (New York, 1893), 269).
19 *Confessions of a Young Man* (The Traveller's Library, 1928), 75.
20 'What is a Realist?', *The New Review* XVI (March 1897), 327–8.
21 Ian Gregor and Brian Nicholas, *The Moral and the Story* (1962), 99.
22 *Ibid.*, 107–8.
23 *Family Letters*, 77; Korg, *George Gissing*, 44.
24 *The Unclassed*, 201.
25 While on holiday in Italy in 1889 Gissing attended a lecture on Zola and was very amused by the lecturer's devotion to his subject; 'He glorified Zola, as an example of all that is noble in the literary life, and worked himself up to an extravagance of passion. I laughed much. As I was coming out, I heard someone call the lecture *"potente"*' (*The Letters of George Gissing to Eduard Bertz 1887–1903*, ed. Arthur C. Young (1961), 50).
26 *The English Novel in Transition*, 85–106.
27 *English Criticism of the Novel 1865–1900* (Oxford, 1965), 5.
28 *Ibid.*, 26.
29 *The Theory of the Novel in England, 1850–1870* (1959), 149

6   *Rudyard Kipling and cockney archetypes*

1   Frierson, *The English Novel in Transition*, 86; Jane Findlater, 'The Slum Movement in Fiction', *Stones from a Glass House* (1904), 79.
2   Stang, *The Theory of the Novel in England*, 177.
3   E. J. Milliken, *'Arry Ballads* (1892), 1.
4   *The History of Punch* (1895), 379.
5   Charles Carrington, *Rudyard Kipling* (1955), 147.
6   'Mr. Kipling's Stories' (1891), in Eliot L. Gilbert (ed.), *Kipling and the Critics* (1965), 4.
7   'The Young Kipling' (1891), *ibid.*, 16–17.
8   *Rudyard Kipling*, 105–6.
9   'Mr. Kipling's Stories', *Kipling and the Critics*, 4.
10   'The Madness of Private Ortheris', *Plain Tales from the Hills* (Macmillan's Uniform Edition), 286–96 *passim*. Unless otherwise indicated, all subsequent page references to Kipling's prose works are to the Uniform Edition.
11   'Soldiers Three', in Andrew Rutherford (ed.), *Kipling's Mind and Art* (Edinburgh, 1964), 235.
12   Noel Annan, 'Kipling's Place in the History of Ideas', *ibid.*, 102. Kipling's attitude towards the French naturalists was as ambiguous as Gissing's; he seems to have read them avidly in private and mocked them in public, or rather mocked the readers who took them too seriously. The problems involved in talking of the French naturalists exerting a direct influence upon Kipling are examined by Louis L. Cornell, *Kipling in India* (1966), 119–21.
13   *Wee Willie Winkie*, 332.
14   *Ibid.*, 329.
15   'On Greenhow Hill', *Life's Handicap*, 71–96 *passim*.
16   *The Light that Failed*, 34.
17   'The Last of the Stories', *Abaft the Funnel* (New York, 1909), 318.
18   Carrington, *Rudyard Kipling*, 140.
19   'In Partibus', *Abaft the Funnel*, 193–6.
20   *Something of Myself* (1937), 56.
21   'One View of the Question', *Many Inventions*, 73.
22   *Something of Myself*, 79.
23   *Ibid.*, 81.
24   'The Record of Badalia Herodsfoot', *Many Inventions*, 295–326 *passim*.
25   *The Immortal Dickens*, 29.
26   *Abaft the Funnel*, 267.
27   *Ibid.*, 273.
28   *Rudyard Kipling*, 351.
29   *Life's Handicap*, 68.
30   *Something of Myself*, 81.
31   As the approximate date of 'Dawn Their Eyes' suggests, 'Sam Hall' belongs properly to the Song and Supper Rooms (the song was

T

especially popular at the notorious Cyder Cellars), but W. G. Ross
went on to become one of the early stars of music hall. See W.
Mcqueen-Pope, *The Melodies Linger On* (1950), 47-9.

32 See M. Willson Disher, *Victorian Song* (1955), 125-37.

33 McQueen-Pope, *The Melodies Linger On*, 66.

34 E.g. J. W. Rowley, Walter Laburnam and Hyram Travers. See
William Matthews, *Cockney Past and Present* (1938), 94; Harold Scott,
The Early Doors (1946), 214.

35 Matthews, *Cockney Past and Present*, 92.

36 *A Choice of Kipling's Verse* (1941), 18.

37 H. Chance Newton, *Idols of the Halls* (1928), 111.

38 J. B. Booth, *Old Pink 'Un Days* (1924), 338.

39 *Ibid.*, 339-40.

40 J. B. Booth, *Pink Parade* (1933), 138.

41 J. B. Booth, *The Days We Knew* (1943), 59.

42 Transcribed from a gramophone record, *The Great Days of Music
Hall*, EMI, MFP 1146. Coborn's act interestingly bridged the old and
new styles. Like the earlier singers he alternated between coster and
heavy swell songs (his most famous number being 'The Man Who
Broke the Bank at Monte Carlo'), but through his friendship with
Albert Chevalier he had access to the new-style coster numbers.

43 Albert Chevalier, *A Record by Himself* (1895), 121. Symmons's
famous phrase first appears in *Black and White*, 18 June 1892.

44 *Mr. Albert Chevalier's Humorous Songs* (1894).

45 *Ibid.*

46 *Ibid.*

47 *Star*, 2 May 1891, quoted Chevalier, *A Record by Himself*, 116-17.

48 *Morning Leader*, 30 May 1893, *ibid.*, 123.

49 *Rudyard Kipling* (1900), 29-30.

50 'Credat Judaeus', *Schoolboy Lyrics* (Lahore, 1881), 38-40. Other
poems in this collection show the young Kipling's interest in the circus
and theatre, especially 'Overheard' and 'From the Wings'.

51 J. B. Booth, *The Days We Knew*, 27-35 *passim*. I have been unable
to find an exact date for 'Kafoozelum' which Kipling so admired.
From this correspondence it appears that Booth himself did not know
the song as at one point he seems to have asked Kipling for the words
(p. 34). In *Pink Parade* (p. 164), Booth lists 'Kafoozalum' with songs
of the 'old army'. 'The Village that Voted the Earth was Flat' (1913),
A Diversity of Creatures, 161-213, is Kipling's most explicit examination
of the emotional power of music-hall songs. This story also contains
Kipling's tribute to Nellie Farren: '"Did we love her?" I answered. "'If
the earth and the sky and the sea' – There were three million of us,
Dal, and we worshipped her"' (p. 187).

52 When referring to this passage J. B. Booth makes the same point.
'"Observed" is the vital descriptive word; the old songs at their best
were "observed", and, within their limits, which were the limits of the
old halls, the singers were indubitable artists' (*The Days We Knew*, 29).

53 Kipling's admiration for the music hall was reciprocal; many of

his poems were 'performed' in the halls. Charles Coborn was very proud of the fact that he was the first music-hall artist to sing 'Tommy'. See *The Man Who Broke the Bank* (1928), 203. There was also a reaction against Kipling in the music hall. Albert Chevalier, angered at the way Kipling's songs were used to inspire militarism during the Boer War, wrote a parody of 'The Absent Minded Beggar' which contained the lines: 'Through the roll of the drums hear the cry from the slums; and pay! pay! pay!' (Chevalier, *Before I Forget* (1901), 166–7).

54 *Pickwick Papers*, Ch. XVI.
55 'In the Matter of a Private', *Soldiers Three*, 77.
56 'Tommy', *Barrack Room Ballads*.

7 *Arthur Morrison and the tone of violence*

1 'Arthur Morrison', *The Bookman* VII (January 1895), 107.
2 For Morrison's early years and his association with the People's Palace, see P. J. Keating, 'Arthur Morrison: A Biographical Study', introduction to *A Child of the Jago* (1969).
3 'A Street', *Macmillan's Magazine* LXIV (October 1891), 460–3 *passim*. By the time this article was republished as the introduction to *Tales of Mean Streets*, Morrison's style had grown even more terse. The quotations given here are from the original. In the *Mean Streets* introduction Morrison also significantly omitted a paragraph containing the sentence: 'A Palace of Delight was once set in the midst of this street, but Commissioners brandished their pens over it and it became a Polytechnic Institution.'
4 *Ibid.*, 462.
5 Interview with Morrison, *Daily News*, 12 December 1896.
6 *Spectator* LXXIV (16 March 1895), 360.
7 'What is a Realist?', *New Review* XVI (March 1897), 326–36.
8 *The Cockney* (1953), 39.
9 Introduction to Robert Tressell, *The Ragged Trousered Philanthropists* (Panther Books, 1965), 8.
10 *Daily News* interview.
11 'What is a Realist?', 328.
12 *Ibid.*, 330.
13 *Tales of Mean Streets*, 37.
14 *Ibid.*, 32.
15 *Ibid.*, 36–7.
16 *Ibid.*, 45–6.
17 *Spectator* letter.
18 See the *Daily News* interview, and 'The Methods of Mr. Morrison', *Academy* L (12 December 1896), 531.
19 See T. Harper Smith, 'A Child of the Jago', *East London Papers* II, (April 1959), No. 1.
20 *Life in Darkest London* (1891), 14.
21 *A Story of Shoreditch* (1896), 98–9.

22 In a letter to the *Fortnightly Review* LXVII (February 1897), 324.

23 *Daily News* interview.

24 Cf. Jay's methods of dealing with his criminal parishioners with those of Father Sturt: *Life in Darkest London*, 35–43, *A Child of the Jago*, Ch. XIV. Also Jay's and Morrison's treatment of gang feuds: *A Story of Shoreditch*, Ch. VI, and *A Child of the Jago*, Ch. IV.

25 *A Child of the Jago* (1896), 1.

26 *Ibid.*, 2, 5, 9, 78.

27 See Jane Findlater, 'The Slum Movement in Fiction', *Stones from a Glass House*, 67–73: Robert Blatchford, 'On Realism', *My Favourite Books* (1901), 222–53 *passim*.

28 *A Child of the Jago*, 112.

29 *Ibid.*, 20.

30 *The New Fiction and Other Essays* (1897), 13. It was the title essay of this collection, challenging the 'realism' of Morrison's Jago portrait, that forced him to publish his defensive article 'What is a Realist?'.

31 *A Child of the Jago*, 51–2.

32 *Ibid.*, 47.

33 *Ibid.*, 141.

34 *Ibid.*, 4.

35 *Ibid.*, 313.

36 *The Summing Up* (1938), 166.

37 *Liza of Lambeth*, Collected Edition of Maugham's Works (1934), 1. All page references are to this edition.

38 *Ibid.*, 5.

39 'Badalia Herodsfoot', *Many Inventions*, 296.

40 *A Child of the Jago*, 281. A similar phrase had been used earlier by Jay: 'only married, not churched' (*Life in Darkest London*, 110).

41 *Liza of Lambeth*, 89.

42 *Ibid.*, 114.

43 *Ibid.*, 109.

44 *Ibid.*, 134.

45 *Ibid.*, 145–6.

46 *Ibid.*, 160.

47 *Ibid.*, 168.

48 *Ibid.*, 30.

49 *Ibid.*, 42–3.

50 *Wine on the Lees* (1899), 58.

51 *Ibid.*, 65.

52 *Ibid.*, 101.

53 *No. 5 John Street* (1899), 11.

54 *Ibid.*, 28–9.

55 *Ibid.*, 31.

56 K. Douglas King, 'Lil: an Idyll of the Borough', *The Child who will Never Grow Old* (1898), 143–56 *passim*.

57 The extreme crudity of Nell's spelling is a further example of Edith Ostlere misunderstanding an important aspect of the slum novels. The use of phonetics to indicate illiteracy rather than the sound of a

voice has a long ancestry in fiction, though the late-Victorian novelists
in the main rarely used phonetics for this purpose. Gissing's
explanation why he does not faithfully reproduce the letter that Carrie
Mitchell sends to Arthur Golding, is particularly relevant: 'The
handwriting was extremely bad, so bad in places as to be almost
undecipherable, and the orthographical errors were abundant. I have
chosen to correct the latter fault, lest the letter should excite
amusement' (*Workers in the Dawn*, II, 285–6).
58   Edith Ostlere, 'Any Fla-ars or Po-t Ferns', *From Seven Dials*
(1898), 1–33 *passim*.

8   The Cockney School

1   Henry Nevinson, *Changes and Chances* (1923), 117.
2   *Neighbours of Ours* (Bristol, 1895), 285.
3   *Ibid.*, 5–6.
4   *Ibid.*, 6.
5   'The St. George of Rochester', *Neighbours of Ours*, 45–85 *passim*.
6   'Sissero's Return', *Neighbours of Ours*, 114–50 *passim*.
7   Quoted Arthur St John Adcock, *The Glory that was Grub Street*
(1928), 276.
8   *Harry the Cockney* (1913), 2.
9   *The Glory that was Grub Street*, 270–6.
10   *Slings and Arrows* (1916), 179–81.
11   *Charles Dickens: The Apostle of the People* (1908), 52.
12   *The Charles Dickens Originals* (1912), 206.
13   *Charles Dickens: The Apostle of the People*, 96–8.
14   William Pett Ridge, *A Breaker of Laws* (1900), 133.
15   Edwin Pugh, *Mother-Sister* (1900), 283.
16   *Ibid.*, 1.
17   'The Slum Movement in Fiction', *Stones from a Glass House*, 85–6.
18   In the nineties Jacobs published four books: *Many Cargoes* (1896),
The Skipper's Wooing (1897), *Sea Urchins* (1898) and *A Master of
Craft* (1900), and many further books in the twentieth century. His
early stories of bargees and lightermen are contrived, superficial and of
little interest in the present context, though some of his later work
deserves more attention than it has so far received; his humour, at this
stage of his development, is inferior Jerome K. Jerome.
19   'The Slum Movement in Fiction', 85.
20   William Pett Ridge, *Mord Em'ly* (1898), 24.
21   *Ibid.*, 54.
22   *Ibid.*, 33.
23   See Raymond Williams, *Culture and Society*, Part III, Ch. 6.
24   *Outside the Radius* (1899), 7–8.
25   *The Hooligan Nights*, vi.
26   Edwin Pugh, *A Street in Suburbia* (1895), 66.
27   *Polly of Parker's Rents* (1899), 180–1.
28   *Mother-Sister*, 201.

29 *Ibid.*, 231.
30 *Mord Em'ly*, 15.
31 *Ibid.*, 56.
32 William Pett Ridge, *A Son of the State* (1900), 7–8.
33 *The Hooligan Nights*, 62–3.
34 Edwin Pugh, *Mother-Sister*, 33.
35 *Ibid.*, 97–8.
36 William Pett Ridge, *Mord Em'ly*, 20.
37 *The Hooligan Nights*, 176.
38 *A Son of the State*, 110–11.
39 *Ibid.*, 231.
40 In *King Circumstance* (1898), 153–62.
41 Annie Wakeman, *The Autobiography of a Charwoman* (1900), 108.
42 The way that the Cockney novelists unconsciously employ the structure of their novels to play down the political power now possessed by the working classes, can be usefully compared with Gissing's attitude. Gissing reasoned that the advent of democracy had given novelists the right to criticize the working classes; the right to be, in short, anti-democratic. In this he is similar to W. H. Mallock whose trilogy, *A Human Document* (1892), *The Heart of Life* (1895) and *The Individualist* (1899), is the most explicit statement of the anti-democratic attitude in late-Victorian fiction.
43 Annie Wakeman, *The Autobiography of a Charwoman*, 16.

9   Industrialism, urbanism and class conflict

1 Disraeli, *Sybil*, Bk. II, Ch. X.
2 *Bleak House*, Ch. XVI.
3 *Ibid.*, Ch. VII.
4 *Ibid.*, Ch. LXIII.
5 *Little Dorrit*, Ch. XII.
6 *Ibid.*, Ch. XXIII.
7 *Ibid.*, Ch. XII.
8 *Ibid.*, Ch. XXV.
9 *Illustrations of Political Economy*, Vol. III, Ch. X.
10 A. B. Hopkins, *Elizabeth Gaskell: Her Life and Work* (1952), 81.
11 Louis Cazamian, *Le Roman Social en Angleterre 1830–1850* (Paris, 1903), 357.
12 *Alton Locke*, Ch. XLI.
13 *Felix Holt*, Ch. XXVII.
14 *Ibid.*, Ch. XLV.
15 'Address to Working Men, by Felix Holt', Thomas Pinney (ed.), *Essays of George Eliot* (1963), 416.
16 'The Natural History of German Life', *ibid.*, 269.
17 *Sybil*, Bk. V, Ch. 1.
18 *Ibid.*
19 *Mary Barton*, Ch. XVI.
20 *Helen Fleetwood*, Ch. XX.

21 *Mary Barton*, Ch. III.
22 *Ibid.*, Ch. XV.
23 *Ibid.*, Ch. XVI.
24 *Sunshine and Shadow: A Tale of the Nineteenth Century*, published serially in the *Northern Star*, beginning 31 March 1849.
25 Thomas Frost, *The Secret*, Ch. IX, published serially in *National Instructor*, beginning 25 May 1850.
26 George Bernard Shaw, introduction to *Hard Times* (1912).
27 Hall Caine, 'Memoir of W. E. Tirebuck', published as a preface to Tirebuck's *'Twixt God and Mammon* (1903); John Hogben, foreword to Tirebuck's *Poems* (1912). Some further information is contained in Hall Caine, *My Story* (1908).
28 *Miss Grace of All Souls* (1895), 195.
29 *Ibid.*, 3–4.
30 *Ibid.*, 16.
31 *Ibid.*, 24.
32 *Ibid.*, 4.
33 *Ibid.*, 148.
34 *Ibid.*, 341.
35 Preface to the American edition of *The Condition of the Working-Classes in England* (1892), in *Marx and Engels on Britain* (Moscow, 1962), 31.
36 Engels, letter to E. Bernstein, 22 August 1889, *Marx and Engels on Britain*, 566–7.
37 E.g. Grant Allen, *Philistia* (1885); Olive Birrell, *Love in a Mist* (1900); and Gertrude Dix, *The Image Breakers* (1900). Despite the authors' familiarity with Socialist ideas, these novels are best classified as working-class romances. A more light-hearted, and readable, novel in the same vein is Bernard Shaw's *An Unsocial Socialist* (written 1883). Two novels by James Adderley which treat of upper-class conversion to Christian Socialism are also best mentioned here: *Stephen Remarx: The Story of a Venture in Ethics* (1893), and *Paul Mercer: A Story of Repentance Amongst Millions* (1898).
38 *A More Excellent Way* (1888), 166.
39 *Ibid.*, 189.
40 *Ibid.*, 277.
41 See above, Ch. I (I).
42 *In Darkest London* (1890), 189–90.
43 *Out of Work* (1888), 2.
44 *Ibid.*, 1, 28.
45 *Ibid.*, 6, 7–8.
46 *In Darkest London*, 45.
47 *Out of Work*, 106. This attitude Margaret Harkness shared with the novelists of the Cockney School. The working-class love scenes in their novels do not almost inevitably lead to brute violence as they do in Gissing, Morrison and Maugham, but the Cockney novelists do occasionally place strange interpretations on the horse-play of working-class courtship. In a short story by Edwin Pugh, a young

factory girl on holiday tells her middle-class boyfriend that she has never been kissed: 'No. The blo- young men I know don't – 't ain't much in their line. We 'as different ways, you see. Some 'as one way, some 'as anuvver. We go in for fumpin' more' ('Eurus: An Episode', *King Circumstance*, 23). Mord Em'ly also is embarrassed when a young man tries to kiss her. She pushes him away saying that she 'ain't particular keen on it' (William Pett Ridge, *Mord Em'ly*, 251).
48   Cf. 'The public houses that flanked its entrance vomited forth their cargoes of depravity and vice, and the air rang with the oaths of women who sell their babies for two shillings or eighteenpence' (*In Darkest London*, 17). Margaret Harkness was, however, aware that these people constituted a minority: 'People who live in Shoreditch, or St. George's-in-the-East, are apt to be confounded with their poorer neighbours by the uninitiated' (*Out of Work*, 42).

10   The phonetic representation of Cockney

1   *The Nether World*, I, 94.
2   Lucien Leclaire, *A General Analytical Bibliography of the Regional Novelists of the British Isles 1800–1950* (Paris, 1954), 12. See also Leclaire's companion volume to his bibliography, *Le Roman Régionaliste dans Les Îles Britanniques 1800–1950* (Paris, 1954), 17–44.
3   It is, of course, easy to find regional and dialect types in drama and fiction before the nineteenth century. What is new about the regional novel is that the characters are seen mainly in relation to a localized environment. According to Leclaire it is Maria Edgeworth to whom 'revient l'honneur d'avoir donné en prose ce que Crabbe produisait en vers' (*Le Roman Régionaliste*, 22). Lionel Stevenson makes the same point, that *Castle Rackrent* (1800) is 'the first real local-colour story imbued with the distinctive customs and outlook of a particular region' (*The English Novel: A Panorama* (1960), 180). Writers on the cockney have also claimed for him a long ancestry in literature. See William Matthews, *Cockney Past and Present*, 1–61; Julian Franklyn, *The Cockney*, 3–26. The main difference here is one of class. Walker's *Critical Pronouncing Dictionary* (1791) defines the cockney as 'A native of London, any effeminate, low citizen'. The strange word is 'effeminate'; but this can be explained by the etymology of 'cockney'. See Franklyn, 47–52.
4   There are, however, important exceptions to this general rule. The substitute working-class hero is an obvious example, but a working-class woman who has a central love interest in the novel may also, against all claims of realism, speak Standard English, as do Mary Barton and Lizzie Hexam.
5   In 1909 an L.C.C. conference on the teaching of English in elementary schools decided that 'The Cockney mode of speech, with its unpleasant twang, is a modern corruption without legitimate credentials, and is unworthy of being the speech of any person in the capital city of the Empire'. This conclusion was challenged by

Mackenzie Macbride, who, in *London's Dialect* (1910), set out to show
that 'though the Cockney dialect has been accused of being a workhouse
child of unknown parentage it can produce its birth certificates for a
thousand years, certificates of which the oldest member of the House
of Lords would be proud' (pp. 29–30). Many later writers, including
William Matthews and Julian Franklyn, have endeavoured to prove the
same. Although the issue has never been satisfactorily resolved, most
philologists today would in the main agree with Ernest Weekley:
'There are probably still many people who believe that all dialect,
whether of the rustic labourer or the old-fashioned Cockney, is
"corrupt English." There are certainly very few who realize that the
exact opposite is the case, and that "standard English" is "corrupt
dialect"' ('Mrs. Gamp and the King's English', *Adjectives and Other
Words* (1930), 139–40).

  6   *East London*, 97.
  7   *The Nether World*, II, 95.
  8   *Ibid.*, III, 5. That Gissing regarded lower-class speech as corrupt
'Standard' can be seen in a letter he wrote while on holiday in Italy:
'As regards the language, there is a serious difficulty. With educated
people I can make myself understood, and can understand perfectly
well; but then one rarely has to do with a man who can be called
educated, and the masses of the people speak an unintelligible jargon
. . . they cut off nearly all grammatical terminations, and almost
always a final *o* or *i* . . .' (*Letters to Eduard Bertz*, 15).

  9   *As We Are and As We May Be*, 32.
  10   Andrew Mearns and W. C. Preston, *The Bitter Cry of Outcast
London* (1883), 3.
  11   *How the Poor Live and Horrible London*, 117.
  12   Pugh, *King Circumstance*, 216; Maugham, *Liza of Lambeth*, 8;
Kipling, 'In the Matter of a Private', *Soldiers Three*, 77; 'The
Incarnation of Krishna Mulvaney', *Life's Handicap*, 6.
  13   Morrison, *Tales of Mean Streets* and *A Child of the Jago, passim*;
Kipling, 'The Drums of the Fore and Aft', *Wee Willie Winkie*, 334;
'The Record of Badalia Herodsfoot', *Many Inventions*, 304; Nevinson,
Neighbours of Ours, 73; Pugh, *Man of Straw*, 68; Pett Ridge, *Mord
Em'ly*, 202. In *Put Yourself in His Place* (1870) Charles Reade makes
great play with what he calls 'Dash Dialect'.
  14   The slum novelists of the nineties used less slang than might have
been expected. The reason for this is probably that the very strong
'slang' tradition in the English novel related primarily to the criminal
classes, although, following the example of Egan, many mid-Victorian
novelists (e.g. Ainsworth, Disraeli, Lytton, L. Oliphant) showed that
each of the classes possessed its own slang terms. See Eric Partridge,
Slang Today and Yesterday (1933).
  15   Dickens's use of phonetics in this respect is traditional. They are
used either to emphasize meaningless expletives (e.g. Mr Mantalini,
'demd', 'demmit'); or to exaggerate an aristocratic drawl (e.g. Sir
Frederick Verisopht, 'pla-an', 'deyvle'). Dickens also sometimes

phoneticizes specific words used by characters who are not working class but who play mean or vicious roles in their novels. Wackford Squeers talks of 'elbers' meaning 'elbows' and also occasionally transposes 'v' and 'w'; and Uriah Heep's inability to manage the aspirate on 'humble' is a similar example.

16 *Martin Chuzzlewit*, Ch. XXV.

17 'Mrs. Gamp and the King's English', *Adjectives and Other Words*, 145.

18 *Pickwick Papers*, Ch. XXIII.

19 *Bleak House*, Ch. XLVI.

20 *Pickwick Papers*, Ch. XXXIV.

21 Charles Yellowplush is a footman and in the class structure of Victorian England would hardly have been considered working class. Like 'Arry' he is given a cockney accent because he is 'low' or 'vulgar'.

22 Dickens was more attracted to malapropisms than to alternative spellings of the kind Thackeray uses. Both techniques are employed to inform the reader that the user is uneducated, but the malapropism enabled Dickens to establish (as he does in the v/w example from *Pickwick Papers* quoted earlier) a genial tone; 'But I will say, and I would if I was led a Martha to the Stakes for it', Mrs Gamp, *Martin Chuzzlewit*, Ch. XXVI.

23 Jorrocks is presented to the reader as a 'city Sportsman' and a 'smoke-dried cit' who is a 'substantial grocer in St. Botolph's Lane, with an elegant residence in Great Coram Street, Russell Square' (i.e. he works in the East End of London and lives in the West). His money raises him above the working classes but his vulgarity prevents him from rising very high. The lasting symbol of his vulgarity, of which he is blissfully unconscious, is his cockney accent. Jorrocks is often considered to have been the original model for Mr Pickwick, but in some respects he is nearer to Sam Weller: 'Well, sir, a werry pleasant plan too, especially for the innkeeper – and all werry right for a gentleman of fortune like you. My motto, however, is "Waste not, want not," and my wife's father's motto was "Wilful waste brings woeful want," and I likes to have my money's worth' (*Jorrocks' Jaunts and Jollities*, Ch. VI).

24 E. J. Milliken, *'Arry Ballads* (1892), 12.

25 'English and American Dialects' (1900), *Three Plays for Puritans* (Standard Edition, 1931), 292. Shaw did not feel, however, that his debt to Tuer was extensive. He later wrote that he became interested in phonetics at the end of the 1870s and that his masters were Alexander J. Ellis and Henry Sweet (preface to *Pygmalion* (1912), 195).

26 *The Kawkneigh Awlminek* (1883), 2. It is by no means clear when exactly cockneys stopped transposing v/w. Almost all novelists writing before 1880 use it extensively: after this date it hardly appears in fiction. This would seem to support the views of Tuer and Shaw that it had survived only as a literary convention. As a complete change in working-class speech patterns in such a short time is unlikely, it is reasonable to assume that Dickens kept alive a speech

characteristic that was dying out in real life. Walker thought the v/w transposition a 'blemish of the first magnitude' and stressed that it was a common fault among Londoners, 'and those not always of the lower order' (*The Critical Pronouncing Dictionary* (1791)). H. C. Wyld has claimed that although the v/w transposition is as old as the fifteenth century, it was not limited to London (*A History of Modern Colloquial English* (3rd ed., Oxford, 1956), 180). Many writers have noted that while the habit had largely disappeared by the late-Victorian period, it was still possible to hear it used by older cockneys. See Ernest Weekley, 'Mrs. Gamp and the King's English', *Adjectives and Other Words*, 149; William Matthews, *Cockney Past and Present*, 181.

27   *Thenks awf'lly* (1890), vii. Tuer is obviously referring here to the Yellowplush-'Arry tradition. Dickens knew perfectly well when and when not to use the aspirate: 'In England, Angleterre, England, We Aspirate the "H" and We Say "Horse." Only our Lower Classes say "Orse!"' (Mr Podsnap, *Our Mutual Friend*, Ch. XI). The addition of aspirates is justifiable in certain circumstances; when, for instance, the cockney is embarrassed, trying to impress, being pompous or mocking the upper classes. Thackeray did not understand this, Kipling did: '"You har my noble preservers," sez 'e. "You har a honour to the British Harmy," sez 'e' ('The Three Musketeers', *Plain Tales from the Hills*, 75).

28   Tuer, *The Kawkneigh Awlminek*, 32.

29   Matthews, *Cockney Past and Present*, 65.

30   Joseph Saxe, *Bernard Shaw's Phonetics* (1936).

31   Andrew Tuer, *Old London Street Cries* (1885), 30–1, 73–4. Liaison and elision, when employed consistently, produce a sound impression which is continuous and not bound to the enunciation of individual words. This receives little attention in earlier working-class fiction, but becomes the dominant feature of Tuer's Cockney. One striking example is in the pronunciation of names. Tuer instances Emma Ran (Emma Ann), *Old London Street Cries*, 50. Other examples from fiction are Gissing's Pennyloaf (Penelope), *The Nether World*; and Morrison's Lizerunt (Elizabeth Hunt), *Tales of Mean Streets*.

32   E. J. Milliken, *'Arry Ballads*, 2.

33   'The Incarnation of Krishna Mulvaney' (1889), *Life's Handicap*, 20.

34   'My Lord the Elephant' (1892), *Many Inventions*, 48.

35   'The Record of Badalia Herodsfoot', *Many Inventions*, 299.

36   *How the Poor Live* (1883), 21.

37   *Out of Work*, 110.

38   *Workers in the Dawn*, I, 154.

39   *Ibid.*, 16–17.

40   See, for instance, *The Nether World*, II, 4. In a speech of ten lines only one word ('ijiot') is not spelt in the normal Standard English manner.

41   'Lou and Liz' (1893), *Victim of Circumstances* (1927), 226–7.

42   *Mr. Sprouts: His Opinions* (1867), 7.

43   *No. 5 John Street*, 216.
44   'Squire Napper', *Tales of Mean Streets*, 224.
45   *Liza of Lambeth*, 77.
46   *The Hooligan Nights*, 190.
47   *Neighbours of Ours*, 144–5.
48   *Mother-Sister*, 29.
49   *Ibid.*, 35.
50   Harry Lander, *Lucky Bargee* (1898), 135.
51   J. Dodsworth Brayshaw, 'Satan', *Slum Silhouettes* (1898), 1.
52   *The City of the World* (1912), 69.
53   'Mr. H. G. Wells is the only author with whom I am acquainted who seems to realise this. His public-school men talk of 'i'on bahs' meaning 'iron-bars' (*Charles Dickens: The Apostle of the People*, 279–80). Bernard Shaw also argued that if the cockney's accent was to be treated phonetically then it was only just to treat upper-class characters in the same manner. See 'English and American Dialects', *Three Plays for Puritans*.
54   For a perceptive analysis of the class factor involved in the rise to pre-eminence of the Standard English accent, see Raymond Williams, 'The Growth of Standard English', *The Long Revolution* (1961).

Bibliography

1 English fiction

The dates given in this section are those of first publication. Where the edition quoted in the text is of a later date this has been indicated in the first footnote reference.

Ackworth, John, *Clog Shop Chronicles*, 1896
Adcock, Arthur St John, *East End Idylls*, 1897
  In the Image of God, 1898
Adderley, James, *Paul Mercer*, 1898
  Stephen Remarx, 1893
Ainsworth, W. Harrison, *Jack Sheppard*, 1839
Allen, Grant, *Philistia*, 1885
Baker, H. Barton, *Margaret Grey*, 1896
Balfour, Clara, L., *Lyndon the Outcast*, 1883
  Scrub: or The Workhouse Boy's First Start in Life, 1860
  Toil and Trust: or The Life Story of Patty the Workhouse Girl, 1860
Barlee, Ellen, *Locked Out: A Tale of the Strike*, 1874
Barrie, James, *Sentimental Tommy*, 1896
Barry, William, *The New Antigone*, 1887
Besant, Walter, *The Alabaster Box*, 1900
  All Sorts and Conditions of Men, 1882
  Children of Gibeon, 1886
Birrell, Olive, *Love in a Mist*, 1900
Black, Clementina, *An Agitator*, 1894
Blatchford, Robert, *A Son of the Forge*, 1894
  Julie, 1900
Boulton, Helen, *Josephine Crewe*, 1895
Bramsbury, H. J., *A Working Class Tragedy*, serialized in *Justice*, 1888–9
Brayshaw, J. Dodsworth, *Slum Silhouettes*, 1898

292   BIBLIOGRAPHY

Breton, John Le, *Unholy Matrimony*, 1899
  'Charlotte Elizabeth' [Mrs Tonna], *Helen Fleetwood*, 1841
Crockett, S. R., *Cleg Kelly: Arab of the City*, 1896
Cummins, Maria, *The Lamplighter*, 1854
Curtois, M. A., *Athlos*, 1886
Dawson, W. J., *London Idylls*, 1895
  The Redemption of Edward Strahan, 1891
Dickens, Charles, *Complete Works*
Disraeli, Benjamin, *Coningsby*, 1844
  Sybil, 1845
Dix, Gertrude, *The Image Breakers*, 1900
Egan, Pierce, *Life in London*, 1821
Eliot, George, *Felix Holt, the Radical*, 1866
  'Address to Working Men, by Felix Holt', *Blackwood's*, January
  1868
Farjeon, Benjamin, *Blade o' Grass*, 1874
  Toilers of Babylon, 1888
Fenn, G. M., *Adventures of Working Men*, 1881
Frost, Thomas, *The Secret*, serialized in *National Instructor*, 1850
Gaskell, Mrs Elizabeth, *Mary Barton*, 1848
  North and South, 1855
Gilbert, William, *De Profundis*, 1864
  Dives and Lazarus, 1858
Gissing, George, *Demos*, 1886
  The Nether World, 1889
  Thyrza, 1887
  The Unclassed, 1884
  Workers in the Dawn, 1880
Gleig, Charles, *When All Men Starve*, 1898
Greenwood, James, *Almost Lost*, 1883
  Behind a Bus, 1895
  Dick Temple, 1877
  Fair Phyllis of Lavender Wharf, 1890
  Handsome Jack, 1888
  Jerry Jacksmith of Lower London, 1890
  The Policeman's Lantern, 1888
  A Queer Showman, 1885
  The True History of a Little Ragamuffin, 1866
Harford, Henry [W. H. Hudson], *Fan*, 1892
Hocking, Joseph, *All Men are Liars*, 1895
  The Madness of David Baring, 1900
Hocking, Silas K., *Cricket*, 1880
  Her Benny, 1879
Howell, Constance, *A More Excellent Way*, 1888
James, Henry, *The Princess Casamassima*, 1886
Jenkins, J. E., *Ginx's Baby*, 1870
Jerrold, Douglas, *St. Giles and St. James*, 1851
Jones, Ernest, *Woman's Wrongs*, 1855

Keith, Leslie, *Nobody's Lad*, 1880
  Our Street, 1892
Kimmins, G. T., *Polly of Parker's Rents*, 1899
King, K. Douglas, *A Bitter Vintage*, 1899
  The Child who will Never Grow Old, 1898
  The Scripture Reader of St. Marks, 1895
Kipling, Rudyard, *Abaft the Funnel*, New York, 1909
  Life's Handicap, 1891
  The Light that Failed, New York, 1890; London, 1891
  Many Inventions, 1893
  Plain Tales from the Hills, Calcutta, 1888; London, 1890
  Soldiers Three, Allahabad, 1888; London, 1890
  Wee Willie Winkie, Allahabad, 1888; London, 1890
Lander, Harry, *Lucky Bargee*, 1898
Law, John [Margaret Harkness], *A City Girl*, 1887
  In Darkest London, 1890
  A Manchester Shirtmaker, 1890
  Out of Work, 1888
Leathes, Mrs Stanley, *All Among the Daisies*, 1881
  On the Doorsteps, 1880
Leslie, Emma, *The Seed She Sowed: A Tale of the Great Dock Strike*, 1891
Lytton, Bulwer, *Paul Clifford*, 1830
MacDonald, George, *The Vicar's Daughter*, 1874
Marston, L., *Miss Mollie and her Boys*, 1890
Martineau, Harriet, *Illustrations of Political Economy*, 9 vols., 1832–4
  Poor Laws and Paupers Illustrated, 4 parts, 1833–4
Maugham, W. Somerset, *Liza of Lambeth*, 1897
Mayhew, Augustus, *Kitty Lamere*, 1855
  Paved with Gold, 1858
Montagu, Frederic, *Mary Ashley: The Factory Girl*, 1839
Moore, George, *Esther Waters*, 1894
  A Mummer's Wife, 1885
Morris, William, *News from Nowhere*, 1891
Morrison, Arthur, *A Child of the Jago*, 1896
  The Hole in the Wall, 1902
  Tales of Mean Streets, 1894
  To London Town, 1899
Murray, David Christie, *A Capful o' Nails*, 1896
  A Life's Atonement, 1880
  Old Blazer's Hero, 1887
Nevinson, Henry, *In the Valley of Tophet*, 1896
  Neighbours of Ours, Bristol, 1895
Nicholson, Renton, *Cockney Adventures*, 1838
  Dombey and Daughter, 1850
Ostlere, Edith, *From Seven Dials*, 1898
Paull, M. A., *The Pearl of Billingsgate*, 1890
  Step by Step, 1882

Prowse, R. O., *A Fatal Reservation*, 1895
Pugh, Edwin, *King Circumstance*, 1898
    The Man of Straw, 1896
    Mother-Sister, 1900
    A Street in Suburbia, 1895
    Tony Drum: A Cockney Boy, 1898
Reade, Charles, *Put Yourself in His Place*, 1870
Reynolds, G. M. W., *Mysteries of London*, 1846–8
Ridge, William Pett, *A Breaker of Laws*, 1900
    Mord Em'ly, 1898
    Outside the Radius, 1899
    A Son of the State, 1900
Roberts, Morley, *Maurice Quain*, 1897
Robinson, F. W., *The Hands of Justice*, 1883
    Lazarus in London, 1885
    Mattie: A Stray, 1864
    Owen: A Waif, 1862
    Young Nin, 1898
Rodney, Harley, *Hilda*, 1898
Rook, Clarence, *The Hooligan Nights*, 1899
Sergeant, Adeline, *An East London Mystery*, 1892
    My Nelly's Story, 1882
Shaw, George Bernard, *An Unsocial Socialist*, 1884
Sims, George R., *The Case of George Candlemas*, 1890
    The Coachman's Club, 1897
    In London's Heart, 1900
    The Ring of Bells, 1886
    Rogues and Vagabonds, 1885
    The Small Part Lady, 1900
    The Social Kaleidoscope, 1881
    Stories in Black and White, 1885
    Three Brass Balls, 1882
    Tales of Today, 1889
    Twinkletop's Crime, 1891
Steuart, John A., *Wine on the Lees*, 1899
Tirebuck, W. E., *Dorrie*, 1891
    Miss Grace of All Souls, 1895
Trollope, Mrs Frances, *Jessie Phillips*, 1844
    Michael Armstrong: The Factory Boy, 1840
Wakeman, Annie, *The Autobiography of a Charwoman*, 1900
Ward, Mrs Humphry, *Marcella*, 1894
    Robert Elsmere, 1888
    Sir George Tressady, 1896
Wheeler, Thomas Martin, *Sunshine and Shadow*, serialized in
    Northern Star, 1849–50
Whiteing, Richard, *The Island*, 1888
    Mr. Sprouts: His Opinions, 1867
    No. 5 John Street, 1899

Winchester, M. E., *Adrift in a Great City*, 1893
  A Nest of Skylarks, 1898
Winthrop, A. T., *Wilfred*, 1880
Wintle, W. J., *Paradise Row*, 1896
Wood, Mrs Henry, *Danesbury House*, 1860
  A Life's Secret, 1867
Wright, Thomas ['The Journeyman Engineer'], *The Bane of a Life*,
  1870
  Grainger's Thorn, 1872
  Johnny Robinson, 1868
Yeames, James, *Dollie and Dottie*, 1875
  Told with a Purpose, 1880
Yerlock, Frank, *Phil Flippin's Rise*, 1898

2   *Literary studies*

Adcock, Arthur St John, *The Glory that was Grub Street*, 1928
Altick, Richard D., *English Common Reader*, Chicago, 1957
'Arthur Morrison', *Academy* LII, 4 December 1897
'Arthur Morrison', *Bookman* VII, January 1895
'Arthur Morrison', *Bookman* XXVIII, July 1905
'Arthur Morrison', *Daily News*, 12 December 1896
Aydelotte, William O., 'The England of Marx and Mill as Reflected in
  Fiction', *Journal of Economic History* supplement VIII, 1948
Baker, Ernest, *A Descriptive Guide to the Best Fiction*, 1903
  and Packman, James, *A Guide to the Best Fiction*, 1932
Becker, George J. (ed.), *Documents of Modern Literary Realism*,
  Princeton, 1963
Bell, Jocelyn, 'A Study of Arthur Morrison', *Essays and Studies*, 1952
Besant, Walter, *Autobiography*, 1902
Blatchford, Robert, 'On Realism', *My Favourite Books*, 1901
Boege, Fred W., 'Sir Walter Besant: Novelist', Parts 1 and 2,
  Nineteenth-Century Fiction X, March 1956: XI, June 1956
Boll, Theophilus, *The Works of Edwin Pugh*, Philadelphia, 1934.
Bovill, E. W., *The England of Nimrod and Surtees*, 1959
Boynton, Percy, *London in English Literature*, Chicago, 1913
Brome, Vincent, *Four Realist Novelists*, 'Writers and their Work', 1965
Brook, G. L., *English Dialects*, 1963
Brown, Malcolm, *George Moore: A Reconsideration*, Seattle, 1955
Caine, Hall, 'Memoir of W. E. Tirebuck', preface to Tirebuck, *'Twixt
  God and Mammon*, 1903
Camp, Charles W., *The Artisan in Elizabethan Literature*, New York,
  1924
Carrington, Charles, *Rudyard Kipling*, 1955
Cazamian, Louis, *Le Roman Social en Angleterre 1830–1850*, Paris, 1903
Chaloner, W. H., 'Mrs. Trollope and the Early Factory System',
  Victorian Studies IV, December 1960
Chancellor, E. Beresford, *The London of Charles Dickens*, 1924

Chandler, F. W., *The Literature of Roguery*, 2 vols., 1907

Cherry, Douglas R., 'The English Social Novel 1870–1900' unpublished doctoral dissertation, University of Toronto, 1953

Chesterton, G. K., 'Slum Novelists and the Slums', *Heretics*, 1908

Child, Harold, 'Caricature and the Literature of Sport', *Cambridge History of English Literature* XIV, 1916

Collins, Philip, *Dickens and Crime*, 1962
Dickens and Education, 1963

Cornell, Louis L., *Kipling in India*, 1966

C.R., 'The Methods of Mr. Morrison', *Academy* L, 12 December 1896

Crackanthorpe, Hubert, 'Reticence in Literature', *Yellow Book* II, July 1894

Dalziel, Margaret, *Popular Fiction 100 Years Ago*, 1957

Davis, Robert Gorham, 'The Sense of the Real in English Fiction', *Comparative Literature* III, summer 1951

Decker, Clarence R., *The Victorian Conscience*, New York, 1952
'Zola's Literary Reputation in England', *PMLA* XLIX, December 1934

Domville, Eric, 'Gloomy City or the Deeps of Hell', *East London Papers* VIII, December 1965
'The Presentation of the London Working Classes in Fiction 1880–1914', unpublished Ph.D. thesis, University of London, 1965

Donnelly, Mabel C., *George Gissing: Grave Comedian*, Cambridge, Mass., 1954

Edel, Leon, *Henry James: The Middle Years 1884–1894*, 1963

Eliot, George, 'The Natural History of German Life', *Essays of George Eliot*, ed. Thomas Pinney (1963)

Eliot, T. S., *A Choice of Kipling's Verse*, 1941

Ellis, Havelock, 'Zola: The Man and His Work', *Savoy* I, January 1896

Elwin, Malcolm, *Old Gods Falling* (1939)

Empson, William, *Some Versions of Pastoral* (1935)

Fanger, Donald, *Dostoevsky and Romantic Realism*, Cambridge, Mass., 1965

Fielding, K. J., *Charles Dickens: A Critical Introduction*, 2nd. ed. rev., 1965

Findlater, Jane, 'The Slum Movement in Fiction', *Stones from a Glass House*, 1904

Ford, George H., *Dickens and His Readers*, Princeton, 1955

Forster, John, *The Life of Charles Dickens*, 1893

Franklyn, Julian, *The Cockney*, 1953

Frierson, William C., 'The English Controversy over Realism in Fiction', *PMLA* XLIII, June 1928
The English Novel in Transition 1885–1940, New York, 1965

Gallienne, Richard Le, *Rudyard Kipling*, 1900

Gilbert, Eliot L. (ed.), *Kipling and the Critics*, 1965

Gissing, George, *Charles Dickens*, 1898
The Immortal Dickens, 1925

Letters to Members of his Family, ed. Algernon and Ellen Gissing, 1927
Letters to Eduard Bertz, ed. Arthur C. Young, 1961
Gosse, Edmund, 'The Limits of Realism in Fiction', *Questions at Issue*, 1893
Graham, Kenneth, *English Criticism of the Novel 1865–1900*, Oxford, 1965
Gregor, Ian and Nicholas, Brian, *The Moral and the Story*, 1962
Gulbenkian, V. R., 'The Slum Movement in English and American Fiction 1880–1900', unpublished doctoral dissertation, Western Reserve University, 1951
Hemmings, F. W. J., *Émile Zola*, 2nd ed. rev., Oxford, 1966
Hicks, Granville, *Figures of Transition*, New York, 1939
Hollingsworth, Keith, *The Newgate Novel 1830–47*, Detroit, 1963
Hopkins, A. B., *Elizabeth Gaskell: Her Life and Work*, 1952
Howe, Irving, *Politics and the Novel*, Ohio 1957
Hulin, Jean-Paul, 'Exotisme et Littérature Sociale au Début de L'Ere Victorienne', *Études Anglaises* XVI, 1963
Jackson, T. A., *Charles Dickens: The Progress of a Radical*, 1937
James, Henry, *Notebooks*, ed. F. O. Matthiessen and Kenneth B. Murdock, New York, 1961
James, Louis, *Fiction for the Working Man 1830–1850*, 1963
Jerome, Jerome K., *My Life and Times*, 1926
Keating, P. J., 'Arthur Morrison: A Biographical Study', introduction to Morrison, *A Child of the Jago*, 1969
Kettle, Arnold, 'The Early Victorian Social-Problem Novel', *The Pelican Guide to English Literature*, Vol. VI, 1958
Kipling, Rudyard, *Something of Myself*, 1937
Korg, Jacob, *George Gissing: A Critical Biography*, 1965
Kovalev, Y. V. (ed.), *An Anthology of Chartist Literature*, Moscow, 1956
Leclaire, Lucien, *A General Analytical Bibliography of the Regional Novelists of the British Isles 1800–1950*, Paris, 1954
Le Roman Régionaliste dans Les Îles Britanniques 1800–1950, Paris, 1954
Macbride, Mackenzie, *London's Dialect*, 1910
Martin, R. B., *The Dust of Combat: A Life of Charles Kingsley*, 1959
Matthews, William, *Cockney Past and Present*, 1938
Maugham, W. Somerset, *The Summing Up*, 1938
A Writer's Notebook, 1949
Milliken, E. J., *'Arry Ballads*, 1892
Moore, George, *Confessions of a Young Man*, 1888
Morrison, Arthur, letter to the *Spectator* LXXIV, 16 March 1895
'What is a Realist?', *New Review* XVI, March 1897
Murray, David Christie, *The Making of a Novelist*, 1894
Nevinson, Henry, *Changes and Chances*, 1923
Nicholson, Renton, *Autobiography of a Fast Man*, 1863
'Novel of Misery, The', *Quarterly Review*, October 1902

Orwell, George, 'Charles Dickens', *Inside the Whale*, 1940
Partridge, Eric, *Slang Today and Yesterday*, 1933
Price, R. G. G., *A History of Punch*, 1957
Pugh, Edwin, *Charles Dickens: The Apostle of the People*, 1908
　The Charles Dickens Originals, 1912
　Slings and Arrows, 1916
Ridge, William Pett, *I Like to Remember*, 1925
　A Story Teller: Forty Years in London, 1923
Roberts, Morley, *The Private Life of Henry Maitland*, 1958
Rutherford, Andrew (ed.), *Kipling's Mind and Art*, Edinburgh, 1964
Saxe, Joseph, *Bernard Shaw's Phonetics*, 1936
Shaw, George Bernard, 'English and American Dialects', *Three Plays for Puritans*, Standard Edition, 1931
　Preface to *Pygmalion*, Standard Edition, 1931
Sichel, Edith, 'Two Philanthropic Novelists: Mr. Walter Besant and Mr. George Gissing', *Murray's Magazine* III, April 1888
Sillitoe, Alan, introduction to Robert Tressell, *The Ragged Trousered Philanthropists*, Panther Books, 1965
Sims, George R., *Glances Back*, 1917
　My Life, 1916
Smith, Sheila M., 'Willenhall and Wodgate: Disraeli's Use of Blue Book Evidence', *Review of English Studies* n.s. XIII, 1962
　'Propaganda and Hard Facts in Charles Reade's Didactic Novels', *Renaissance and Modern Studies* IV, 1960
Smith, T. Harper, 'A Child of the Jago', *East London Papers* II, April 1959
Spearman, Diana, *The Novel and Society*, 1966
Spielmann, M. H., *The History of Punch*, 1895
Stang, Richard, *The Theory of the Novel in England 1850–1870*, 1959
Stevenson, Lionel, *The English Novel: A Panorama*, 1960
Stoffel, C., ''Arryese', *Studies in English: Written and Spoken*, 1894
Swinnerton, Frank, *George Gissing: A Critical Study*, 1912
Thompson, E. P., *William Morris: Romantic to Revolutionary*, 1955
Thomson, Patricia, *The Victorian Heroine: A Changing Ideal 1837–1873*, 1956
Thorp, Margaret, *Charles Kingsley*, 1937
Tillotson, Kathleen, *Novels of the Eighteen-Forties*, 1954
Traill, H. D., *The New Fiction and Other Essays*, 1897
Tuer, Andrew, *The Kawkneigh Awlminek*, 1883
　Old London Street Cries, 1885
　Thenks awf'lly, 1890
Vooys, Signa de, *The Psychological Element in the English Sociological Novel of the Nineteenth Century*, Amsterdam, 1927
Warburg, Jeremy, *The Industrial Muse*, 1958
Webb, R. K., *Harriet Martineau: A Radical Victorian*, 1960
Weekley, Ernest, 'Mrs. Gamp and the King's English', *Adjectives and Other Words*, 1930
Whiteing, Richard, *My Harvest*, 1915

Wilson, Angus, *Émile Zola*, 2nd ed, 1964
Wolff, Renate C., 'Currents in Naturalistic English Fiction 1880–1900',
   unpublished doctoral dissertations, Bryn Mawr, 1951
Wright, Edgar, *Mrs. Gaskell: The Basis for Reassessment*, 1965
Wyld, H. C., *A History of Modern Colloquial English*, 3rd ed., Oxford,
   1956
Zola, Émile, *The Experimental Novel and Other Essays*, trans. Belle M.
   Sherman, New York, 1893
   'Germinie Lacerteux', *Mes Haines*, Paris, 1866

3   *Economic and social history*

Adderley, James, *In Slums and Society*, 1916
   The Parson in Socialism, Leeds, 1910
Ausubel, Herman, *In Hard Times*, New York, 1960
Barnett, Henrietta, *Canon Barnett*, 2 vols., 1918
Bayly, Mrs Mary, *Ragged Homes and How to Mend Them*, 1859
   Mended Homes and What Repaired Them, 1861
Beames, Thomas, *The Rookeries of London*, 1850
Besant, Walter, *As We Are and As We May Be*, 1903
   East London, 1901
Booth, Charles, *Life and Labour of the People*, Vols. 1 and 2, 1889, 1891
Booth, J. Benion, *The Days We Knew*, 1943
   Old Pink 'Un Days, 1924
   Pink Parade, 1933
   (ed.), *Seventy Years of Song*, 1943
Booth, William, *In Darkest England and the Way Out*, 1890
Briggs, Asa, 'The Language of "Class" in Early Nineteenth Century
   England', *Essays in Labour History*, ed. Asa Briggs and John Saville,
   1960
   Victorian Cities, 1963
Burke, Thomas, *The Streets of London*, 1940
Burns, Dawson, *Temperance in the Victorian Age*, 1897
   Pen Pictures of Some Temperance Notables, 1895
Chevalier, Albert, *Before I Forget*, 1901
   Humorous Songs, 1894
   A Record by Himself, 1895
Coborn, Charles, *The Man Who Broke the Bank*, 1928
Cole, G. D. H. and Postgate, Raymond, *The Common People 1746–1946*,
   University Paperbacks, 1964
Collier, Richard, *The General Next to God*, 1965
Cullen, Tom, *Autumn of Terror*, 1966
Currie, Sir Edmund Hay, 'The Working of the People's Palace',
   Nineteenth Century XXVII, February 1890
Denison, Edward, *Letters and other Writings*, ed. Sir Baldwyn
   Leighton, 1872
Disher, M. Willson, *Victorian Song*, 1955
   Winkles and Champagne, 1938.

Dyos, H. J., 'The Slums of Victorian London', *Victorian Studies* XI, September 1967
Felstead, S. Theodore, *Stars Who Made the Halls*, 1946
Fergusson, Sir Louis, *Old Time Music Hall Comedians*, Leicester, 1949
Foster, Sir William, *East London*, Historical Association Pamphlet No. 100, 1935
Garland, Thomas C., *East End Pictures*, 1885
Garwood, John, *The Million-Peopled City*, 1853
Gavin, Hector, *Sanitary Ramblings*, 1848
Glass, Ruth, 'Urban Sociology in Great Britain: A Trend Report', *Current Sociology* IV, 1955
Godwin, William, *London Shadows*, 1854
   Town Swamps and Social Bridges, 1859
Greenwood, James, *In Strange Company*, 1873
   Martyrs by Proxy, 1885
   A Night in a Workhouse, 1866
   Odd People in Odd Places, 1883
   On Tramp, 1883
   The Seven Curses of London, 1869
   Tag, Rag and Co., 1883
   The Wilds of London, 1874
Hadden, R. H., *An East End Chronicle*, 1880
Haddon, Archibald, *The Story of Music Hall*, 1935
Harrison, Brian, 'Drunkards and Reformers: Early Victorian Temperance Tracts', *History Today* XIII, 1963
Heasman, Kathleen, *Evangelicals in Action*, 1962
Hoggart, Richard, *The Uses of Literacy*, 1957
Hollingshead, John, *Ragged London in 1861*, 1861
How, Frederick, *Bishop Walsham How*, 1899
Inglis, K. S., *Churches and the Working Classes in Victorian England*, 1963
Jay, Rev. A. Osborne, *Life in Darkest London*, 1891
   The Social Problem and Its Possible Solution, 1893
   A Story of Shoreditch, 1896
Jones, Henry, *East and West London*, 1875
   Fifty Years, 1895
Knapp, John M. (ed.), *The Universities and the Social Problem*, 1895
Lansbury, George, *My Life*, 1928
London, Jack, *The People of the Abyss*, 1903
Lynd, Helen, *England in the Eighteen Eighties*, 1945
Mcqueen-Pope, W., *The Melodies Linger On*, 1950
Mander, Raymond and Mitchenson, Joe, *British Music Hall*, 1965
Marsh, Catherine, *English Hearts and English Hands*, 1858
Marx, Karl and Engels, Frederick, *On Britain*, Moscow, 1962
Mayhew, Henry, *London Labour and the London Poor*, 4 vols., 1861
Mayor, Stephen, *The Churches and the Labour Movement*, 1967
Mearns, Andrew and Preston, W. C., *The Bitter Cry of Outcast London*, 1883

Morrison, Arthur, 'Christmas Eve in the Streets', *Palace Journal* V, 25 December 1889
    'On Blackwall Pier', *Palace Journal* III, 8 May 1889
    'Whitechapel', *Palace Journal* III, 24 April 1889
    'A Workman's Budget', *Cornhill* LXXXIII, April 1901
Mowatt, C. L., *The Charity Organization Society*, 1961
Newton, H. Chance, *Idols of the Halls*, 1928
Odell, Robin, *Jack the Ripper in Fact and Fiction*, 1965
Pike, G. Holden, *Golden Lane : Quaint Adventures and Life Pictures*, 1876
Pimlott, J. A. R., *Toynbee Hall : Fifty Years of Social Progress*, 1935
    The Poor in Great Cities, 1896
Pugh, Edwin, *The City of the World*, 1912
    Harry the Cockney, 1913
Pulling, Christopher, *They Were Singing*, 1952
Ranyard, Mrs Ellen, *The Missing Link : or Bible-Women in the Homes of the London Poor*, 1859
Reason, W. (ed.), *University and Social Settlements*, 1898
Rogers, Joseph, *Reminiscences of a Workhouse Medical Officer*, 1889
Rose, Millicent, *The East End of London*, 1951
Scott, Harold, *The Early Doors*, 1946
Shaw, Capt. Donald ['One of the Old Brigade'], *London in the Sixties*, 1908
Sherwell, Arthur, *Life in West London*, 1897
Simey, T. S. and M. B., *Charles Booth : Social Scientist*, 1960
Sims, George R., *How the Poor Live*, 1883
    How the Poor Live and Horrible London, 1889
Sinclair, Robert, *East London*, 1950
Smith, Charles Manby, *Curiosities of London Life*, 1853
Smith, Sir Hubert Llewellyn, *The History of East London*, 1939
Stafford, Ann, *A Match to Fire the Thames*, 1961
Walker, Henry, *East London : Sketches of Christian Work and Workers*, 1896
Webb, Beatrice, *My Apprenticeship*, 1926
Wheatley, Henry S., *Hogarth's London*, 1909
Wightman, Mrs J. B., *Haste to the Rescue*, 1862
Williams, Raymond, *Culture and Society*, 1958
    The Long Revolution, 1961
Wohl, Anthony S., 'The Bitter Cry of Outcast London', *International Review of Social History* XIII, 1968
Woodruffe, Kathleen, *From Charity to Social Work*, 1962
Wright, Thomas ['The Journeyman Engineer'], *The Great Unwashed*, 1868
    Our New Masters, 1873
    Some Habits and Customs of the Working Classes, 1867
Yeames, James, *Life in London Alleys*, 1877
Young, A. F. and Ashton, E. T., *British Social Work in the Nineteenth Century*, 1956

Index